Stealing First in a Two-Team Town

The White Sox from Comiskey to Reinsdorf

Richard Carl Lindberg

Sagamore Publishing
Champaign, IL

Production supervision and interior design: Brian J. Moore
Dustjacket and photo insert design: Michelle R. Dressen
Editor: Susan M. McKinney
Proofreader: Phyllis L. Bannon

Special thanks to photographer Mark Fletcher for his research
and assistance in providing photographs for this project.

Library of Congress Catalog Card Number: 94-65137
ISBN: 0-915611-93-7

Printed in the United States.

In memory of my mother, Helen Lindberg, who took me
to my first White Sox game.

— Contents —

Who's Who in *Stealing First*

The Comiskey Family

1. Charles A. Comiskey, former star first baseman of the St. Louis Browns of the American Association and the founder and first president of the Chicago White Sox. Born in 1859, died in 1931.

2. John Comiskey, father of Charles A. Comiskey born in Ireland in 1827. City alderman of the 10th Ward, and a power broker in 19th Century Chicago politics. Died in 1900.

3. John Louis Comiskey, the only son of Charles Comiskey who inherited the Chicago White Sox upon his father's death in 1931. Lou Comiskey guided the White Sox until his own passing in 1939.

4. Grace Reidy Comiskey, wife of Lou Comiskey who supervised the affairs of the ballclub from 1939 until 1956. She bequeathed majority interest in the White Sox to her surviving daughter Dorothy thereby precipitating a lengthy court battle with Dorothy's brother Chuck.

5. Charles A. Comiskey II, grandson of the founder and the only son of Lou Comiskey and his wife Grace. Served as team vice-president for much of the 1950s until control of the ballclub passed out of the family in 1959.

Baseball Pioneers

1. Theodore "Ted" Sullivan, player, manager, owner, league organizer, and early baseball mentor of Charles Comiskey while Comiskey was a student at St. Mary's in Kansas. Signed Comiskey to his first professional contract in 1879 with the Dubuque Rabbits. Died in 1929.

2. Christian Von der Ahe, flamboyant owner of the St. Louis Browns of the American Association from 1881-1898. He hired Comiskey to manage the Browns in 1885. He lost his team in 1898 after going bankrupt. Died in 1913.

3. John T. Brush, National League executive and Indianapolis clothing store owner who invested in several teams including the New York Giants and the Cincinnati Reds. An arch-rival of Ban Johnson, Mr. Brush hired Charles Comiskey to manage his Redlegs in 1892, an unhappy arrangement that lasted only three seasons. Died in 1912.

4. Byron Bancroft "Ban" Johnson, Cincinnati sportswriter appointed president of the Western League (forerunner of the American League) in 1894. Formed a short-lived friend-ship with Charles Comiskey and was instrumental in help-ing Comiskey relocate his St. Paul team to Chicago in 1900. His differences of opinion with the White Sox owner how-ever, resulted in a life-long feud that was never resolved to the satisfaction of either party. Deposed as president of the American League in 1927, Johnson passed away four years later.

5. Andrew Freedman, vain and corrupt New York politician who purchased the Giants in 1895, and held on to them until 1902. Conspired with John Brush to create a baseball monopoly in 1901 whereby all teams would be jointly owned through shares of stock held in trust by the owner. Often called the most hated man in baseball, Freedman ran his team into the ground and the term "Freedmanism" came to symbolize the avaricious greed of owners in the 1890s. Died in 1915.

6. Albert Goodwill Spalding, a star Chicago pitcher of the 1870s, Spalding served as president of the local National League team the White Stockings (now called Cubs) from 1882-1891. Held in low regard by Comiskey in later years, Spalding was a powerful voice in National League affairs until his death in 1915.

7.   James Hart, team president of the Chicago National League ballclub from 1892-1905, and a strident foe of Charles Comiskey. Hart attempted to block the transfer of Comiskey's team to Chicago in 1900, and failing to do so he imposed harsh terms on the new ballclub including a clause that prohibited Comiskey's team from using the name "Chicago" in its business dealings.

8.   Adrian "Cap" Anson, star batsman for the National League White Stockings (Cubs) in the 1870s and 1880s. Owned part of the Cubs in the 1890s before leaving the team in 1897 to pursue other ventures including a failed attempt to start a rival league in 1900—a diversionary move that helped pave the way for Ban Johnson and Comiskey to re-christen their Western League the "American League." Died in 1922.

Evolution of the Professional Baseball Leagues

1.   National Association of Professional Baseball Players, (1871-1875). Forerunner of the modern National League that failed because of a lack of strong central leadership, monetary losses, and the presence of gamblers who corrupted the players and influenced the outcome of games.

2.   National League, (1876-present). Founded by Chicago White Stocking owner William Hulbert, the National League was organized on the principal that there should be strong management at the top, with membership restricted to cities of 75,000 people or more. In the 1890s, the monopolistic practices of some N.L. owners contributed to a serious morale breakdown, and opened the door for the formation of the American League in 1900.

3.   American Association, (1882-1892). Confederation of Midwestern cities who offered professional baseball at cheaper prices, beer in the grandstand, and games played on Sundays. These liberal attitudes ran against the grain of the National League and resulted in baseball's first real "trade war."

4.   Player's League (The Brotherhood), (1890). Protesting the injustices of a "reserve clause" that bound an athlete to one team for life, a confederation of disgruntled players belonging to the Brotherhood of Baseball Players organized its own professional league. Charles Comiskey piloted the Chicago team which he called the "White Stockings" for John Addison, a local businessman who later sold his interests in the team to Albert Spalding for $15,000 when the league folded after just one year of play.

5.   Western League, (1894-1899). A strong Minor League rooted in the Midwest and founded in November, 1893, by veteran baseball men who vested their faith in Ban Johnson to build the confederation to prominence as the organization's first president. Charles Comiskey pooled his life savings to purchase the Sioux City team in 1894, which he transferred to St. Paul in 1895, and from there to Chicago five years later when the Western League changed its name to the American League and went into open competition with the Nationals.

6.   American League, (1900-present). Upgraded to Major League status in 1901 by Ban Johnson and Charles Comiskey, the American League endured as baseball's second bonafide professional association. The league prospered under the stern and autocratic rule of Johnson, and would survive a challenge from the Federal League in 1914-1915, and the devastating consequences of the 1919-1920 Black Sox Scandal.

The Teams & Their Nicknames

1.   The National League ballclub: was organized as the Chicago White Stockings in 1870 to mount a challenge to the Cincinnati Red Stockings, baseball's first professional touring team. In 1876, the White Stockings were admitted to the National League and maintained this nickname until 1890 when they were called "Colts" because so many veteran players went to the Brotherhood League, leaving behind only the younger men. They became the "Orphans" in 1898

after Albert Spalding fired Cap Anson. During the Spanish-American War they were nicknamed "Roughriders," then later "Remnants" after Charles Comiskey stole several of their best players in 1901. Around 1902, the nickname "Cubs" gained popularity but it would take several more years before this designation became accepted.

2. The American League ballclub: There was little doubt in Charles Comiskey's mind that his Chicago team would be called White Stockings in honor of the team of professionals he had watched as a boy in Dexter Park back in 1870. Comiskey made his announcement to the press that his American League team would be called the White Stockings shortly after announcing his intention to "invade" Chicago on February 25, 1900. The local newspapers shortened the name to "White Sox" in 1902 to save on column space.

Ownership Chronology After the Comiskeys

1. Bill Veeck, owned the Sox twice; 1959-1961, and again from 1976-1980.

2. Arthur C. Allyn, Jr., son of a Chicago-based investment broker who was associated with Bill Veeck in his earlier baseball ventures purchased the White Sox from Veeck in 1961 and sold the team to his brother in 1969.

3. John Allyn, younger brother of Arthur involved in the Chicago Mustangs soccer team in the late 1960s purchased controlling interest of the Sox in 1969 and owned the team until 1975 when he sold the ballclub to Bill Veeck.

4. Jerry Reinsdorf, chairman of the Balcor firm in Skokie, Illinois, purchased the White Sox from Veeck with his partner from law school, Edward M. Einhorn in 1981.

— Foreword —

Those of us who call ourselves White Sox fans can easily conjure up images in our minds' eyes. Minnie, Chico, and Little Looie. The Go-Go Sox and '59. Bill Veeck, the Old Roman, and Comiskey Park, both the new and the old. South Side Hitmen.

Memories are like fine wine. They are to be savored and usually get even better with age.

Stealing First in a Two-Team Town tells the story of the White Sox, mostly through the eyes of its ownership down through the years, and for good reason. Team owners, starting with Charles Comiskey, right on through the current owner, Jerry Reinsdorf, inject their own personality on a ballclub, give it direction, vision. In many cases, the game on the field tells only a small part of the whole story.

Rich Lindberg gives us a look at the White Sox through many stories that have seldom, if ever, been heard. There's the Old Roman himself, Charles Comiskey, who was so moved by the euphoria of winning the World's Championship in 1906 he gave his team a combined $15,000 bonus. By the time he mailed out 1907 contracts, however, the euphoria had been replaced by Comiskey's penny-pinching "sensibility," and contracts offered "took into account" the bonuses and were for less than players anticipated. This was the same Comiskey, however, who in 1917 donated 10 percent of his club's gross receipts to the Red Cross for relief in war-torn France.

Lindberg "peeks" into the past through stories that seldom are offered as part of White Sox history, so after 93 seasons as an American League franchise, the team's story is told not only from the historical perspective, but also anecdotally. You get a different view of The Old Roman, the man who solved the problem of 200 peepholes drilled in the outfield fence of his St. Paul franchise. He simply built a second, inner fence six inches in front of the peephole-infested fence that was cutting into his business.

If nothing else, what follows here traces a mercurial White Sox history. But from Comiskey's first maneuvers to build the original Comiskey Park, to Reinsdorf's more complicated efforts to make new Comiskey Park a reality, one thing becomes evident — history, at times, does repeat itself.

—Ken "the Hawk" Harrelson

— Acknowledgments —

For more than 16 years I have been actively engaged in accumulating, cataloguing, and documenting Chicago White Sox lore. What began in 1978 as a labor of love for a little-known paperback titled *Stuck On the Sox*, has since become a major research project culminating in the publication of this volume of team history.

Along the way I discovered that it is entirely possible for a professional baseball team to "lose" its history. And that is the fate that had befallen Chicago's South Side ballclub up until a few years ago when the team's media relations department first called on me to supply them with statistical data and historical anecdotes to expand the contents of its spring media guide and roster book in order to keep pace with other Major League teams who had painstakingly charted and more carefully preserved their histories over the years.

Ownership changes, a steady front office turnover, and the retirement of media statistician Don Unferth, who stored all this information in his remarkable memory, had a debilitating effect on the team's ability to supply quick answers to fans and media about player records, game data, and historical events that pour in every day. In the early 1980s, I discovered (to my great surprise), that the historical archive did not extend much further back in time than 1951.

Of course, a cynic might argue that White Sox history didn't amount to all that much before Minnie Minoso's arrival in 1951. I beg to differ. Though largely ignored by an East Coast literary establishment that heaps praise on the Boston Red Sox and the Brooklyn Dodgers in a glut of new books published each year, the history of the Pale Hose is fraught with its own elements of drama, tragedy, and comedy. It is a wonderfully colorful and vivid story.

But statistics and a knowledge of trivia alone do not paint a complete portrait of this or any other baseball team. And frankly, I have grown weary of the number-crunching obsessions of the "S.A.B.R.-metricians" who devise convoluted new formulas each year to re-interpret past and present player performance. The credibility of the baseball historian and the value of his discipline suffers as a result.

Major League baseball is a game played by men from all walks of life with a unique story to tell. In many ways, baseball has reflected the transformation of an agrarian society into an urban one. The growth of the professional game has paralleled the rise of the modern city and the corresponding decline of the industrial north—the "Rustbelt"—and is reflected in the westward migration of older teams like the Giants, the A's, and the Dodgers, to more lucrative ports-of-call.

Charley Comiskey's ballclub mirrors the growth and surprising development of Chicago as an urban colossus in the early years of the twentieth century. The struggles of the Comiskey family and its successors to survive and prosper against difficult odds in an archaic stadium is the premise of this book and I would like to take a moment to acknowledge some important people who have assisted me in my baseball-related projects over the years.

For their research help and the many kindnesses shown me over the years, I am indebted to the following members of the White Sox family and front office both past and present: Doug Abel, Chuck Adams, John Allyn, Jr., Tim Clodjeaux, Chuck Comiskey, Mary Dosek, Danny Evans, Doak Ewing, Dan Fabian, Nancy Faust, Bob Finnegan, Rob Gallas, Ken Harrelson, Roland Hemond, Paul Jensen, Barb Kozuh, Christine Makowski, Mike McClure, Minnie Minoso, Dana Noel, Joe Pinoti, Howard Pizer, Adelle Powell, John Ralph, Scott Reifert, Jerry Reinsdorf, Paul

Reis, Tim Romani (I.S.F.A.), Sue Selig, Eric Soderholm, Jeff Szynal, Joyce Ulleweit, the late Don Unferth, Ken Valdiserri, Mike Veeck, Stuart Wade, and John Wasylik.

Sox fans: how I wish I could acknowledge all the wonderful fans who have taken the time to contact me relating their experiences, memories, and common frustrations. But I can only single out a few, and I will begin with Sox Fans On Deck, the real unsung heroes of the 1988 stadium crisis who crusaded for the team while others merely argued: first, Tom Murphy, a friend whose research contributions were invaluable to this project; S.F.O.D. founder John Pontikes; Cindy Gortowski, Jens Lauesen, George Skuros, Harvey Anderson, Jeff Bolker, Dean Geroulis, and the late Judith C. Helm.

Many thanks to photographer Mark Fletcher who supplied valuable material for this book; Stew Thornley and Dave Anderson of Minneapolis; David Stephan of Los Angeles; L. Yager Cantwell for his many wonderful stories of his grandfather, the original Woodland Bard, and fellow journalists George Castle, Les Grobstein, Bruce Levine, Jerry Kuc, Bruce Miles, Bill Motluck, and Joe Rozanski.

Special thanks to my agent Connie Goddard. Also, Bob Norris, an ex-Chicago Cardinal; Bob Foster, Oak Lawn's finest; Jo Gayle; Howard Bulgatz; Dennis Bingham; Joe Schiavo; Jane Johnson; Pete and Mike Donoghue; George Carlson; Barbara Gregorich; Pete Bjarkman; Teri Cortesi; my publisher, Joe Bannon, Jr.; Robert Krupp; Jimmy Pistorio; Tom Barabus—friends for life; C.C.P.A. founder John Flood—who has always fought for higher principles; my wife, Denise, and my brother, Chuck Lindberg.

Tony Inzerillo

Smiles all around as (from left) Peter Bynoe, Thomas Reynolds, and Tim Romani, prepare to break ground at the site of the new Comiskey Park, May 7, 1989.

Mark Fletcher

While construction at new Comiskey Park was underway in 1991, old Comiskey Park was coming down.

— Prologue —

The Bonfire of the Comiskeys

June 30, 1988, Illinois State House

Red faced, frantic, and exhibiting the visible strain of his 12 years in office, Governor James R. Thompson nervously paced the aisles of the House of Representatives as he tried to pull one last rabbit out of his hat before the gavel banged down on the spring legislative session, and the last flickering hope that Charles Comiskey's baseball team might remain in its South Side ancestral home.

"An optimist," Oscar Wilde once wrote, "expects his dream to come true." And on this pleasant summer evening in the Illinois State Capitol, James Thompson exuded optimism. He alone believed that the funding bill to construct a new state-of-the-art facility for the White Sox, thus staving off a certain exodus to St. Petersburg, Florida, could be passed . . . even as the clock inched ever closer to the midnight gavel. Governor Thompson was full of dreams and hope. He did not want his political epitaph to record that he failed to save an 88-year-old civic institution for the people of Illinois.

Big Jim, as he was commonly known to friend and foe alike, made his bones in the U.S. Attorney's Office in the early 1970s by sending former Illinois Governor Otto Kerner and a half-dozen corrupt Chicago politicians to jail. Political opponents on the

Democratic side who were at frequent loggerheads with the state's chief executive often cried foul. Thompson, they charged, answered to only one authority: the limits of his own ambitions. As governor, Big Jim helped re-build Illinois with massive public works projects like the new Arlington Park Race Course, a government building in the heart of downtown Chicago, and other projects that drained state coffers.

Deal cutter that he was; back-slapping, make-you-feel-real-good Jim was often forced to conduct business in the smoke-filled rooms of Illinois politics. And yet for all his wheeling and dealing, there was not a hint of scandal attached to this man, and the voters had dutifully returned him to office three times since his first gubernatorial triumph in 1976. Thompson was a seasoned alley fighter, and he had been mustering support for this bill for weeks. But it seemed to be a foregone conclusion that nothing short of a miracle could save the White Sox now. Baseball-hungry Floridians savored the arrival of the South Side team, and at the St. Petersburg Chamber of Commerce, 2,200 Florida White Sox T-shirts were selling briskly at $10 a pop. All that remained to be done, they presumed, was to wait for the ink to dry on the 15-year lease agreement between the Sox owners and the proprietors of the new 43,000-seat Florida Sun Coast Dome.

The other matter . . . that meaningless vote in the Illinois Legislature was mere formality. The Sox were coming, and this sleepy resort community populated by senior citizens and snow-belt refugees was excited about the possibilities of baseball in the Spring.

James Thompson however, had other ideas.

* * *

Minutes before the House and Senate leaders emerged from their caucuses to convene the evening session, the sharpest thinkers in Springfield predicted failure for the amended $150-million stadium package that would build the new house of Comiskey. Republicans who supported the measure gloomily informed Thompson that they could guarantee only five votes. House Speaker Michael Madigan, a Democrat bitterly opposed to Thompson on matters of fiscal policy, yet strongly committed to keeping the Sox in his home town, could muster between 30 and 40 votes—far short of the cumulative 90 votes needed for passage. In other words, situation hopeless, but never impossible.

Who could justify a heavy outlay of scarce tax monies toward a dubious project such as this when the chronically underfunded public school system could barely afford to pay teacher salaries and keep its doors open at the same time?

Among certain lawmakers there was a consensus of opinion that White Sox owners Jerry Reinsdorf and Eddie Einhorn were carpetbagging rascals playing both ends against the middle. State Senator Roger Keats from Chicago's northern suburbs for one, was convinced that Einhorn didn't give a damn about remaining in Chicago.

The media, as usual, was apathetic to the Sox plight. They didn't particularly care for the owners very much either. As *Chicago Tribune* columnist Mike Royko reminded readers in his nationally syndicated column: ". . . the fans don't like Einsdorf and Reinhorn, or whatever their names are . . . I expect Einhorn and Reinsdorf to be greedy—you can't get mad at a skunk if it stinks." Still, ardent Cub fan Royko believed it was his civic duty to launch a crusade. He implored readers to send Florida their socks . . . their tired, thread-worn socks from the bottom of the laundry hamper. And so bundles of hosiery postmarked Chicago, arrived in the Sunshine State within days of Royko's call to arms.

* * *

In the last critical moments of the legislative session, just where *were* Jerry and Eddie? At the impending hour of the South Side's baseball Armageddon Reinsdorf was attending a B'nai B'rith sports banquet where his son was being presented an award. "I remember everyone coming up to me and asking what was going to happen and I said I honestly don't know," the Sox president relates. "But I'm remaining optimistic." Later he returned to his home in Highland Park; a posh bedroom suburb of Chicago far removed from Springfield or the gritty South Side neighborhood his partner and sidekick Einhorn had hoped to abandon.

* * *

"Right up to June 29 we still didn't have a lease agreement with the White Sox," recalls Tim Romani, Assistant Executive Director of the Illinois Sports Facilities Authority, who had weathered a steady stream of opposition from community-based leaders who fought against the new stadium. "We still had a deadlock in the deal over the amusement taxes and failure of the legislature to appropriate." The Sox were playing hard ball. And without Jerry's name on the lease, Governor Thompson would march into battle firing a pop-gun.

To resolve technicalities in the lease Reinsdorf agreed to flip a coin three times with Thomas Reynolds, a Thompson ally who also served on the Authority. "When it comes to negotiations, you never know who's going to win. But when it comes to flipping a coin, *always* go with the Irish," advised Reynolds to his young colleague, Romani.

Tom Reynolds called all three flips of the magic coin correctly, which allowed the document to be finalized and hand-delivered to Springfield from Chicago the following morning just hours ahead of the vote. Big Jim could now go to the naysayers and say "The White Sox are committed, are you?"

If Jerry and Eddie were strangely silent during the last days, the Sports Authority, represented by its Executive Director, Peter C.B. Bynoe, and legal counsel Julian D'Esposito, was not. They had been pressing the flesh with balky legislators for two straight days. "The ability to present information was our responsibility," Romani said. "The Governor could not explain the fine points of the deal as well as we could. We negotiated and assisted in the drafting of the legislation that called for a 2% lodging tax to pay for stadium construction. Our feeling was that in nine or 10 years the state would recover every penny that initially went into the project. It was a hard sell to the downstaters. They were skeptical."

An appeal to civic pride. Economic necessity. Call it what you will, Bynoe and Romani were the men in motion and they pulled out all stops. They could not hope to complete a project of this magnitude until the public got behind them. And up until the eleventh hour, the Sox fans were as silent as the great Sphinx.

Beloved Bill Veeck was dead. Jerry and Eddie were detested. And the blathering of a grassroots organization known as Save Our Sox (S.O.S.) worked to the detriment of the legislation. The S.O.S. message was laden with sarcasm and anger. "Screw Jerry. Screw Eddie. Save our park and maybe we'll get a new team!," in essence is what it boiled down to.

In the real world, things aren't quite as simple as that. So, borrowing a page from Abraham Lincoln when he tried to goad General George McClellan into doing something more positive than strutting around the parade grounds while the Confederate Army was scratching at the door, South Sider James Richards said: "Excuse me S.O.S., if you're not using your name at the moment, may I borrow it for awhile?" Richards rallied the troops and secured private financing for a day-long bus caravan to Springfield waving a Save Our Sox banner. The intrepid group stormed the front lawn of the capitol building. They grilled bratwurst, sang Irish folk tunes, and button-holed their legislators outside chambers.

The Chicago contingency was greeted by Governor Thompson and Speaker Madigan, but the two antagonists refused to appear on the same dais together. Madigan waited in the wings to address the gathering until after Thompson retreated into the capitol rotunda. When he finally spoke, Madigan echoed the Governor's message: "We'll fight for you on this. It's the right thing to do."

A glimmer of hope in a mood of pessimism.

* * *

Four o'clock p.m. June 30. "This thing was given the last rights. It wasn't going to be called for a vote. There was no interest in it anymore," Romani said.

Then the Governor's limousine pulled up to the capitol steps. As Thompson stepped out of his car, the Sox stadium bill was uppermost in his mind. To complete an end around run past a hostile legislature and pass this thing would be his lasting legacy. If the late Richard J. Daley was remembered as the mayor who built Chicago's necklace of super highways and beautiful downtown skyline, James Thompson would seal his place in history as the man who laid the bricks and mortar of the new Comiskey Park.

Thus far, the Governor was having a bad session. The majority of his legislative agenda including a Republican-sponsored income tax hike was already dead. Thompson needed the tax increase to trade for votes with lawmakers outside Chicago; notably the legislators from Southern Illinois, where the St. Louis Cardinals and the Cubs were considered the home teams.

As he made his way up the stairs to confront his opponents, members of the Illinois Sports Facilities Authority were there to greet him and to seek encouraging signs that their efforts to date were not in vain. The mood was somber; defeat hung in the air, Romani vividly recalls. But then the Governor, appearing sure of himself predicted victory. "There's no reason this bill can't be passed," he said. "We've got to resurrect it, however we can. Now if you'll excuse me . . . "

Privately, the Governor harbored grave doubts about the bill's chances in the General Assembly. But the troubled look on Tim Romani's face was disturbing to Thompson. "This is a youngster who had come to work for me out of college and who had been at my side for a year and a half before he went to graduate school," Thompson said. "And I could see the absolute look of disappointment and I said to myself, 'I'll be damned if we're going to let this fall.'"

Big Jim raced upstairs to huddle with James "Pate" Philip, the powerful Senate Republican leader from suburban DuPage County who had effectively nixed any hope the White Sox once had of moving to the Village of Addison, within his up-scale white-collar district. The conference with Philip lasted into the early evening hours before there was a renewed stirring of interest. Governor Thompson recalls the frank discussion he had with Philip. "I said 'Pate, we're going to pass this bill.' He said 'You're crazy!' I said Pate, we're going to pass this bill, because it's very important to me and it's important to the state and you're going to help me.' And then he asked me: 'Do you really want to do this?' I said 'I really want to do this.' He said 'Okay, I'll help.'"

Governor Thompson travelled from office to office talking with legislators. He called the party leaders into his chambers for a half hour. Then they would report back to their caucuses for debriefing. Afterward there were more closed door meetings. A full court press was on.

***

In Chicago, a disconsolate gathering of 18,168 die-hards turned out in Comiskey Park to pronounce last rights. The New York Yankees, and their ageless left-hander Tommy John, appropriately, provided the opposition this evening, but the game on the field was incidental to the larger drama in the State House 189 miles to the south.

In the Depression and war years, the Comiskey family had always counted on the arrival of the Yankees to help them square accounts in the ledger books. The big weekend series in July lured 30,000-40,000 each day. Only the weatherman and the booming bats of Babe Ruth, Lou Gehrig, and Joe DiMaggio diminished the enthusiasm of Sox fans in those lean, losing decades.

Then the "Go-Go"ing White Sox of the 1950s restored pride to a franchise devastated by the Black Sox Scandal and three decades of losing baseball. The vintage White Sox of that fabled era rekindled passion for the game among South Siders. Days of childhood passed all too quickly however, and the mythic memories of ballpark days and the players those fans watched became priceless heirlooms handed down to their children.

Sentiments of the past, the well-worn tales of pin-stripe glory from the era of Ike, Sputnik, and black and white TV had a hollow tint to it this evening. Memories of a time and place sometimes turn bitter. "It's gonna pass . . . I got a feeling . . . it's gonna pass," whispered North Sider John Pontikes, one of the founders of the Sox Fans On Deck (S.F.O.D.) group.

Pontikes had been thrust into the spotlight quite unintentionally. When fan apathy threatened to doom Governor Thompson's sincere efforts to save the team, "Big John," as he was known to his friends in Section 130, organized a petition drive that garnered 30,000 signatures supporting passage of the bill.

S.F.O.D. members probably didn't like Jerry and Eddie any more than the S.O.S. faction. But they *loved* the White Sox, and by God, if it meant tearing down old Comiskey Park to save the franchise, so be it.

Between innings of this lackluster contest between the faded Yankees and the fifth-place White Sox, Pontikes left his seat and proceeded under the grandstand to seize upon any speculative rumor he might overhear in the beer concession line. Just a little straw to grasp at that might support his unflagging optimism that come morning, the fifth-place laggards who were bowing meekly to Tommy John would still be *his* laggards. "I feel it in my bones," but Big John's voice was sagging and it was only the sixth inning.

* * *

For much of the 1988 season, the Florida media had been dogging the trail of the Chicago White Sox. Reporters from the *St. Petersburg Times* began covering the team as if it was their own. There were more media requests flowing through Tim Romani's office from Florida than Chicago.

In the ancient Comiskey Park press box—a cramped relic from Bill Veeck's first ownership—the Florida writers elbowed their way past the local scribes toward the choice seating without so much as a whimper of protest. The vultures were circling, and nobody in the Fourth Estate, as the members of the press are sometimes called, seemed phased by it except, perhaps, Les Grobstein, a reporter from WLS Radio.

To Les, an unrepentant Cub fan, it was a matter of civic outrage. He was the one reporter in town who felt a keen sense of anger toward the importuning Floridians. He kept assuring the visiting delegation that the White Sox were not going any-where . . . except, perhaps, across the street into a new ballpark. Since the White Sox did not even know where they would be playing in 1989, it is fair to assume that Les was communing with the spirit world on his forecasts.

Just in case Grobstein happened to be wrong, Media Relations Director Paul Jensen had prepared a set of press releases to be distributed just as soon as word was received from Spring-field. The first statement from the team expressed regret over the reluctant decision to sever ties with the City of Chicago. The second one expressed ownership's pleasure to recommit its resources to the South Side in a spacious new park scheduled to open in 1991.

* * *

At 11:35 p.m., long after the lights of old Comiskey Park were turned off and the last of the malingering fans stumbled out of

McCuddy's tap across the street from the park, the bill was called for a vote in the State Senate. Inside Miller's Pub, another preferred watering hole of the sports addicts in Chicago, a patron was nervously scribbling on his napkin as the local TV station cut away to Springfield for live reports. South Sider George Vergos was trying to figure out a license plate number if indeed it was going to be Florida. "St-Pt-Sox?" What do you think?" he asked, holding up the napkin. Of course such a message could also mean "Stay Put White Sox!"

"I'll be with them wherever they are!" he added. Miller's Pub, located under the rumbling el tracks along Wabash Avenue in the Chicago Loop was where Bill Veeck would go to quaff his brew with legions of admiring fans. He had his own bar stool near the front door—Veeck's Corner.

* * *

The Senate roll call began. In the dying seconds of the legislative session four opponents, one Republican and three Democrats reportedly, changed their votes. Among them was Senator Dawn Clark Netsch, an avid White Sox fan who frequently attended games at Comiskey Park in the company of her husband, Walter. Senator Netsch allowed sentiment to override conviction. School reform would always be with us. This was a one-time thing for future generations of kids. Yes, by all means save the White Sox.

Out of practical necessity, Senator Richard Newhouse, a black Democrat from Chicago, was persuaded to support the bill on the condition that minority contractors would receive 24% of the construction jobs on the new park. He voted yes—but said it was "hollow" because school reform failed.

Governor Thompson had the required 30 Senate votes. The bill glided through with a bare minimum. Pate Philip, and his counterpart across the aisle, Democrat Phil Rock had put aside partisan differences and had rallied behind the Governor at long last.

The Illinois House presented a more formidable challenge. "Everybody in the entourage—Rock, Tom Reynolds, Pate Philip, Gayle Franzen, and the Governor, dashed across the third floor of the capitol to witness the final outcome," Romani remembers. "We all held our breath."

Governor Thompson removed his suit jacket, loosened his tie, and rolled up his sleeves. Here stood a towering figure in state politics; the longest reigning chief executive in Illinois history who would compromise when necessary or confront. Jim Thompson required no less than a miracle this evening, but he could not leave that miracle to chance. Tonight he would confront.

His legislative assistants knew where the swing votes were. "As I walked in, the spotters would call to me, 'Here! Here!' Those were the people who needed to hear it from the boss," Thompson said. "I was driven by the clock and by the notion this was the second time I was doing this. And thirdly, it was not only the right thing to do, it was an easy thing to do. But time was running out."

A chorus of "Na Na Hey, Hey, Kiss (them) Goodbye!" echoed across the room. The downstaters were confident they could defeat the stadium bill. What a chance for them to chip away at the stranglehold of power enjoyed by the Chicagoans! The historic differences between the big city and the small towns and farmlands of Southern Illinois crystallized the frequent problems of gridlock in the General Assembly. Chicago, some believed, should be cut loose from the rest of the state.

Jabbing his finger into the chest of legislators from Vermilion, Ogle, Boone, and LaSalle Counties, Thompson drove home the point that the revenue-generating potential of the new stadium would also benefit downstate. When that tack failed, the Governor called in his chips. The accumulated favors of the past 12 years now came due. "Horse trading alone was a small part of it," Thompson reveals. "In fact, horse trading alone would not have gotten it done." Still, there were some who attached a price tag to their vote.

The Governor recalls that a prominent suburban legislator asked for his endorsement for Secretary of State in the next primary election in return for a yes vote on the stadium bill. "I said absolutely no! He said well, okay, I just thought I'd try."

Walking down the Democratic side of the aisle, Thompson encountered Representative Wyvetter Younge of East St. Louis, who had pushed the red light button signalling a no vote. "I said Wyvetter, why are you a no? And she said, oh, did you want me to be green, Governor? And I said yes! She said okay, and this was when the clock was ticking!" Other legislators were not so easily swayed.

"What in Heaven's name are we doing at this hour with our top-ranking politicians on this floor when we can't take care of our children!" screamed Representative John Dunn of Decatur. "We can't take care of the poor and we can't take care of the people who need our help!" It was an emotional moment when reason and logic collided with passion. The image of Thompson moving from desk to desk engaged in short but furious debates with long standing political adversaries filtered back to Chicago—and Florida—via TV and radio. The telling outcome was at hand; the history of the 88-year-old franchise swung on a thread as the final roll call at last began.

The clock pushed dangerously close to midnight. After 12:00 a.m., any measure still before the body would require a three-fifths majority, or 71 votes to pass. And that was not going to fly.

Seconds left and still six votes shy of a majority. Speaker Madigan conferred with Alton Democrat James McPike, keeper of the gavel. It was made clear to McPike that the gavel would not fall until Madigan *wanted* it to fall. There was still a chance.

Meanwhile, Thompson continued to work the floor. Feverishly he negotiated with the downstaters until one by one they caved in. "Even though I was a Governor from Chicago and I wore Chicago on my sleeve, I had always delivered from downstate," Thompson points out. "So they trusted me to take care of them and I didn't have to promise future things because my past history demonstrated I would always look out for downstate, whether it was roads, or buildings, or whatever."

At 12:03, or 11:59 (depending on whether or not the legislator happened to be wearing a Chicago watch), Representative James Stange of Oakbrook cast the 60th and deciding vote for passage of the stadium bill. The final score on the electronic tote board showed 60 in favor, 55 opposed. It was a political resurrection. The deal was done.

Angry legislators tossed reams of paper into the air. This sly piece of maneuvering to make the clock stand still . . . only Chicago could perpetrate such an outrage.

Mike Madigan's Irish eyes were twinkling. "I don't think there is a judge in the nation, especially in Illinois who would challenge this."

* * *

The reporters from Tampa-St. Pete dispatched to Illinois to file their stories sat in stunned silence. They had badly underestimated the resolve—the chutzpah of the rust belt politician when it came to matters tugging at the heart strings. The only na na hey-heying sung at 10 minutes past midnight was performed by Les Grobstein to the departing Florida delegation as they tried to flag down a cabbie outside the ballpark in the dead of night.

The Florida White Sox T-shirts would have to be packed away in moth balls for the time being.

* * *

It was a moment to savor for bone-weary White Sox fans who had endured three grueling seasons when the only issue worth hot-stoving was the stadium crisis. At last, a new beginning and much hope for the future. "In my experience in state government, this was the highest political drama I've ever experienced," Romani would later say. "An incredibly emotional issue."

How strange the timing. How unbelievable the outcome. A new day of White Sox baseball was dawning on the 78th anniversary of the grand opening of Charles Comiskey's "Baseball Palace of the World." True, the old shrine was consigned to the wrecking ball—and with it an irretrievable link to a troubled past would disappear forever. But since so much of this history bespoke of failure, scandal, and heartache, how much of a loss was it really? It was a question that begged an answer; and one not likely to be solved anytime soon by the skybox moguls occupying the supersuites, or the slogan-chanting organizers purporting to represent the best interests of the South Armour Square community, which was about to be laid to waste by the construction firms.

Neither side could rightfully assess what the White Sox and old Comiskey Park had meant to generations of fans passing through the turnstiles—the real baseball purists who had taken this team to its heart. The game's historic place in our culture has lately taken a back seat to the agenda of the greed mongers and their opposite counterparts seeking personal aggrandizement through the hot rhetoric of personal confrontation.

This moment had been coming for a long time, but nobody seemed prepared for the eventualities, least of all the Chicago baseball fan who witnessed the priorities suddenly rearranged before his stunned eyes in the 1980s when modern realities finally caught up with Chicago, and the candy store philosophy of management on *both* sides of town vanished forever.

The corporate ownership that was about to demolish this field of faded glory reflected the slow transformation of the game from its humble agrarian roots into a marketing pitchman's cornucopia.

It was a foregone conclusion that the White Sox would have a new stadium to present to the public. The seeds of this drama were sewn many, many, years before. Why it hadn't happened sooner remains the real mystery.

Fireworks at new Comiskey, 1993.

Charles A. Comiskey
"The Old Roman"

Chapter
— One —

Young Man in a Hurry

April 3, 1900, Chicago

Elbowing his way past an early-morning throng of Loop office workers, delivery men, and newsboys who were jostling for position on the crowded thoroughfare known as Dearborn Street, a tall, striking man outfitted in a fashionable chesterfield overcoat and a wide-brimmed tan fedora hurried along to keep a pressing engagement. The very future of his new team — of American League baseball — hung on a thread.

There was urgency in his step and a look of concern on his face as he bobbed and weaved through the mass. Towering 17 stories above the street at the northeast corner of Van Buren and Dearborn, one of the city's most fashionable business addresses, was the majestic, cream-colored Fisher Building. Daniel Burnham's magnificent structure embodied form and utility. Here, Chicago's most ambitious and clever entrepreneurs clamored for office space on the upper levels in order to survey the panoramic sweep of the city at their feet.

The age of miracles was at hand — and the spirit of the pioneers was keenly felt by men of vision in the arts, commerce, business, and professional sport; an industry barely a quarter-century old, but experiencing the same familiar growing pains as the burgeoning cities. In Chicago, this feeling surged through a man's veins like hot current.

Charles Albert Comiskey, a prominent man in his own right, was aware that the only limitations to vision are those that are self-imposed. Despite attaining a degree of fame in the sporting world as a star first baseman and player-manager for the World Champion St. Louis Browns of 1886, Charley Comiskey toiled in the shadow of his illustrious father, Alderman John Comiskey, right here in the old home town.

Comiskey, at age 41, well imagined that all of that was sure to change, once the local baseball fans previewed his new team, about to begin play on a re-sodded South Side weed patch that had once served as the home of the Wanderers Cricket team. Comiskey had only recently announced his intentions to re-locate his cash-starved St. Paul team of the Western League to Chicago, in a back room power move that startled the most sharp-eyed observers of the national game. Comiskey, it seemed, had pulled a fast one on James Hart, the president of the Chicago Colts, the star-studded National League team of "Cap" Anson, Albert Spalding, and Jimmy Ryan. Of late, some of the wise guys around town began referring to Hart's boys as the "Colts" or "Orphans" after Comiskey stole their moniker of former years, "White Stockings."

There were few people who frankly believed Comiskey was up to the challenge of placing a second team in Chicago to compete with Hart's aggregate for the fan's money. No less a man than the beloved "Pop" Anson had fronted a group intent on breaking the National League monopoly in Chicago and else-where.

But in the busy weeks following the historic announcement on February 24 that the St. Paul Saints (or Apostles by some accounts), would transfer to Chicago to begin play under the banner of the re-christened "American League," Comiskey had already leased his playing field at 39th and Wentworth, and was steaming ahead with his plans to construct a sheltered wooden grandstand and bleacher without a professional contractor to show him how such things were to be done. The entire construction project was scheduled to be completed by opening day, now less than three weeks away.

If successful, and Comiskey had no reason to believe other-wise, he would savor the satisfaction of proving to Mr. Hart that he alone had designed and built Chicago's first new stadium since the National Leaguers moved from the lakefront into their new home on the West Side in 1885. If he could not meet this self-imposed deadline, well . . . that simply couldn't happen.

In these last few weeks before the "White Stockings" were to make their debut, Mr. Hart had done his level best to prevent his fellow N.L. magnates from allowing the intruder into the lodge, even if they had promised to play by the rules as a minor league, subservient to the terms of the sacrosanct National Agreement. As any plundering mogul understood, promises, verbal or otherwise, were made to be broken. "A thousand times, no!" Hart screamed. And a thousand times the moguls preached appeasement. "They shall see! They will be sorry!" warned Hart.

Hart heard the sound of the wolf scratching at the back door.

* * *

On this bright, pleasant April morning, when every idle minute was time misspent, Charles Comiskey confronted a new crisis: one that required the immediate intervention of his friend and mentor, the dour-faced American League president Byron Bancroft Johnson.

Perspiring and out of breath from his early morning canter to the league office on the fifteenth floor, Comiskey swept through the anteroom and deposited his six-foot frame into a soft leather chair. Facing Johnson, the "Old Roman" as Comiskey was sometimes referred to in the local press, scribbled the sum of $1,500 on a blank check. "Ban," Comiskey drawled, "will you send somebody around to the bank and get this cashed for me? I want to pay the workmen off for what they are owed."

Johnson peered at the check through a pair of prince-nez reading glasses. Here sat the imperious American League president; coldly calculating, loathing his enemies, reserving sentiment for the very few. His strained friendship with Comiskey was already entering its eighth year. These two strong-willed men set aside their personal differences to begin challenging a weakened and politically corrupt National League, about to collapse under the weight of interlocking ownership, disgruntled players, and sagging attendance in financially troubled markets. These two men were about to save baseball from its self-destructive tendencies, but could they be saved from themselves?

"Great Scott!" Johnson roared. "This is a legal holiday, and not a bank in town is open. You should know that. Can't you put this off until tomorrow?" Johnson, an incorrigible misanthrope smoothed back his thinning hair, parted down the middle.

"No, it cannot wait," replied the young magnate. "I don't care if it is election day. These men expect to receive their money today, and they are going to have it. Let's go out and see if we can cash this check somewhere else." The Old Roman was desperately trying to avoid the embarrassment of missing his first Chicago payroll, and jeopardizing the venture over a technicality. That morning the solemn faced union steward of the carpenter's local rapped on Comiskey's door. He handed over a time sheet expecting to receive the full amount in cash. As they spoke, his men were applying the final touches to the pine enclosure that circled the cricket field.

Comiskey had assured the steward that he would have their money by sunset, and harangued the man about the importance of continuing the work. It had been a hellish winter, and the snow and cold had delayed construction and set the project back by weeks. The unions obliged Comiskey's request that the workmen put in double time and Sundays.

Time is money, and for the moment both were in short supply. Charles Comiskey had salted away $30,000 in cash over the years, through frugal management and a keen eye for the ledger sheet. However, much of that sum was earmarked to repay old debts in St. Paul, and for the lease agreement on the 39th Street Grounds with the First National Bank.

American League monies were forthcoming. The benefactor in the deal was Charles Somers of Cleveland, a coal and utilities baron, who was part of that class of businessmen who harbored a strong desire to fulfill a vicarious longing to become a sportsman. With no new worlds to conquer in the realm of finance, men like Charles Somers could easily be persuaded to part with their money in return for the publicity, the ego gratification, and the chance to become little boys again, reliving a time in their lives when peer acceptance equated with athletic prowess.

Before Johnson and Comiskey were through with Mr. Somers, they would pry loose seed money to start new teams in Cleveland, Philadelphia, and Boston. But for now, Ban Johnson's office safe was quite empty, and the only alternative was to find themselves a Somers-surrogate in the streets of Chicago, who would cash the Old Roman's check. Johnson tagged along, because he recognized that Comiskey's momentary problem was also an *American League* problem.

In the wood-paneled saloon of the Great Northern Hotel where the baseball men sometimes gathered to hoist a stein, Comiskey found such a benefactor who cheerfully exchanged a set of crisp $100 bills for the check. "Well," the Old Roman intoned, "I guess there won't be any trouble now, Ban. I will just drop into one of the downtown hotels and change six or seven of these centuries into small bills. Then I will go out and pay off the men."

That was easier said than done. The search for bills of smaller denomination to satisfy the hod carriers consumed much of the afternoon. Comiskey and Johnson "dropped in" on the boys at the Grand Pacific, the Stratford, and Vogelsaang's restaurant, where for the price of a few bottles of French champagne, the commercial men and travelling drummers obliged Comiskey with change.

At 4:00, the two men parted. The Old Roman returned to the South Side and Johnson to his office. Appearing at the South Side Grounds a short time later, Comiskey beckoned the foreman to lead the army of tradesmen into the semi-privacy of the club-house. At the moment the clubhouse office was mobile; perched atop a set of enormous wooden rollers for transport across the diamond to the northwest corner of the field.

The White Sox owner lit a cigar and smiled pleasantly as a wisp of smoke curled lazily toward the ceiling. "Come forward men, be quick! My pockets are filled with money, and I have plenty to share today!" Comiskey winked at the head groundskeeper, a beefy German man who kept a watchful eye on the frozen turf being groomed for baseball.

"Mr. Comiskey, by the rules of the union, there's eleven dollars and sixty-seven cents a coming to me and what's more, there's an hour and a half extra time!" The ruddy-complexioned Irish construction worker named Finnegan fiddled nervously with a weatherbeaten derby as Comiskey scanned the paymaster's ledger sheet to verify the amount. He peeled off a fifty from the fat bankroll and handed it over. "Here you go Finnegan, how will that do you?"

The Irishman frowned. "For the love of hivens, is ye kidden me ye are?" There was a look of panic to his face. "Does ya think I'm a bank president? Change is it? Why man, I have only four cints in me pocket now, and one of them coppers is plugged!" It was getting late in the day, and the rough hewn carpenters grumbled among themselves when they realized what was happening.

"Now hold on a second there, Finnegan," Comiskey calmly advised. Motioning to the groundskeeper, the Sox owner asked for a few more minutes of their time. "See if you can get this cashed," he said, handing over two fifties. Twenty minutes later the German came back with a hat full of silver dollars. When that too was gone, Comiskey sent the flushed grounds keeper out a second, and then a third time. "Mine gracious, dis is awful!" he moaned. "Der feller at the drug store say himself that if I don't stop running a crap game he vil have me arrested!"

Before the last man was paid off, Comiskey's groundskeeper had made the rounds of every saloon, grocery store, and barber shop within a quarter mile of the ballpark. In this Bridgeport community, where thousands of Irish famine immigrants came to dig the Illinois and Michigan Canal and slaughter the steers shipped from the western rail heads in Kansas, life had been a grim struggle. The stench of the stockyards less than a mile south of the ballyard choked the air, and the poorest among them subsisted on a diet of cabbage in their squalid hovels along the banks of the Chicago River. In this religious, highly secular community, where a man's social life centered around the saloon — and the church — where atonement could be made on Sunday for Friday night's debauchery, the coming of a ballteam represented a modest beacon of hope. Mr. Comiskey offered them a different kind of neighborhood diversion from the drudgery of the work week. The ballyard would be a place to go to on a Sunday; for a game they so dearly loved at popular prices. They knew his father to be a man of honor. He was one of them. He was Irish, and he had their best interests at heart.

"I need a nickel for carfare to go home!" Comiskey padlocked the door to the clubhouse before he realized that all he left in his pocket was a fifty—and no change.

The hapless groundskeeper, whose name is lost to history, threw up his hands in disgust. "Dey vil mob me if I ask for more change!" he bellowed. "I'm going home now, dat's what I'm going to do. What do you think of that?"

Exhausted by his day's labors, Comiskey strolled into a Bridgeport cafe, where he was certain to be recognized. The Old Roman smiled agreeably and chatted for a few moments with one of the patrons. He pressed a complimentary pasteboard into the hand of a packinghouse worker, and invited the rest to sip a free mug of lager. Comiskey laid down his fifty, hoping for carfare change. "Say Charley, this don't go see, the drinks for this bunch comes out to a dollar twenty see?" the barkeep warned. But Charley Comiskey's fifty was already on the mahogany bar and the boys had gathered 'round. "Why, I'll stand you off till tomorrow, but don't go four-flushin' around here with any more of that long green." Johnny McCuddy frowned at the Sox owner. He slapped a towel down on the cook stove. "A good thing's a good thing and you're my friend see, but if ya' ain't got the price of carfare I'll stake ya'. And if you're thirsty I give you another gargle. But I'll be blamed if I'll change another hundred for ya', or whatever ya' got in dem pockets!"

"I'll remember you Johnny, that you can be sure. And the name is 'Commy.' I like my pals to call me Commy," he said, his Irish eyes twinkling. Comiskey accepted the loan of a nickel and doffed his hat to his genial host, whose little place on 39th Street was near and dear to the Bridgeporters. "Ah there's nothing like being independent of your neighbors," Commy mused. "I'll be seeing you good people on April 21st — that's when we give them West Siders a run for it."

"To your health Commy! To your health!" Johnny McCuddy tucked the half century under the change tray and slammed the register shut.

With a wave of his hand, Comiskey stepped through the portals and walked slowly past the frame worker cottages, two flats, and store fronts in and around 39th and Wentworth. The spire of old St. George's scraped the sky of this grand old Irish town — Bridgeport — still known by its name of former years, Lee's Place, to the old timers. These South Side people were the salt of the earth, and he was proud to be counted among them, even if the family homestead was located on the West Side.

So many happy memories of days gone by. So much to look forward to with this new team and all. The South Siders would rally to his cause and he would never disappoint them if he could help it. Ah, noblesse oblige!

The Goddess of Fortune had indeed smiled on him for another day—as it always would. Of that he had little doubt. How good it would be to slide down into a steaming tub tonight and drift away . . . and remember the way it used to be.

James Hart, president of the Chicago Cubs for much of the 1890s, fought hard to keep Comiskey and the White Sox out of Chicago.

Byron Bancroft "Ban" Johnson was appointed president of the Western League (forerunner of the American League) in 1894. Johnson formed a short-lived friendship with Charles Comiskey and was instrumental in helping Comiskey relocate his St. Paul team to Chicago in 1900.

Theodore "T.P." Sullivan was a baseball mentor to Charles A. Comiskey. Sullivan was one of Comiskey's camp followers and helped plan the Sox 1913 World Tour.

Chapter
— Two —

Baseball from the Buckboard

Long before Charley Comiskey's White Sox were even a notion in his mind, baseball was being played at Dexter Park in Chicago by the city's original White Sox. Dexter Park was a handsomely outfitted baseball grounds that accommodated 2,000 people with space for a like number of carriages parked out beyond the oval track where the thoroughbreds ran. With its ornate balconies, awnings, and spacious clubhouse, baseball games at Dexter Park in the summer of 1870 had become a gala social event, attended by the leading politicians, industrialists, and dashing military figures like General Philip Sheridan, fresh from his Indian campaigns in the west.

The crowds were good humored — "occasionally noisy but perfectly orderly at all times," according to one contemporary account. Because Dexter Park was located in a remote location, far removed from the tenements surrounding the business district, management succeeded in keeping away the rabble of boys who "make baseball matches perfectly hideous with their yelping," gloated a reporter from the *Chicago Times*. Baseball, even in its infancy, was never viewed as an egalitarian endeavor.

The dignitaries gathered at the West Side park to preview the Chicago White Stockings, Chicago's first professional baseball team which was organized at great expense — and fanfare — by local entrepreneurs for the express purpose of defeating the champion Cincinnati Red Stockings. The Ohio team had waltzed through the 1869 season with a perfect 60-0 record, and was a tremendous marquee attraction wherever it played. Civic pride, coupled with the undeniable profit motive, demanded that the local promoters spend $20,000 of their own money assembling the finest local talent to play in a public grounds ideally suited to the temperament of the emerging national game. In the decade preceding the formation of the White Stockings, baseball had evolved from a leisure-time amateur sport practiced by street corner loungers with time on their hands to a highly profitable entertainment industry that charged admission and paid salaries to the participants.

The success of the Red Stockings in their celebrated 1869 national tour convinced the local moguls of the public's willingness to pay to see a top-drawer team compete with a visiting nine. "The Chicago club is a $20,000 article, and for that money a dozen of the best players in the country may be had!" grumbled one out of town reporter witnessing the day's events.

The *Chicago Times*, a Democratic journal of a decidedly liberal bent when it came to publicizing the local amusements around town, beat the drum the loudest for the White Stocking management to go out and procure the right kinds of players that would place the team on equal footing with the Cincinnatians.

The White Stockings did not disappoint. The partisans were soon impressed by the skill and alacrity by which the local club dispatched the Forest Citys of Rockford, and the New York Mutuals. The high point of the season came on September 7, when the visiting White Stockings prevailed by a 10-6 score in Cincinnati. The weakened Red Stockings had experienced earlier defeats in the course of the 1870 campaign, but for the moment the Chicago promoters were agloat. The victory was an important one, because it placed the professional game on solid ground in their corner of the world.

Reflecting back on it in later years, Charles Comiskey liked to say that he got into baseball because it was born in him. If that is true, his baptism surely occurred in Dexter Park during the storied 1870 season.

Amid the society matrons and their downtown high hats perched atop Landau carriages, Four-by-Fours, and Dog carts parked in the spacious outfield pasture, 11-year-old Charles

Comiskey bobbed and weaved toward the front of the line, in order to steal a glimpse of the well-heeled "ringers" attired in azure blue caps, snow white uniforms, and matching stockings.

Cuthbert, King, Hodes, McAtee, Craver, Pinkham, Flynn, Treacy, and Myerle. The Chicago nine who proudly strutted out onto the field at Dexter Park those warm afternoons in 1870 are long forgotten today, and baseball historians of this era would be hard pressed to provide us with much scintillating detail about them, but they were larger than life to one Charley Comiskey who imagined himself in their place.

Charles Comiskey was born into a semi-privileged world. His presence in the suburban setting of Dexter Park that season confirmed that here lived a boy who never experienced deprivation or economic want at anytime in his young life. The Comiskey brood included six boys and one girl born to Mary (Kearns), and her husband John, immigrant Irish from Crosserlough, County Caven.

The elder Comiskey established himself in Chicago in 1854, at a time when the Irish were just beginning to shed the stigma of the nativist anti-foreign, anti-Irish "Know Nothing" prejudice that had darkened the doorstep of the first potato famine immigrants who began arriving in the 1840s. The notion of public service, so abhorrent to many of the blue-blood nativists, left a vacuum in city politics. The Irish answered the call, and within a few years, sons of the *auld sod* occupied positions of importance in county government. At various times in his career, John Comiskey served as Clerk of the County Board of Commissioners, superintendent of the water meter department, and with the coming of the Civil War, he organized the famous Irish Brigade out of Chicago.

In 1857 he was elected alderman from the Tenth Ward, on the near west side, becoming an eloquent spokesman for the predominantly Irish constituency he served. "Honest" Johnny Comiskey, without a hint of scandal to his name, chaired the first aldermanic investigation into the politico-criminal tie-up that existed within the Chicago Police Department in 1868. The Alderman's relentless cross-examination of the downtown gambling bosses and powerful vice merchants earned him respect and bi-partisan support from the opposition. Republican mayors always considered Comiskey dependable; which in itself was quite a token of respect, especially during the post-Civil War years when big city Democrats were excoriated for their tolerance of social drinking, gambling, and other forms of behavior considered unacceptable by the silk-stocking crowd.

An oft-told tale that has been given much credence by Gus Axelson, Warren Brown, and other writers who have profiled Charles Comiskey's life over the years, tells of the father's stern opposition to baseball. In fact, John Comiskey harbored no particular objection to baseball whatsoever. The alderman appreciated sport, the camaraderie of athletics, and the good will between fellows, evidenced by his own participation in the first annual City Hall baseball game, played at Dexter Park that same magical summer of 1870. Left fielder Comiskey led his Democratic colleagues in a stunning 34-5 rout of the Republicans while his wide-eyed son looked on.

No doubt John Comiskey conceded early on that Charley and his older brother Jim were not likely to inherit his aldermanic seat, much less show an interest in politics. Fearing perhaps that his son might succumb to idleness, Charley considered an apprenticeship in the building trades for a time, but these notions were temporarily brushed aside in the fall of 1873 when Charles was enrolled in St. Mary's College in Kansas. Brother Jim was an upperclassman at the school, and a star ballplayer and boxer in his own right.

If St. Mary's was intended to purge Comiskey of his baseball ambitions, it was a poor choice. Sports were vigorously promoted by the administration, and an older boy named Theodore P. Sullivan became Charley Comiskey's early mentor. Sullivan, (destined to become one of the Old Roman's closest friends, a Midwest talent scout during the White Sox years, erstwhile advisor, and the brains behind the celebrated World Tour of 1913) played for the school varsity, but organized a freshman baseball team. Comiskey was installed as the catcher.

There is no Hall of Fame plaque in Cooperstown bearing the name Ted Sullivan, a forgotten 19th century star, but perhaps there should be. The mustachioed "T.P." coined the word "fan" after the St. Louis baseball fanatics kept hounding him with their advice and fawning attention. Sullivan laid the foundation of several minor leagues, including the Texas League, and the Western and Southern Leagues, and possibly conceived the idea of baseball's first ladies day. Yet he was forever fated to toil in Comiskey's long shadow, and today is simply a footnote figure.

Having completed his preparatory schooling at St. Mary's, Kansas, and the Christian Brothers College in Prairie du Chien, Wisconsin, Comiskey returned to Chicago in 1876 still lacking the requisite skills for a useful trade. It was at this time, when the lad was well into his teens, that Alderman Comiskey attached a greater sense of urgency to his son's search for future avocation. For these reasons, Comiskey senior engaged Charley in his own lucrative construction business, not so far outside the realm of politics.

In the years following the great Chicago fire of October 1871 that leveled the central business district, there was a crying need for able-bodied men to rebuild Chicago; plumbers, contractors, masoners, lumber shovers, and dray drivers. Political insiders, such as John Comiskey, who tinkered in various business enterprises including private banking and the shipment of cattle to and from the Chicago markets, naturally had the first crack at the pork-barrel contracts doled out by the County Board. Steeped in patronage and graft, the Board was controlled by Irish ward bosses, political hacks of the very worst sort, and well-connected gambling bosses like Michael McDonald to the "friends" of the Democratic Party, of which John Comiskey most certainly was counted. Chicago is an insider's town. It has always been that way.

It was not unusual therefore, that the alderman should want to take care of his son and establish him in worthwhile endeavors—a city job. Accordingly, he found him a job driving a brick wagon to and from the fire district. On a hazy summer day in 1876, Comiskey detoured well off his beaten path in order to take in a ballgame being played at Jackson and Laflin Streets between two West Side semi-pro teams, the Libertys and their arch-rivals the Franklins, made up of newspaper printers. Manager Ike Fleming of the Libertys noticed the gangly youth standing near his dray, and according to popular legend, invited Comiskey into the game when his own pitcher faltered. Standing in the field eyeballing the young apprentice were the three fearsome looking O'Day brothers — one of whom went on to become a famous National League umpire — Hank O'Day.

Charley Comiskey played hard — and performed well. So well in fact that he did not notice the presence of his father who quietly mounted the buckboard and completed the appointed route to Washington and LaSalle Streets for his son. That night the alderman scolded his son about responsibility, but no discouraging words were said about baseball. It was a fine game with many redeeming qualities, and one that was practiced by handsome, strapping Irish lads for the most part.

Irish boys from the working classes played the sandlot game on the streets and back alleys of Chicago's noisy west side, very often amid the rubble of burned out buildings and hay barns. By 1876 Irish immigrant sandlot teams proliferated the city. The Franklins, Libertys, West Ends, Dreadnaughts, and even the "Crooks" were challenged by visiting nines from surrounding suburban towns and as far away as Rockford.

It was a curiosity of the evolving game to observe players of one team hover around the opposing catcher, hurling insults and taunts so that he might become rattled. Yet after each game, the members of the winning team would give the losers three rousing cheers before repairing to the local chop house to drink lager and feast.

On many occasions Comiskey and his Liberty mates would travel from their West Side haunts to the new Lake Front Park to preview the White Stockings, now one of the charter members of the recently formed National League. Charley Comiskey, who more or less decided that he wanted to become a pitcher, closely studied the technique and delivery of Albert Goodwill Spalding — one of the bright young White Stocking stars of the professional game in Chicago.

The Libertys on the other hand, were amateurs in every sense of the word; that is, they did not accept payment for playing baseball.

The prospect of earning money for baseball, and thereby justifying his self-worth to the increasingly skeptical alderman, tantalized Comiskey. When Ted Sullivan re-emerged that same year with an offer for him to become the only paid player for a newly formed team in Milwaukee's Third Ward, Comiskey accepted without hesitation. The Milwaukee Alerts as they were commonly known, were owned and operated by Thomas Shaughnessy, one-time president of the Canadian Pacific Railroad.

Comiskey played less than a season in Milwaukee, but it was long enough to establish himself as a paid professional, however modest the sum. After treading water in Rockford and Elgin where he played ball with a watch company team for the duration of the 1877 season, he returned to Chicago. The next year, 1878, Comiskey's foray into the professional game appeared to be all but over. He accepted Ike Fleming's offer to rejoin the Libertys as their pitcher. The underhanded pitching delivery was still in vogue, but even then, Comiskey's ability to deliver the ball with speed and accuracy made him more valuable to the team than the three O'Day brothers combined, or even Fleming, who played first base.

Ted Sullivan summoned his young charge to Dubuque, Iowa, for the 1879 season. A consummate organizer and promoter, Sullivan had an idea that his fledgling Northwestern League might one day emerge as a bonafide threat to the powerful National League. The confederation was one of many such challengers, all seeking a place in the baseball world, however tenuous.

Comiskey's salary for 1879 was nearly double what it had been in Milwaukee —$125. The catch: Sullivan's boys had to work as train butchers. Off days found Comiskey justifying his baseball earnings by selling and distributing magazines and confections on a 20% commission basis to passengers of the Illinois Central line who regularly traversed the Chicago-Dubuque corridor.

These were some happy, carefree times for Comiskey, the three years spent in Dubuque with Ted Sullivan. The two men talked long into the night about baseball, its past, its future directions, and ways to improve the game.

Comiskey (having already converted to a first baseman), is generally credited by baseball historians as being the first player to field ground balls at first base while playing well off the bag. Others claim that this particular piece of defensive strategy was invented years earlier. Though he may not have been the first to play off the base, Comiskey and Sullivan did in fact perfect a new fielding play — one in which the pitcher was taught to cover the bag on ground balls hit well to the right of the first baseman.

The Old Roman began courting his future wife, Nan Kelly, in Iowa and through careful observation of Sullivan's acumen for promotion, Comiskey finally had a pretty good idea of his future course in the pro game.

The Dubuque Rabbits won a league title but failed to whip up a level of interest to sustain them in the counting house. The league faltered after only one year, but the prairie team lasted through the 1881 season, taking on all comers. The tiny Iowa city brushing up against the Illinois border remained in the Old Roman's heart for years to come. Well into the 1950s, the Sox maintained a minor league affiliate in Iowa. Chuck Comiskey, the grandson, served his baseball apprenticeship there. And in 1932, the city fathers dedicated a public park in Dubuque named Comiskey Field.

While Ted Sullivan was cooking up delirious new schemes to enthrall the good folk of Dubuque, Alfred H. Spink and his brother William were busy with some baseball plans of their own down in St. Louis. They had just acquired the lease to an empty lot used by German immigrants for sharpshooting events and amateur baseball. Al Spink was anxious to bring baseball back to St. Louis with the financial backing of one Chris Von der Ahe, a cartoonish St. Louis bar keeper whose saloon was only a short distance from the baseball park at Sullivan and Spring Streets. Von der Ahe shrewdly recognized that social drinking and baseball were conducive to the recreational tastes of the working class ethnic Germans and Irish who patronized baseball; a marvelous mix.

In return for the concession rights, Chris Von der Ahe eagerly invested in the Spink brothers' athletic venture known as the Sportsman's Park and Club Association. Within a year's time, a team was fielded with the help of Cincinnati sportswriter O.P. Caylor. Players were invited to St. Louis from the nearby region for a one-day tryout. Those who survived the cuts were promised a salaried berth on the team. However, it was made clear that paychecks would be handed out only after all operating expenses had first been met.

It was the habit of this team to defy the prevailing conventions by booking Sunday games with Midwestern challengers, charge 25-cent admission (jitney ball), and serve beer in the grandstands. Opposing players were reimbursed for their overnight expenses aboard a "Sullivan," or day coach, as it was commonly known in those days.

Ted Sullivan accepted an invitation from the Spink brothers for the afternoon of July 16, 1881, and led his Dubuque Rabbits into the Mound City for a first-class showdown with the newly formed "Browns." The game was a one-sided rout, with St. Louis coasting to a 9-1 victory. More importantly though, it was the first time Comiskey's team had actually played a game inside an enclosed stadium. And so began an association with a city that brought an otherwise washed-up sore-arm pitcher who was barely making ends meet, to national prominence.

Comiskey had done little to impress Al Spink or Von der Ahe, if his 1-4 batting performance that afternoon was taken into consideration. The following winter, however, when his fortunes were about at their lowest ebb (the Northwestern League had folded and Commy was back to hawking candy and novelties on the train), a letter came from Spink inviting him to play for the St. Louis Brown Stockings of the American Association, a bonafide challenger to the National League's previous lock on the pro game. The Association placed teams in discarded National League cities, charged lower admission prices, opened their gates on Sunday, and were not nearly as priggish on the issue of drinking in the ballpark as Hulbert's National League. When they began enticing National League players with higher salaries and better working conditions, baseball's first major trade war ensued.

Charles Comiskey's salary was only $75 a month (he was accorded living accommodations inside the ballpark), but the chance to play professional ball without pre-conditions was an irresistible lure. Comiskey accepted without hesitation, but to his dismay, the manager installed him in right field. After threatening to bolt the team unless he was transferred back to the infield, Manager Ned Cuthbert acquiesced.

From the grandstand, eccentric owner Chris Von der Ahe looked on approvingly at the pugnacious Comiskey. "Der Boss President," or "Der Boss Glupp" as he was often referred to, was an occasionally meddlesome owner whose gruff exterior belied a kindly nature. He once chartered a train load of caviar and champagne for his boys and would name his various real estate holdings after his favorite players. Of course, he was known to fine other players for making errors, and he would blacklist a man for failing to keep his uniform clean.

Ted Sullivan was bound to turn up sooner or later, so it came as no surprise that he took over the management reins from Cuthbert in 1883. His genius was never more evident than in St.

Louis. Sullivan acquired the nucleus of a destiny-bound team, among them; Tom Deasley, Tony Mullane, Bill Gleason, Walter "Arlie" Latham, and Hugh Nichol.

Sullivan drew up the blueprints, but it was Comiskey who reaped the glory. The Browns of 1883, though not yet championship material, were a solid, competitive club in a league that was gaining new stature and popularity among fans. How different would things have been, if manager Sullivan could have rode out the storm with Von der Ahe, and put up with his antics a might longer? But T.P. walked out on "Der Boss Glupp," at the tail end of the 1883 season in order to accept a position with the short-lived Union Association, which was to last all of one year.

With Ted Sullivan gone, the door was thrown open to Comiskey, who seized the opportunity. Jimmy Williams, future president of the Western League, guided the Browns through the 1884 season, until Von der Ahe lured Comiskey back from Dubuque (where he was promoting a local harness racing venture during the off-season), with a contract to manage on a permanent basis.

Chris Von der Ahe paid among the highest salaries in baseball at the time, and he supported his boys right down the line. Charles Comiskey, a scrappy, management-oriented player was to become his special favorite, and was given a free hand in running the team any way he saw fit. His success as a field leader of a team that Ted Sullivan had assembled brought fame and fortune to Von der Ahe. Manager Comiskey won four consecutive league titles in St. Louis, spanning the 1885-1888 seasons. More importantly, Commy was a congenial sort of man who succeeded where others failed in keeping the owner at arm's length from the team and its day-to-day field operations.

Comiskey's Browns met Cap Anson's Chicago White Stockings in the forerunner of today's World Series, played in October, 1885. The flagship franchise of the N.L. was pitted against the league champions of a confederation held in very low repute by the *Chicago Tribune*, and other journalistic endeavors supporting the senior circuit. Nevertheless, the Association had emerged as a strong challenger, and the success of the new league was born out on the field.

The Browns and White Stockings played a seven-game series for a $1,000 pool to be divided among the winners. The emotionally charged 1885 series featured several brawls and a near riot after Comiskey threatened to take his players off the field following an unfavorable umpire's judgment in Game Two. In that contest, Anson pulled his men off the field in protest. The St. Louis fans spilled out onto the diamond and a forfeit was declared. The 1885 series ended in a three-three draw.

The next year, the two blood rivals squared off again with more conclusive results. Pool selling on the outcome of the 1886 championship series ran heavily in favor of the White Stockings. Chicago gambler Dick Roche wagered $20,000 on Anson's team—no small amount for those times. Indeed, pool selling, or wagering on the outcome of a game, was already a lucrative venture in cities where professional baseball was played. Up and down "Gambler's Row," on Randolph Street in Chicago, the local fans wagered on their favorite players, runs by inning, and the outcome of the contest. The sporting fraternity, the saloon culture, and the ward bosses of the teeming inner city neighborhoods who supported baseball in its incipiency, enjoyed placing friendly bets. They saw nothing wrong with the game, alcohol served in the park, or in debate over the outcome of a contest.

The threat of the fix was always a present danger, long before the 1919 Black Sox Scandal. The baseball magnates recognized it, but took only half-hearted measures to circumvent the evil business . . . on occasion. The night before the sixth and deciding game on October 23, 1886, Von der Ahe got wind of a scheme by certain Chicago gamblers to get his players drunk. Instead of reporting the incident to the police, or the Association's governing commission, Von der Ahe conferred with Comiskey, and decided that it was best if they kept the Browns sequestered in a hotel room for the night. The next day, St. Louis walked away champions, and the *Tribune* sulked: "Everyone was wishing that Chicago would begin to rub it in on these presumptuous youngsters from St. Louis." The three Chicago games netted $5,589 in revenue to the owner. The Chicago gamblers meanwhile, took a big hit on this series.

The championship was an early high point of Comiskey's budding career, but it was to be his last taste of pennant champagne until the White Sox were founded in 1900.

Beset by personal and financial problems, Von der Ahe was forced into a position where he had to sell five star players in

1887. Partly because of altruistic reasons (the Browns' success had upset the delicate competitive balance favored by the owners in those days), and to meet mounting operational expenses, Von der Ahe took these extreme measures. In later years, the Dutchman resorted to renting his grounds as a honky tonk and amusement park, featuring a shoot-the-chutes water slide in center field. He sponsored a Wild West show one year, and even dug a horse racing oval on his grounds to capitalize on the thoroughbred craze sweeping America in the 1890s. The racing privilege was granted to promoter Fred Foster in consideration of a $20,000 payment.

The Browns, and for that matter the Association, had become an irritating embarrassment to the baseball moguls, though it can be reasonably argued that an owner like Von der Ahe was a master showman well ahead of his time. More than anything, Chris recognized baseball as a vehicle for entertainment.

Innovator or carnival huckster, Chris Von der Ahe presaged Bill Veeck by fifty years, but never received the accolades or emotional support from the fans and media. The *Sporting News*, that great arbiter of the national game and font of wisdom, decried Von der Ahe's promotional tactics, and referred to him as a "maggot," when they undoubtedly *meant* to say "magnate."

Despite the departure of Curt Welch, Bill Gleason, and star hurler Bobby Carruthers, the Browns were still good enough to win the A.A. Pennant for the fourth straight year in 1888 only to lose to New York in the 10-game post-season final. Still, it was not enough for Comiskey to want to remain on board Von der Ahe's leaky ship past the 1889 season. The Old Roman harbored a warm, personal affection for the Dutchman. He was a regular visitor to Von der Ahe's bedside shortly before Von der Ahe expired in 1913, his fortune depleted and his wife gone. Comiskey paid the funeral expenses.

However, sentimental ties to Von der Ahe were not enough to sustain Comiskey, who joined a faction of disgruntled ballplayers in rebellion against the hated reserve clause, which contractually bound a player to a team for life, or until ownership traded or released the athlete in question. The measure was enacted in 1883 between the American Association and the National League. The uneasy alliance forged between the two rival professional leagues served several useful purposes. It effectively eliminated free market competition, legitimized the owner's "black list" of wayfaring players, and legally bound an athlete to the same team for the duration of his career. For the time being at least, the reserve rule stabilized the industry from the owners' perspectives, but it did little to improve the lot of the players.

Under the aegis of John Montgomery Ward, the National Brotherhood of Players decided to form their own league. Teams were to be located in Boston, Brooklyn, New York, Chicago, Philadelphia, and Pittsburgh. The Brotherhood, otherwise known as the Player League, adopted a non-conflicting schedule of games, and sought friendly relations with the Nationals. They were naive to believe this was possible under the governance of N.L. president Nicholas Young and the powerful owner of the Chicago franchise, Albert Spalding. As was the case with the American Association, the National League did not countenance the presence of an upstart, especially one comprised of rebellious players violating the spirit of the National Agreement. They responded in kind by boycotting independent teams who engaged the Brotherhood in exhibition games and by scheduling their clubs to play on the same day as the Brotherhood when two teams shared a market, as in Chicago.

Considered by latter day historians to be somewhat of a company man, it seemed unusual at the time for the well-paid Charles Comiskey to bolt the American Association for John Addison's unproven Chicago entry, even with Von der Ahe's mounting financial problems. "I couldn't do anything else and be on the level with the boys," he explained in later years.

Far from being a casual participant, Comiskey joined the brotherhood for much more than a canter in a new baseball park. He was a member of a militant faction of players seeking to destroy the National League at all costs.

Charles Comiskey inked a three-year contract to play and manage a "picked nine" for John Addison, a wealthy Chicago contractor who erected a sheltered grandstand near the corner of 35th and Wentworth that in every respect was far in advance of stadiums that had come before. Addison was a smart operator and a sportsman at heart. However, Addison's role in player development was limited because the structure of the Player's League required that four players from each team serve on the board of directors. Comiskey and his old pal from St. Louis days, Arlie Latham, were two of the player delegates for Chicago.

Comiskey selected the players and undoubtedly had a hand in naming the team, which not surprisingly was to be called "White Stockings" by the press and fans. Even with some of the luminous stars of Von der Ahe's championship teams playing in a comfortable new stadium that was conveniently located near a half-dozen Chicago street car lines, the White Stockings were a bust.

After an early flurry of success at the gate, interest in the Player League games waned by mid-season. Head to head competition in National League cities hurt their chances for sustained success, and the dilution of talent sorely reduced the quality of play. By mid-season, Player League owners were resorting to shoddy gimmicks to lure fans to their parks. The New York team worked a prize package arrangement with one of the 5¢ newspapers dispensing a free ticket to a Brotherhood game in their Sunday edition. Thirteen thousand of the 100,000 newspaper subscribers showed up to witness the contest.

The professional game in America was approaching a low ebb following a period of steady, if not spectacular growth through much of the 1880s. The squabbles between the Player's League, the Association, and the Nationals exposed the bitter divisions between labor and capital; the fast-buck mentality of businessman investors, the racial exclusivity of the game, the intransigence of big-market magnates like Spalding, and the venal greed of certain players who assumed all along that the fans would blindly support them in their bid for higher salaries and greater fringe benefits during these depression-ridden times. The future of baseball was never gloomier than it appeared to be in the early 1890s. The troublesome issues confronting modern-day baseball and the men who claim to have the "best interests of the game" at heart, are markedly similar to the logic put forth by their great grandfathers of a hundred years ago in every regard.

Albert Spalding, for one, bristled at the very idea of compromise, or working toward the betterment of baseball. The present difficulties, he observed in May 1890: ". . . will simply be a case of dog eat dog and those with bulldog tendencies will live the longest. Money will be necessary in plenty to carry on the fight, and the league is prepared to go into its pocket whenever necessary."

Echoes of the 1990s. "The Player's League," he continued, "is no longer the Brotherhood. It is an organization of speculators from Wall Street, who, in back of 100 ballplayers are making an effort to win some money from the game. The National League is not a speculative body; its backers are conservative business-men who never go out on flyers."

Instead they strove toward building monopoly. At season's end, the ill-advised Player's League was suing for peace. The league was a financial and artistic failure, and Colonel Edwin McAlpin, president of the Brotherhood aggregate, was desirous of reaching an accommodation in the form of a consolidation with the hard-liner Spalding, who, like the Tribune Company in later years, seemed to be calling the shots for baseball. Spalding quite naturally wanted to absorb as many star Brotherhood players into the National League in order to strengthen its position for the coming showdown with the Association, once the Player's League was out of the picture.

As the outlaw league inched ever closer to merging with the Nationals, John Addison became frantic to sell his team to Spalding for the modest outlay of $25,000. By mid-November, Spalding and Addison had completed their deal after wrangling over figures and terms. The injury-riddled Chicago team, which had finished the season in fourth place, was done for, and for that matter, so was the league, once Colonel McAlpin resigned his post. From St. Louis, Charles Comiskey angrily reacted upon hearing the news. "Why, they had the National League done for," he snorted, "and at their mercy. The National League was in such a bad way that a child could have pushed the organiza-tion over, but nothing would do the Player's League people but a compromise! They ran after the National League instead of keeping quiet, and solicited a compromise."

In Chicago, A.G. Spalding coldly responded to Comiskey's admonitions. "The Player's League is deader than the proverbial door nail! It is now undergoing the embalming process!" The liberal use of the metaphors of death and dying suggest that the national game in the '90s (the 1890s) was not so much sport, but a grim Darwinistic struggle between blood combatants. The surreal image of baseball as a rhapsody of the agrarian ideal was myth making at its finest. Was it ever as pure and good as the dreamers and poets first imagined?

Charles Comiskey, right, and P.J. Prunty, a local business figure.

Chapter
— Three—

A Maverick Owner in an Outlaw League

Out of the ashes of the Brotherhood came more turmoil and devastation. The National League chewed the bones of the expired Player's League at a meeting of the owners held in New York on November 13, 1890. The owners of the Cincinnati franchise were expelled for violating the cardinal principles of the National Agreement — they had previously negotiated the sale of their team to the Player's League — and from that meeting emerged John T. Brush, an Indianapolis clothing manufacturer, as the head of a consortium that assumed control of the Redlegs. Brush was the new "strong man," and a key figure in the factional warring that paved the way for the American League nine years later.

Stung by the collapse of the Player's League, and Addison's weak-wristed sell-out to Spalding, Comiskey licked his wounds and returned to Von der Ahe's Browns for a final go-around. The American Association had emerged from the "war" weaker than what it was going in, and feeling betrayed by the Nationals. The Association dropped out of the National Agreement in February 1891, lowered admission prices to a quarter, and put into practice a novel idea well ahead of its time: the revenue sharing of gate receipts between the rich and poor clubs. Such an idea, even today, strikes some owners as "socialism."

These drastic measures were not enough to save the American Association from folding in December 1891. Four of its better teams, Baltimore, St. Louis, Washington, and Louisville, were absorbed into the National League for $135,000. Peace brought a stronger National Agreement, an unwieldy 12-team N.L. configuration, a sense of false confidence among the magnates, and the seeds of the American League challenge.

It was a paradox of the times that the dissenting Comiskey, whose heart was filled with so much malice for the Nationals, should move into the enemy camp without a whimper of protest. But then, his three-year contract to manage the Cincinnati Redlegs for Mr. Brush was one of those strange occurrences that must be considered an economic necessity. Comiskey had a wife and a 10-year-old son, John Louis, to feed and no other viable prospects short of retirement from the game.

John T. Brush was somewhat of an anomaly among baseball owners of the day. Here was a literate, exceptionally well-read, bookish individual who maintained a close personal friendship with the poet James Whitcomb Riley. The *Literary Digest*, a leading journal of the time, described Brush in later years as a "great baseball legislator," whose "monument on the island of Manhattan is the great stadium, the Polo Grounds," which he was to open on June 28, 1911 for the benefit of the Giants team he would purchase in 1902.

Brush was viewed in somewhat different terms by the generation of players he dealt with on and off the field. He was an early proponent of "syndicate ball;" the simultaneous ownership of more than one team. He had purchased the original Indianapolis entry in the National League four years before assuming control of the Cincinnati Redlegs as a consequence of the Brotherhood war. With two teams in hand, serious accusations were leveled against Brush that his purchase of the Reds was a scheme to develop talent for the Indianapolis club. The charges were brought before the public by Byron Bancroft Johnson, the sardonic sports editor of Murat Halsted's *Cincinnati Commercial Gazette*.

Brush foisted the salary limit rule on the league, and fathered the notorious "Classification Plan" of 1888, which equated salary to a player's personal habits; his self-discipline, temperance, and forthrightness. In short, Mr. Brush was the quintessential National League owner of the troubled nineties and presumably someone Comiskey would have no use for, if his public statements concerning the labor-management dealings of the N.L. were creditable. However, this was not the case. The Old Roman would describe Brush to his biographer Gus Axelson thusly: "Regardless of the enemies he made—our own league was solid against him, including myself—I still think of him as one of the biggest men the game has produced." Fortunately for baseball, Ban Johnson viewed Brush and his cohorts with greater skepticism.

Ban Johnson had been attached to the staff of the *Commercial-Gazette* for nearly six years when he first made Comiskey's acquaintance in 1892. The sour-faced plutocrat who was to give long-term direction to an obscure minor league that was to crack the N.L.'s hegemony, was attending the Cincinnati Law School when Halsted tabbed Johnson for a part-time correspondent's position, covering suburban news for the paper. Looking back on it: "I had always believed a boy should make his own way. And after a year as a law student, I'd decided I'd seek labor in the newspaper field." Whatever else could be said about Ban Johnson, he was a square-jawed individualist, honest, and hard as granite. He was not a man given over to duplicitous acts. Johnson had his friends — and a like number of enemies. Once crossed, he could neither forgive nor forget.

As a full-time journalist, Johnson covered local politics and the police beat before the city editor moved him over to sports. During the time Johnson was making an enemy of Brush, he was building his friendship with Charles Comiskey, whose dispirited leadership of the Redlegs translated into three lackluster finishes. Cincinnati was never a factor in the 12-team race with the Old Roman at the helm.

Now in his tenth year of professional baseball, Comiskey was well past his prime. Never an overpowering hitter, his batting average had slipped precipitously in the National League. His playing time in 1893 was limited to just 64 games.

Retirement was very much on Comiskey's mind when Brush persuaded him to finish out his contract, which had one year left to run. Accordingly, owner Brush sent Comiskey to the South; ostensibly on a scouting errand to come up with some new recruits for the organization.

Charles Comiskey had a remarkable capacity for playing both ends against the middle, while somehow remaining in everyone's good graces. During his baseball safari through the south lands, the notion of starting up a new league and becoming a magnate himself began to take shape. Comiskey's meetings with Southern League executives who complained bitterly about the low state of the game, dwindling revenues, and faltering support from the National League oligarchy sparked a broader discussion concerning renewed expansion into vacated Midwestern territories.

Mr. Brush was none the wiser when Comiskey returned to Cincinnati, and reported back to Johnson what he had heard. Over a round of highballs at the "Ten Minute Club" on Vine Street, an idea first took hold and was given direction by Commy. The Redlegs manager—in theory at least—proposed that the Western League (a lineal descendent of Ted Sullivan's original Northwestern "prairie" league) begin anew for the 1894 season. The original Western Association was a National Agreement confederation, but it had "blown up" prior to the 1893 season.

Interested baseball men—men rich in experience—could be brought to the table, Comiskey argued. Ban Johnson listened thoughtfully to the proposal, but was coy and very aloof. "I like my newspaper associates, and conditions in Cincinnati," came his reply. Johnson was both a pragmatist and a visionary. He harbored grave doubts, reserved judgment on the matter, argued the technicalities with Comiskey, but was to allow the Old Roman to place his name in nomination for an executive position within the rejuvenated Western League at the first organizational confab held at the Grand Hotel in Indianapolis, November 20, 1893.

Present at this historic meeting to organize the forerunner of the modern American League, were delegates from eight cities who each posted a $1,000 surety bond in order to join the confederation for its maiden season; George Ellis, Grand Rapids; H.H. Drake, Sioux City; John Barnes, Minneapolis; James Manning, Kansas City; William Sparsig, Indianapolis; Michael Killilea, Milwaukee; and Dennis Long of Toledo who held the proxy vote of George Vanderbeck, a wealthy industrialist seeking a franchise for Detroit.

Comiskey, representing no one, sat in on the morning sessions. What he said on behalf of his friend Johnson is not a matter of public record, but it is fair to say that his words were mixed with slight-of-hand praise for Mr. Brush, whose agent, William Sparsig, represented the Indianapolis owner in absentia. John Brush was in New York at the time, and had left no specific instructions concerning the election of a league president. Sparsig went along with Comiskey's urgings, and voted in favor of Johnson. The infant league had bestowed upon their leader the title of president, secretary, and treasurer at a salary of $2,500 per annum. For the moment, Comiskey's uncertain future seemed assured now that his star was permanently hitched to Ban Johnson, who at that point still attached greater weight to his sportswriting duties.

His first year in organized baseball convinced Johnson that the business side of it "was mainly a matter of grief." The Western League was a cash-poor operation from its inception. The Sioux City franchise, under veteran manager William Henry Watkins, won the first pennant, but suffered the same fate as Ted Sullivan, when Comiskey's friend tried to bring big-time baseball to Dubuque. That is, the city was too small and inconsequential to support a ball team on a cash-paying basis.

The challenge facing Johnson was to come up with the right demographics, and solicit the help of wealthy backers willing to pay for the relocation costs to move an unprofitable franchise to a better market. Ban Johnson's most important task those first few years was to entice new investors to build the wooden grandstands, and assume the costly overhead associated with running a team. In the first five years of its existence, the Western League played musical chairs with its teams. The Sioux City team was shifted to St. Paul at the end of the 1894 season. Dennis Long moved his Toledo club to Terre Haute midway through the 1895 campaign without seeking the proper authorization from Johnson, who then expelled him when all was said and done. In 1898, Grand Rapids and Columbus merged into one team representing both cities under the direction of Tom Loftus, a former teammate of Comiskey and one of his closest friends from his Dubuque days.

It was a bewildering task, this business of running a league under the stringent guidelines set forth by the National League moguls who promulgated the National Agreement. Western League owners were subject to the unrestricted "draft" of their players by National League teams. A star-calibre player could be summoned to an N.L. team on a moment's notice. A Western League "mogul" received $500 compensation for each player drafted off his roster, but scant attention was given to how this might affect the outcome of the yearly pennant races in the junior circuit, or to ways in which it might upset the delicate team parity that Johnson had fought so hard to achieve.

Throughout its short-lived existence, the Western League sought important modifications to the National Agreement of 1883 from the N.L. owners—modifications they believed were essential for any chance of success. Johnson wanted to restrict the drafting of players to two per year from each club, and build in a provision that no player could be taken until serving at least a two-year apprenticeship in the Western League. It was only at the eleventh hour of the Western League's existence in 1900, when the N.L. magnates were faced with the prospect of a strong challenge from an outside group, that were they willing to yield any concessions to Ban Johnson on these hard and fast rules.

The N.L. was reaping the harvest of monopoly in the early 1890s, but as the economic recession deepened across the country, gate revenues fell off, the gulf between the rich and poor teams widened, and the destructive influence of several of its owners crippled the league.

Andrew Freedman was a Tammany Hall politician who was allowed to purchase the New York Giants in 1895. Freedman's misspent power, corruption, and greed were a crime against baseball, its players, fans, and media. His chicanery and behind-the-scenes machinations are too numerous to recount here, but suffice to say he conspired with fellow magnates to drive down player salaries, and to pool the assets of all National League teams into a gigantic "trust," much like the beef or railroad monopolies that drew the ire of the muckraking journalists of the period.

The intention of the National League moguls was to build monopoly on top of monopoly, since the National League already had its interlocking ownerships. John Brush, who was Freedman's ally in this scheme, held stock in the Giants ballclub while owning the Cincinnati Redlegs and Ban Johnson's Indianapolis team. And Albert Spalding, the truculent owner of the Chicago White Stockings dipped his hands into the Giants ballclub, while installing James Hart as the "point man" in the Chicago operation.

In fact there were only a handful of autonomous N.L. clubs, and the ones that were free of tampering from a John Brush, Albert Spalding, or Andrew Freedman, languished in the nether regions of the League for much of the decade. The national game was slipping into the abyss, weighted down by greed, jealousy, and a long history of unfair business practices.

Ban Johnson summoned his league executives to a conference at the Wellington Hotel in Chicago nearly one year to the date of the 1893 meeting, in order to notify them of his desire to step down as president and return to the daily humdrum of newspaper work. "Not a soul in the world knew of my intention to resign, so I couldn't understand what these men were talking about," Johnson recalled.

James Manning and George Ellis greeted Johnson in the lobby of the hotel and whispered something about being with him "tooth and nail." "I made inquiry and soon learned that there had been active campaigning to unseat me," he said. It developed that Mr. Brush had been working quietly behind the scenes to depose his enemy and install a candidate more favorable to his interests. "I said to myself that nobody could railroad me out of a job, and I resolved to stick," Johnson vowed.

John Brush introduced resolutions to nominate his man for president, but was voted down 7-1 on each measure. The Western League magnates dispensed with the irksome Brush, who stormed out of the room, his wings clipped and his palace coup foiled. Ban Johnson had been given an important mandate—and renewed sense of confidence in his abilities.

Charles Comiskey waited patiently elsewhere in the hotel until he was summoned to the conference room following their business with Brush. The formal transfer of the Sioux City club to St. Paul was accomplished, and Comiskey was awarded controlling interest. Believing that he was through with Brush, Comiskey invested his last available cent into the purchase of the St. Paul team.

With no further matters of import to be dealt with, Johnson exited the room and went downstairs for a breath of fresh air, not knowing that Brush was loitering in the lobby. Mr. Brush was keenly aware that his manager was meeting with Western League owners this very minute, but he was not certain as to why. "Say Ban, you wouldn't deny me the opportunity to have a word with Commy would you?" Johnson scowled. He knew that Comiskey was on friendly terms with this man whose interests were contrary to the league, but he was also respectful of Brush's importance in the baseball world. "Certainly not John, you have that right," he replied. Comiskey was summoned from the chambers.

The two men exchanged pleasantries as was their custom, and then Brush offered Comiskey an extension on his expired contract, no doubt hoping to embarrass Johnson and keep the Old Roman in the National League. Despite the poor showing in the standings, Brush recognized Commy to be a capable field manager and tactician. But when Comiskey informed his ex-boss of his plans, Brush sneered and pronounced St. Paul a baseball "graveyard." "It's a dead city Charley. Why, nobody will come out to watch your team."

St. Paul had that reputation. But Comiskey and Johnson presented a united front on this issue, and now more than ever, they were bound to see it through. Shortly afterward, Johnson severed his ties with the newspaper and moved the Western League office to Chicago, where it would remain for the next 17 years.

To the patrons of the "graveyard" city of St. Paul, Comiskey gave a scrappy, aggressive team, and the humble beginnings of a colorful civic baseball rivalry between the Saints and their rivals to the west, the Minneapolis Millers. The Twin Cities teams battled each other for territorial bragging rights into the early 1960s.

Operating on a brutally austere budget, Commy was nevertheless able to fill out his roster with a good mix of seasoned veterans of the pro game, like the crowd-pleasing ambidextrous pitcher Tony Mullane, and Charlie Irwin, former starting third baseman of the Spalding's 1894 White Stockings. Younger players like first baseman Frank Isbell and Roy "the Boy Wonder" Patterson became mainstays of Comiskey's "Hitless Wonder" teams of the early 1900s. It was a hustling, and occasionally mean-spirited ball club that got under the skin of the Minneapolis fans across the river.

Researcher Stew Thornley uncovered this long-forgotten 1896 gem from the files of the *Minneapolis Tribune*: "Manager

Comiskey will be served with a formal notice that the Minneapolis club will not play today's game unless guaranteed that there will be no spiking of Minneapolis players, no interference on the part of the crowd, no throwing of rocks, no throwing of dust and dirt in the eyes of the Minneapolis players, and a few other tricks which the game yesterday was featured by."

Baseball contests in those rough and tumble days were wild and woolly affairs, characterized by frequent brawls between players and fans, unsportsmanlike conduct all around, and a lack of central control by the umpires who were neither respected nor paid much attention to. Comiskey's team were no "Saints" by any stretch of the imagination.

As his first order of business in St. Paul, Commy secured a work permit on April 2, 1895, to build an open-air wooden grandstand at Aurora, Fuller, Dale, and St. Albans Avenues in the Summit-University section outside downtown St. Paul. Alderman John Comiskey, well into his sixties by this time, was brought out of retirement to supervise construction of his son's first ballpark, which comfortably seated 1,500 fans. Construction costs were pegged at $4,000, which Charley paid for out of his own pocket.

The Aurora Avenue Grounds were officially opened on May 17, scarcely a month after construction work first began. A booming brass band, a festive downtown parade, and much pomp and circumstance surrounded the arrival of the Saints, who came marching into their new home for an afternoon contest with the Milwaukee Brewers. Comiskey was elated, brimming with confidence by the presence of 3,000 fans who turned out to watch his team bombard the visitors from Milwaukee by an 18-4 count. Western League games were played in tiny, cramped ballparks that favored the hitters. Given the generally poor quality of pitching throughout the league, it was not unusual for both teams to run up double-digit scores.

However, things went sour for Comiskey after his gala opening day pageant. Improvising St. Paul fans quickly discovered that an adjacent bluff on St. Albans afforded them a splendid, unobstructed view of the game without having to pay their way into the park. Comiskey made some fast computations and soon realized that he was losing upwards of 1,000 paying admissions a week. So he ended their freeloading by raising the height of the outfield fence and building his grandstand.

The neighborhood ragamuffins got around this temporary inconvenience by boring 200 peep holes into the pine fence, and watching the games from this vantage point. "Boys will be boys," Comiskey snorted. The owner, whose nickel-nursing reputation was not yet a matter of public record, gritted his teeth and ordered immediate construction of a *second* outfield fence, strategically positioned six inches *inside* the outer wall.

More troubling to Comiskey was the blue-nose attitudes of the city fathers and the clergy toward baseball games played on the Sabbath. The Saints were playing their arch rivals from Minneapolis one Sunday early in the season when a violent thunderstorm sent the fans in the exposed grandstand scurrying for cover in a church directly across the street. The episode sparked a considerable outcry from conservative theologians, so when Comiskey returned from his next road trip, he discovered to his horror that the Reverend of the neighboring church had prevailed upon the Hon. Judge Otis to grant an injunction barring further Sunday games at the Aurora Avenue Grounds. "I probably would have been better off if they enjoined me from playing anywhere for all time," Comiskey quipped, following his unsuccessful road trip.

Future Sunday games were split between the Minnehaha Driving Park, near Minneapolis, and the St. Paul, West Side Park. The injunction held until the 1898 season long after Comiskey located a new home for the club. "The finest park in the West," as the *St. Paul Pioneer Press* glowingly referred to the Aurora Avenue park after it was rendered obsolete and vacated at the end of the 1896 season. Hoping to attract a larger numbers of Minneapolis fans, Comiskey moved into Lexington Park, a more spacious surrounding ideally situated between the Twin Cities in the Midway District. The park featured an unusually short right field "porch" for the abundance of left-handed hitters on the roster, resulting in numerous high-scoring action-packed games.

To spark attendance, Comiskey sponsored several "ladies days," presuming that the wives and girlfriends would want to bring along their cash-paying male companions. Firemen and police officers were frequently admitted for free, and the patron of the bleacher seat was made to "feel like a king."

During the 1895 State Fair, Comiskey played a league game with Detroit in the middle of the Fair Grounds. Like his early mentor Von der Ahe, Commy strived to present the fans with the best in local entertainment for their money, and went to great lengths to market and promote the team. On August 3, the Twin City Mandolin Club played a one-hour concert in the grandstand prior to the game.

Whatever else may be said about Comiskey's reputation for penury, the Old Roman appreciated the loyalty of the bleacher patrons, and went out of his way to ensure their comfort and enjoyment. This policy remained in force long after he arrived in Chicago.

Good marketing technique was not enough to ensure Comiskey a sizeable return on his investment, however. To his dismay, the Old Roman discovered that St. Paul was not so much a baseball graveyard as it was a one-team city. Two clubs competing in small market cities is an age-old problem for baseball. St. Louis, Philadelphia, and Boston eventually lost their weaker franchises, and expansion has thus far seen fit to ignore them. The issue persists even today in the Bay Area of San Francisco where the Giants and A's fiercely compete for the attentions of an admittedly limited demographic fan base.

In the case of Charles Comiskey's St. Paul team, rising expectations coupled with his desire to achieve baseball supremacy did not measure up to the reality of the situation. Despite fielding reasonably competitive teams—the Saints finished second, fourth, third, fourth, and fifth in the eight-team league during the five years Comiskey piloted the club, St. Paul played second fiddle to the Minneapolis Millers. This remained the case for many years to come, even as these two teams reprised their historic and colorful rivalry in another league.

Charles Comiskey's grand design for a second Major League to rise up and smite the Nationals never wavered. St. Paul was to be his springboard for the plan. Ever since the demise of the Brotherhood, Comiskey harbored a special dislike for the Spalding faction of the National League. The Old Roman had his rivals in Chicago. Brush and Johnson were barely civil. Add to this volatile mix, one Cornelius McGillicuddy (Connie Mack), who was fired from his managerial post in Pittsburgh for spouting off to the ownership, we find a Western League simmering with enmity and ambition; and one primed for a fight to the finish.

St. Paul proved to be a mixed blessing for Comiskey. Minnesotians were kindly disposed to the Saints ballclub, but the limitations of the market and the Old Roman's yearly P/L statements submitted at the annual fall meeting built support for his plan to move the team to Chicago. There was never any doubt that the Western League would invade the Chicago territory — the only question was when.

A combination of external forces in the fall of 1899 moved the gambling Western League duo ever closer to a realization of their ambitions. Adrian "Pop" Anson, the "Grand Old Man" of Chicago baseball, beloved by all, had parted company with James Hart, president of the National League franchise in Chicago.

Anson had been retired from the game for nearly two years, but his name was still good in Chicago. Eager to exploit the publicity value of this towering figure of Chicago sports and his differences with Hart, a consortium of St. Louis businessmen intent on reviving the dormant American Association convinced Anson, and the fiery baseball manager John McGraw, to join their group. Acting as the spokesman, McGraw announced formation of a seven-city circuit that included Chicago, Boston, Louisville, Milwaukee, St. Louis, Baltimore, and Philadelphia. It was a paper league, operating on a tight budget and false hope, and was only as good as the hard currency put up by its backers; Alfred Spink of the *Sporting News*, and Al Reach, the sporting goods manufacturer.

Their boasting evoked terror among the National League high hats who had decided to circle the wagons and shed four of their unprofitable teams for the coming 1900 season. Anxious to block this latest attempt to break the monopoly, John Brush summoned Ban Johnson to Indianapolis in the early fall to discuss those "modifications" to the National Agreement that the Western League owners had thrown on the table year after year. "We must be able to keep our players two years," Johnson demanded.

Brush, now eager to placate Johnson and forge a close alliance at the hour of threatened invasion, nodded in agreement. "I will even see to it that the drafting price is increased from $500 to $1,000."

"Per player?" Johnson queried.

"Per player, as you say."

The proposed changes to the National Agreement were consummated in a handshake deal, hammered out without official sanction from the league office, or from Nick Young, the brittle president whose title was largely ceremonial. The Brush-Freedman wing was making important concessions without Young's or Spalding's decree.

Johnson broached the subject of realignment. He was interested in moving his Grand Rapids team to the N.L.'s recently vacated Cleveland property.

"Ten thousand dollars. That's the price," Brush interjected. The hapless Cleveland Spiders lost 134 games in 1899, and were barely able to finish out the season. Brush was eager to be rid of the mismanaged, sorry affair, but he didn't want to see a National Agreement territory fall into the hands of Association men.

Then Johnson dropped his cards. "We intend to announce at our next meeting that Chicago will have a Western League team next year under the direction of Comiskey." It was not an unseen development. Brush fully understood Charley Comiskey's intentions. He also knew that James Hart had been going back and forth on this very issue for six years. As early as 1894, Hart petitioned Johnson for a Western League franchise to use as a "farm" for his team.

Nothing much came of the discussions, and Mr. Hart, acting in the best interests of Spalding, was no longer warm to the idea. "The matter will have to be taken up in conference, Ban. I cannot commit to your proposal at the present time," Brush replied.

John T. Brush was inclined to sanction Comiskey's move into Chicago. There was support among the other owners in his faction: the conservative-minded Boston owner Arthur Soden and Col. John I. Rogers of Philadelphia. Behind the scenes however, Brush had floated a secret offer to Comiskey to return to the National League as a stockholder and officer in the St. Louis Cardinals organization. Things are never what they seem in baseball.

To avert a war, Hart was prodded into supporting Johnson's plan. As long as the American Association threat was still viable, President Hart lent encouragement and gave Comiskey no reason to believe that he would attach conditions or stand in the way of the St. Paul transfer. James Hart didn't approve of any of it, and like the mythic Candide who was forced into choosing between two gruesome methods of death, the sullen National League magnate preferred neither of the alternatives presented him.

Events were moving swiftly now. Ban Johnson convened a summit meeting of his owners at Chicago's Great Northern Hotel on October 11, 1899. Five minutes into the conference, W.F.C. Golt of Indianapolis rose from his chair and entered a formal motion into the record to change the name of the organization to the "American League," to reflect the changing demographics of this previously midwestern confederation. Realignment would soon bring Cleveland, Chicago, and Buffalo into the fold for the 1900 season.

Details of the agreement landing the St. Paul team in Chicago were not made public until after the new year, on February 24. The announcement came a week after the bottom fell out of Anson's American Association. Hopes for a second professional league faded when the Philadelphia promoters refused to post the required $5,000 bond. The usual finger pointing and excuses were offered. "I will not start the Association with such cities as Worcester, Newark, and Rochester!" snapped John McGraw.

More haunting, but strangely familiar echoes across the expanse of time: "As the people in the larger cities would not go to see them, and the attendance of the small towns could not pay as the salaries of the players would be the same in those cities, as in the larger towns."

With the new professional team gone by the boards, James Hart reneged on his guarantees of non-interference with Comiskey. He cited the "protection" afforded by the National Agreement. "Nobody has ever been given the right to establish a club in Chicago under the National Agreement in opposition to the Chicago National League baseball club," he explained. "They cannot enter so-called National Agreement territory without violating that instrument," curiously adding: "I know nothing about Comiskey's plan of placing an American League club on the South Side except what I read in the newspapers."

It was a specious argument and indicative of the levels the League had sunk to in recent years as it continued to foist on the luckless populace its own internecine warfare, syndicate ball, and all-around bad manners. "In their greed for gain and their fear of even healthy competition, they have determined to spring the scheme again," commented the *Chicago Inter-Ocean*.

Hart and Spalding stood alone against the Brush-Freedman clique who refused to block the path of Comiskey. James Hart's opposition was groundless, and Comiskey had little to fear from the National League club, which threatened to buy up the Old Roman's top players under the provision of the National Agreement, whose significance almost seemed to override the slabs of the Ten Commandments, in the view of Hart. For the time being, Brush, Soden, Freedman, and Rogers were in Johnson's corner, and promised to checkmate Hart if he attempted to see through his plan. They still feared the possibility of a hostile Johnson joining forces with the Association, and the resumption of an all-out trade war.

For his part, Johnson was eager to promote good will with the League. He met with Hart and offered private assurances that Comiskey's team would play south of 35th Street, and refrain from using the name "Chicago" in its business dealings and publicity. Johnson had conceded nothing to Hart when all was said and done, because Comiskey intended all along to make his mark on the South Side.

The blueprints for the South Side Grounds were borrowed from the original set of plans drawn up by Cap Anson when *he* was formulating the American Association's incursion into the South Side Chicago realm.

The use of a Chicago moniker sewn across the front of the home team's jersey made little difference to the fans, the owner, or the American League, because Hart said nothing about nicknames, and the White Stocking designate was the most famous of them all. Comiskey's team henceforth, would be called "White Stockings," named after his boyhood heroes who cavorted happily around Dexter Park when baseball was new. Later, when Albert Spalding's team carried the White Stocking banner into the battle during the first years of the League, they turned out more stars, earned vast sums of money, and gained a national reputation that exceeded even that of the Cincinnati club. For reasons known only to Spalding, the White Stocking name was discarded in 1893 in favor of "Orphans," and then after a while, "Roughriders."

"I mean to give the patrons of the game in this city the best team that money can buy," Comiskey proudly announced to the press on March 6. "We will stand or fall on our merits as ballplayers." The gentlemen of the press admired his pluck.

The National League breathed a collective sigh of relief, believing it was free of outside invaders once and for all. Cap

Anson was back in Chicago minding his billiards parlor. The Association was dead, and Ban Johnson was appeased. For his own selfish, mistrustful reasons, James Hart intuitively understood an elemental truth that his fellow syndicate ball magnates failed to grasp. The American League, despite its outward promises, neither respected nor would uphold the sanctity of the National Agreement. War was again at hand.

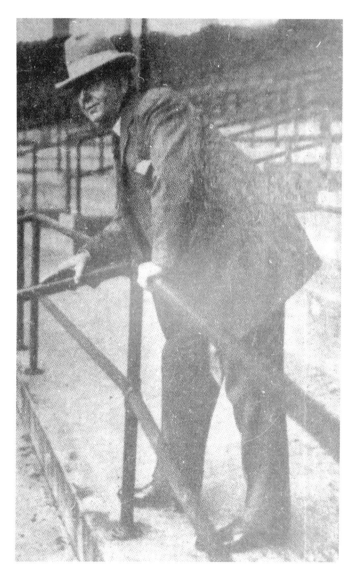

This rare photo shows Charles Comiskey looking out on his new ballpark from an upper deck vantage point, 1910.

44

MONDAY MORNING, OCTOBER 15, 1906.   PRICE TWO CENTS.

WHITE SOX CAPTURE BASEBALL CHAMPIONSHIP OF WORLD BY AGAIN DEFEATING THE CUBS

South Siders' Fourth Victory Won by 8 to 3 Score Before Crowd of Nearly 20,000.

MINER BROWN TO THE BENCH

Comiskey Presents Team With $15,000 Check— Crowd Breaks Down Fences in Order to See Game—Dr. White Holds the Sluggers.

THE CHAMPIONSHIP SERIES.

Score of Final Game—White Sox,
8; Giant Killers, 3.
Games Won and Lost—White Sox,
won 4, lost 2; Giant Killers, won 2,
lost 4
Attendance yesterday...   19,249
Receipts yesterday $26,361
Total attendance (six
· days)   99,845
Total receipts (six
days) $165,246
Players' Share—
Sox (each) $1,138.70
Killers (each) 439.50
Comiskey's present to
Sox 15,000.00
Total for each Sox......   1,920.51
SERIES BATTING AND FIELDING.
Batting.
AB. R. H. SH.SB. Av.
White Sox...186 22 48 5 6 .204
Giant Killers-183 28 37 13 9 .191
Fielding.
PO. A. E. Av.
White Sox.........162 96 16 .944
Giant Killers.....159 81 7 .971

President Charles A. Comiskey of the

DR. WHITE, THE MAN WHO WAS, AND MINER BROWN, THE MAN WHO WASN'T

DR. HARRY WHITE

Chapter
— Four —

The Glories of the Roman Empire

Bitter, bitter winter. The construction crews sat idle. The air was cold, and the grounds were frozen solid. It was a Chicago winter, and not even the cemetery workers could lay the dead to rest until the soil thawed. New Year, 1900 was barely eight days old when the Old Roman's father passed away at the family's west side homestead at 142 Lytle Street. His death was not altogether unexpected; John Comiskey had been ailing for some time. His funeral at the Church of the Holy Family at 12th and May Streets was a showy affair attended by well-wishers from the political and financial world, and the neighborhood. They had come to pay their last respects to a man who looked after their interests at a time when the "Bloody Ninth" Ward was still the Tenth. They remembered Comiskey, the strapping, bearded ward boss, for the many free turkeys he dispensed at Christmas, and the well-paying city jobs that awaited their sons after election day.

In his own inimitable way, Charley attempted to emulate his father with an outward show of affection and concern for the little guy — the "strap hangers," — as the 1890s traction magnate Charles Yerkes condescendingly termed the working people.

Much has been made over the years about the Old Roman's penchant for thriftiness. Modern twentieth century writers and latter day historical revisionists like Eliot Asinof, and film maker

John Sayles have attached contemporary standards to a figure who harkens back to the self-reliant Victorian Age when attitudes toward subordinates were not quite the same as they are today. Comiskey must be viewed within the context of his times, and measured against his peers in order to come up with an accurate historical rendering. Otherwise he emerges as a one-dimensional Dickensesque-villain, and that is unfortunate, as well as misleading.

There is little doubt that he was close with a dollar, but so were the other successful baseball magnates of the day. The profligacy of a Chris Von der Ahe had left an indelible mark on Comiskey and the other owners as to the fate that befalls a spendthrift.

What the historians often overlook is Comiskey's benevolent side. He was one of Chicago's most warmly regarded public figures throughout his lifetime. Commy would frequently reward players down on their luck with cash bonuses, with little or no fanfare coming from the press. He took a chance on players considered over the hill, and provided them with one last crack at fleeting fame. Commy subscribed to the usual Christian charities befitting a man in his position, and would often send food and baseball equipment to the Newsboy's Home. He was a nineteenth-century man in the truest sense of the word, and he had learned much from his father concerning social obligations, altruism, conservative management of a business, and the way a public man ought to conduct himself. And at times he was vain, unforgiving, petty, and occasionally shortsighted. This too, must also be conceded.

This public man endeavored to bring Chicago baseball fans a winner in the spring of 1900, as the inter-league wrangling that characterized the off-season melted away with the advance of the warm weather and opening day. The fans of that era, much like today, were willing to look past the incessant salary squabbles, the jealous owners, and inherent greed of the monopolists provided they could watch baseball.

By any other name, the new American League was still the Western League and subject to the N.L. draft, but even that failed to diminish the spirit shown by the new White Sox in their first year. Without any one big star to lead the way, Manager Comiskey's 1900 misfits were magical. The team was selected from a pool of players cast adrift when the Nationals folded their four weakest teams. Younger players like Roy Patterson, Jack Katoll, and Frank Isbell came down from St. Paul. On paper it didn't look like very much, but once the season was well under way, the White Stockings quickly jelled.

They lost their first game on April 21, while the carpenters were hammering the last nail into the 39th Street Grounds and continued to play sluggishly until mid-June when things began to click for them.

The South Side fans responded enthusiastically to their "hometown" team. Leaving the North and West Side fan base to Hart, Comiskey concentrated his energies on building a sense of "oneness" with the community. He undercut the National League by charging quarter admissions (Hart and Spalding charged the usual league price of 50 cents). And of course, Comiskey was always on hand to meet and greet the fans. Underneath the stands of the tiny wooden park near the Old Roman's office, there stood a bar where the owner held court on game days. With a hearty greeting to all, and a bottomless pitcher of beer, Comiskey's admirers were made to feel like big shots as he listened to their advice. He catalogued their names and occupations in his remarkable memory, and the favored few — the businessmen, the ward bosses, cops, and show people — would analyze baseball strategy with their host until the cover of darkness descended on the park. When it was necessary to adjourn to the neighborhood sample room to continue the discussion, Comiskey paid for the drinks and sat with them — long into the night. The fans were with him, all the way.

The largest crowds of the year turned out on June 18-19 to watch the Sox in a first-place showdown battle with Connie Mack's Milwaukee Brewers. In the stifling 100-degree Chicago heat, Comiskey's team registered a pair of 1-0 shutouts, only to lose a doubleheader the next day. In those heart rending losses, Mack's unknown pitcher, Rube Waddell, twirled 22 masterful innings, besting the Sox 3-2 in 17 innings in the first game, and 1-0 in the darkness-shortened nightcap.

The league pennant was clinched on September 12 when the White Sox crushed Cleveland. Three days later Comiskey was honored by his players and 6,000 applauding onlookers who presented him with a five-foot bat donated by a local sporting goods company. It was appropriate irony in this, his last year as a field manager. The Sox, not so surprisingly, established early precedents by winning big, but finishing dead last in hitting and team offense.

The quality of play, the level of competition, and the enthusiasm of the fans, illustrated to the press that the American League team was a genuine article, and with a shrewd owner it was likely to go far. The first-year success of the White Sox was encouraging to Johnson, Mack, Killilea, and other owners who convened on October 14, 1900 to analyze the season just completed. The five-year National Agreement was scheduled to expire, and Johnson decided that it should not be renewed unless the Brush-Freedmanites made additional concessions and allowed the A.L. to expand into Philadelphia, Baltimore, Washington, and Boston for 1901. A week after this meeting, Johnson received his notice from the National Board to forward the American League's membership fee.

He slipped the notice into his desk and curtly informed the National League that good relations could only be maintained when the American League's eastern expansion was recognized. "I was in Philadelphia at the time," Johnson recalled years later, "Hoping to be summoned by the National Leaguers to whom I wished to explain our stand. They sent back word that I could stay there until hell froze over."

Mulling over these events, the *Chicago Inter-Ocean* scolded the National League: "that gray-headed association of masters of trickery and weird deception . . . is after the dollars first, last, and all the time."

The winter snows brought with them the usual rancorous feelings between the leagues, and fresh rumors of another attempt to bring to life the American Association; the point man this time was editor Frank C. Richter of the *Sporting Life*. It was becoming an annual rite of winter, and the *Inter-Ocean*, expressing the sentiments of many fans who had about enough of the post-season bickering, reported that the National League . . . "is not going to help Frank Richter, nor is it going to waste a shekel if it can help it, in scrapping with Ban Johnson." In other words, every magnate for himself and let the chips fall where they may.

As the century turned, the players had become bolder in their demands for better salaries and working conditions, sensing that the baseball trust was coming apart at the seams. At Comiskey's behest, Clark Griffith, a star hurler for much of the 1890s, travelled to New York to present the demands of his fellow players to the owners.

Griffith was the vice-president of the Player's Protective Association, a toothless union that had preached sedition for much of the 1900 season, but sadly lacked in the resolve to call a strike. Griffith demanded an increase in the maximum wage paid to the upper-echelon players like himself from $2,400 to $3,000 per year. Utility players and rookies were excluded from their protection apparently. "We're going to put it right up to the National League," Griffith explained to Comiskey, "3,000 a year or we strike. If they say no, the National League players will have every right to jump to the Americans and make it a Major League."

Accompanied by three other player representatives, Clark Griffith registered in the Fifth Avenue Hotel, fully expecting to bargain in good faith with Nick Young, the aging National League president. Instead, he was greeted by the hard-line Arthur Soden, now the National League vice-president. Soden accepted their letter of grievance, said he would present it to the owners meeting in an adjoining room, and then pushed the players out the door with well-wishes and kindly words.

Having been given the bum's rush, the players wandered down to the street-level pub to quaff a few beers and talk over the recent developments. As Griffith happened to turn around to signal a waiter, he caught sight of Soden sneaking down the stairwell toward the side entrance of the hotel. Fearing that he might run into the players using the main entrance, Soden had chosen the least conspicuous route. Griffith motioned him over to the table. The red-faced Boston Brave owner mumbled a few indecipherable words before reluctantly agreeing to join them.

"Say Arthur, what do you have in your coat pocket there?" Soden had tucked the players' proposal inside his vest pocket, and the observant Griffith immediately spotted it when he sat down. Soden never intended to present their demands to the league. That was painfully clear.

"Oh, I . . . that's . . . " Before he could spit out a suitable reply, Griffith bolted out of his chair and accused Soden of the double-cross. The White Stocking pitcher stormed out of the room, and raced to the nearest telephone where he called Johnson and Comiskey, who had been waiting in their league office in Chicago for news of the latest developments. "Ban, there's going to be a new major league!" he beamed. "If you can get the financial backing, I can deliver the ballplayers!"

At about this time, the sports-minded shipping magnate Charles W. Somers entered the picture. With Somers bankrolling the operation, there was enough money to float contract offers to 40 top National League stars. After Johnson announced his National League draft, the senior circuit just laughed. Ban Johnson and his stripling league were a joke!

Clark Griffith was sent to the countryside to procure talent. He tramped through several feet of snow in a New York snowstorm in order to ink Fielder Jones of the Brooklyn club to an American League contract. In Carnegie, Pennsylvania, the immortal Honus Wagner, a company player all the way, barricaded himself in the second floor of a pool hall when he heard Griffith was fast approaching. Clark Griffith stood outside in the snow yelling up at the window where he knew Wagner was likely to hide. "Go away you," the Dutchman roared. "If I let you talk to me, I'll jump the Pirates sure!" Wagner was making $2,100 at the time.

The American League had fired the opening shot of what was to become a three-year war to gain acceptance and recognition. The League's tactics in those early weeks were rife with intrigue. "Those were the most trying days of my 34 years in baseball," Johnson recalled. "I or my representatives moved into a city under cover of darkness and out again before daylight. We were watched almost constantly, but seldom did the Nationals' system of espionage prove effective against it." How could it, when one considers the galaxy of stars who jumped to the outlaw American League?

Cy Young, Jake Stahl, Bill Dineen, and Chick Fraser joined without hesitation. The war was lost from the National League side when Nap Lajoie left Col. Rogers' Philadelphia club for Connie Mack's team. Rogers secured a court order restraining Lajoie from playing in Pennsylvania. However, Johnson countered the move by trading him to Cleveland where he went on to star for many years.

Comiskey kept close watch on the caliber of men changing sides. The new league afforded excellent opportunities for reserve players as well, providing they fit the profile and were not outside the baseball color barrier. When John McGraw signed Cliff "Tacks" Lattimer, a Cherokee Indian, to his Baltimore club, Comiskey raised a terrible outcry among the other owners. "This Lattimer is a wild-eyed goat from the jumping flats, and what he will do in the American League will be a fright," Comiskey roared. "I will get a Chinaman of my acquaintance and let him on third! Somebody said this Cherokee of McGraw's is really Charlie Grant, the crack Negro second baseman fixed up with war paint and a bunch of feathers." There had not been a black man playing professional ball since at least 1877, and Comiskey and his fellow magnates made sure that it would remain that way for many decades to come. The anti-monopolists were unanimous in their opinion on the racial issue.

Charles Comiskey struck hard at Spalding, and exacted the revenge he so desperately craved since the break up of the Brotherhood by inducing Griffith, outfielder Sandow Mertes, and pitcher Jimmy Callahan to sign with his ballclub. With Fielder Jones, and catcher Billy Sullivan of the Boston club added to the mix, the Old Roman had four future managers of the ballclub under contract.

Not every National League player was so enamored with Johnson, Comiskey, and company, to the point where they would be willing to risk the possibility of finding their names on a permanent black list one morning. After agreeing in principle to play for Comiskey, two St. Louis Cardinal players, Bobby Wallace and "Snags" Heidrick, jumped back to their original teams, unsure of the American League's chances for long-term success. Comiskey was furious, but there was little he could do. "They say Heidrick has weak legs," the Old Roman retorted, "but I think it is his head that is weak!" The American League was not invulnerable to strong counter measures after all.

The lack of a strong Czar-like ruler to check the ambitions of the American League was never so apparent as now. The Nationals held a trump card, but failed to effectively play it. In their process of self-denial, the N.L. had completely forgotten about the main body of 82 American League holdovers from 1900, who had been signed to contracts running from $900 to $1,200. Players who provided faithful and splendid service the year before found their pay frozen in order for Johnson to reward the 39 "free agents" with boxcar salaries spiraling upward from $2,500 to $6,000 per year. The National League failed to go after these players in counter raids.

Johnson had personally supervised the raids into National League territory for star-caliber talent, but he also looked past the backbone of his own league at the same time. If these underpaid players decided to strike at the eleventh hour, what would Comiskey and Johnson do?

The American League holdovers did nothing to improve their lot, and the new order began inauspiciously on April 24, 1901, when the entire schedule of American League games was washed out by rain storms, save one, the Chicago-Cleveland contest at the 39th Street Grounds. Comiskey's White Stockings, directed by Clark Griffith, inaugurated the second "Major League" with an unremarkable 8-2 win highlighted by seven errors.

Stocked with four blue-chip contract jumpers, the White Stockings (the name was shortened to White Sox in 1902 to accommodate headline space in the newspapers), were uneven favorites to capture the championship. Because Johnson believed that his larger market cities (especially Chicago, where a National League team played) should field reasonably competitive teams, there was some grumbling among the other owners that Johnson was "favoring" Comiskey in league matters. Johnson's offices were, of course, located in the Windy City. The camaraderie between the league president and the owner smacked of cronyism, and now incredibly, the first ominous signs of factionalism surfaced in the new league. The ancient sins of baseball were reprised in a league that seemed to offer the greatest hopes for the long-term salvation of the sport.

Unchecked rowdyism and violence against umpires were nasty characteristics brought over from the National League by the contract jumpers who were unaccustomed to strong disciplinary measures. Johnson had issued strong edicts that his five umpires would be empowered to uphold all rules, and would be supported by the league office. But as the 1901 season progressed, American League games became riotous free-for-alls.

In an August matchup at the 39th Street Grounds, a police detachment escorted umpire Jack Haskell off the field after he called Sandow Mertes out on strikes to end the game and a budding White Sox rally. Two days later, Jack Katoll fired a fastball at Haskell's shins. Then shortstop Frank Shugarts slugged the umpire in the mouth. The red-faced, seething Haskell tore off his face mask and flailed away at Shugarts' head before the police could restore calm and stave off a riot. The two players were led off the field and were booked on assault charges.

While these events unfolded, Johnson and Comiskey were white-water rafting the Flambeau Rapids in Northern Wisconsin. Both men narrowly escaped death when their raft overturned in the middle of the dangerous, churning waters. Comiskey quickly returned to Chicago to attend to the problem while suffering from walking pneumonia. The Comiskey-Johnson alliance drew considerable comment and speculation around the circuit that the A.L. existed for the pleasure of Charley Comiskey and its imperious president, whom many considered to be a camp follower.

Ban Johnson reacted strongly to these insinuations of favoritism and took sterner measures than what the situation warranted by blacklisting Shugarts and suspending Katoll indefinitely. "Let them jump back to the National League if they want!" Johnson exclaimed, in an obvious reference to the umpire-baiting Griffith. "Inexperienced playing managers have made all the trouble this year!"

Comiskey looked past the blacklisting and generally supported Johnson. The A.L. could not sanction brawling, no matter what the circumstances happened to be. But in the next few years, the peevish Johnson seemed to go out of his way to make an example of Comiskey's players. The growing coolness in their personal and professional dealings was underscored by a 1905 incident involving umpire "Silk" O'Laughlin and Sox outfielder James "Ducky" Holmes, who was chased from the dugout for his relentless bench jockeying. After the game was over, Holmes was loitering outside the park when O'Laughlin happened to be leaving. Then a youngster hurled a bottle at the offending umpire, barely missing his head.

Thinking that Holmes was at fault, O'Laughlin warned: "I'll get you for that!" Ducky, a fiery character replied: "I'll be waiting!" The next day, a special courier notified Comiskey of Holmes' three-day suspension. (American League rules required an umpire to submit a written account of such incidents within three days.) Comiskey, already short two outfielders in the midst of a close pennant race with the Philadelphia Athletics, was incensed. "O'Laughlin must have broken into Johnson's home with the report!"

Their public bickering over the years was common knowledge to the sportswriters assigned to cover the team, but the growing coolness between Comiskey and Johnson was kept under wraps by the press. The Holmes affair was just one of many sorry occurrences that strained their close friendship. Comiskey vacated his office at the Fisher Building on May 1, 1906, and moved into the Marquette Building a few blocks away. The American League president immediately refurbished the empty rooms with the polite explanation that Comiskey's adjoining suite was needed for expansion.

The first serious breach in the friendship between the two strong-willed founders resulted from a policy disagreement concerning their strategy toward the rival National League.

American League baseball, despite its obvious shortcomings, proved to be a popular drawing card in cities like Chicago where head-to-head competition sparked fan interest. After the first year of hostilities, the Brush-Freedmanites and the Spalding faction of the National League concluded that the war was being lost. Therefore, they decided that in their own best interests, an independent overture for peace should be attempted.

The slippery Mr. Brush came to Chicago in December 1901 and registered under an assumed name at the Great Northern Hotel, only to be accidentally discovered by James Whitfield, president of the re-organized Western League. The story was leaked to the press that Brush's visit was aimed at an amalgamation of the American League teams with New York, and Cincinnati from his wing. A single ten-team league was proposed, with Cleveland and Baltimore being cut loose and their assets purchased by Brush, who not surprisingly would become a man of some importance in the restructured A.L.

Of course Spalding made essentially the same offer, with *his* teams, but Comiskey was more inclined to deal with Brush. The Old Roman pressed Johnson for immediate adaptation of the Brush plan, hoping to permanently disable the National League. There is little doubt that the A.L. had the power to put the Nationals out of existence. Comiskey strenuously argued for his fellow owners to do so with impunity, but Johnson had lined up the other seven owners who were unanimous in the opinion that the two leagues should work together as nearly as possible to control all interests of baseball. If Freedman's plan were to be adopted, Johnson argued quite convincingly, another rival association would likely spring up in a few short years and claim the abandoned territories.

This was the reply eventually sent to Brush. But when the Pennsylvania courts enjoined Nap Lajoie from playing baseball in their state, the National League withdrew all offers of conciliation from the table, believing that the law was on their side. Had the courts handed down the decision sooner, it is likely that the other A.L. owners would have come around to Comiskey's way of thinking, and the Chicago Cubs and the National League as we know it today would be extinct.

The war would drag on another full year before a formal treaty was signed at the St. Nicholas Hotel in Cincinnati on January 10, 1903. In return for Johnson's promise to refrain from further raids and incursions into National League territory, the A.L. was recognized, the Baltimore team was allowed to transfer to New York City, and nine players whose disputed contracts were tied up in the courts were awarded to the American League owners. A three-man National Commission to carry out the duties of the Napoleon-like figure that baseball so desperately needed was affirmed, and a competitive balance was at long last achieved.

The agreement reflected a curious marriage of monopoly and entrepreneurship, ending 25 years of acrimony between the wealthy owners and players that detracted from the game on the field. With the business of baseball finally relegated to the back rooms and counting houses . . . at last it was time to play ball.

The game embarked upon seven decades of relative calm and prosperity, interrupted only by the short-lived Federal League war of 1914-1915, and the Black Sox Scandal of 1920. But even these events that once again drew sharp attention to the owners' shortsightedness and greed failed to diminish the public's interest and enthusiasm for professional baseball.

* * *

The first decade of the 20th Century was to become the glory years of White Sox baseball. Every day seemed like opening day, and the ill winds of the tempest were far removed.

The White Sox attracted 354,350 paying customers to the tiny confines in 1901, as Comiskey's team carted away a second consecutive American League pennant. For the second year in a row, Commy declined Hart's gracious offer to play a "city series." The American League believed it had nothing more to prove after luring almost 150,000 more fans to its gates than Mr. Hart's team. The newspapers had ceased calling the National League ball club the "Orphans," preferring the moniker "Remnants." If not for Ban Johnson's desire for reconciliation between the leagues, they would not have even been that.

Relying on instinct and a belief that no ballplayer should be paid more than he was worth, Comiskey proved to be a shrewd judge of talent and a most capable money manager who knew how to deliver more bang for his buck. "Just because a Babe Ruth makes a big salary, it doesn't mean a two-dollar busher should," he liked to say.

Star performers such as pitchers Nick Altrock, Guy "Doc" White, and Frank Owen, were signed to contracts after having only limited success in other organizations. With the White Sox, they developed into pitching mainstays who turned the fortunes of the franchise around following disappointing campaigns in 1902-1903.

With his close personal contacts to minor league executives Joseph Cantillon, Clarence Rowland, Tom Loftus, and Ted Sullivan, Comiskey was often tipped off in advance about the availability of top-drawer prospects. Later, when his playing days were through, Frank Isbell, a mainstay at second base for nearly 10 White Sox seasons, would assume this role for Comiskey out in Iowa. That is how winning ballclubs were assembled in the old days.

Comiskey reeled in the biggest prize of them all in 1904 when pitcher Ed Walsh was invited to the spring camp in Marlin Springs, Texas. Ed Walsh had toured Wilkes Barre, Newark, and Meridian with little success. His lack of physical conditioning, and an exaggerated pitching windup that allowed opposing players to run the bases at will made this big Irishman from the Pennsylvania coal fields an amusing, if not eccentric, sight to behold. What saved Walsh from oblivion was his mastery of the spit ball, or "eel ball" as it was then known.

Walsh was to become a three-time 20-game winner. Twice in his career he won both ends of a doubleheader. In the glorious summer of 1908, Big Ed was credited with 40 wins (however, closer scrutiny of the day-to-day box scores of that year reveal the win total to be "only" 36). It was an awe-inspiring performance that endeared him to the legions of South Side Irish who pulled for the Sox. Walsh, despite his yearly contract differences with Comiskey—he held out for $7,500 in the spring of 1909, and his uncertain status with the team made for interesting gossip in the sporting pages—was a crowd pleaser and a figure larger than life to the neighborhood boys. In attendance the day that Walsh twirled the only nine-inning no hitter of his career, was a 7-year-old Washington Park waif who paid his carfare at the 51st Street Station to see the Hose of White battle the "Sox of Red." Years later, author and social critic James T. Farrell would recall in his *Baseball Diary* that afternoon of August 27, 1911, when Big Ed no-hit Boston. "God was helping Ed Walsh. Oh, you Ed Walsh! God wouldn't let him hit Ed Walsh now!"

The White Sox were woven into the day-to-day lives of the "steam heat" Irish of these South Side enclaves; Irish who attended their parish, dreamed of a better life for their offspring, and nervously eyed the changing demographics of the neighborhoods. More than anything they subsisted on fear. Fear of the blacks who were arriving from the Jim Crow south in search of the very things the Potato Famine forebears came to this city for in the previous century. Fear of inevitable change. Fear of the world outside their "fron troom" curtains. Farrell's poolroom hustlers and street corner loungers whom he knew so intimately from the neighborhood imagined themselves playing with "da Sox," ". . . with Walsh." But dreams sometimes turn bitter as the novelist Farrell reminds us in his grim, but masterful *Studs Lonigan* trilogy.

"Say Slug, didn't you have a tryout with the Sox?" asked Fitz. "Long time ago when they had Ed Walsh. Nineteen eleven or twelve. But I was suppose to be there at twelve, and for three days Goddam it, I couldn't wake myself up," Slug said.

* * *

By nature, the fans of Chicago's National League ballclub (Cubs, as they began to be called around 1905), were more aloof and less prone to histrionics than the White Sox rooters. In 1906, a year unlike any other for Chicago sports fans, Comiskey was forced to abandon soda pop sales because the empty glass bottles passed to the fans proved to be effective missiles when aimed at opposing players and umpires.

"The pikers who crowd into the first base bleachers and bet nickels or hurl bottles at them when they lose are responsible for the reputation Chicago has of being the toughest town in either Major League circuit." — *Chicago Tribune*, May 1, 1906.

The boisterous South Sider viewed his team as an extension of his neighborhood, his church parish, indeed, his own identity. And in 1906, the grandest year of them all, Comiskey brought pride to a section of town maligned for its politics, its rough characters, and tolerance of blue-collar vices such as saloon drinking.

Fielder Allison Jones had taken the managerial reins of the White Sox from Jimmy Callahan midway through the '04 season. Next to Ty Cobb, Jones was the most ferocious umpire baiter of the age. His fiery tirades with the arbiters of the game did not go unnoticed by the Chicago fans who appreciated his hell-bent-for-leather style of play, or the league president who banished him one day after he had kicked an umpire. Comiskey protested to Ban Johnson, who just smiled. . . . and sent the Old Roman a fresh catch of fish the next day for his troubles. "What does Johnson want me to do? Play the fish in left field?"

Jones elevated the Sox tempo of play. He taught his men to exploit an opponent's every weakness, the intricacies of the motion infield, which he pioneered, and the "body twist slide," another Jones innovation. He was without question the greatest field manager in team history, those five-and-a-half years he spent at the helm.

He demonstrated this genius by guiding a dissension-ridden, injury-plagued band of "Hitless Wonders" to a surprise pennant in 1906. As late as August 1, the Sox were mired in fourth place, trailing the pack by nine games. As the summer progressed, it appeared as if the Cubs had recaptured the public's fancy. James Hart's inept regime had ended, and the West Siders had rebuilt nicely under the capable direction of Charles W. Murphy. The 1906 edition was destined to win 116 games, still a Major League record.

By comparison, the weak-hitting White Sox batted a miserable .230, good for last place in the A.L. Jones had a poorly defined outfield, a muddled catching situation once Billy Sullivan was hospitalized for food poisoning, and a good luck charm in one Hiram "the Bear" Connibear, the University of Chicago physical conditioning expert who was hired by Comiskey to restore the health of the troops and steer the boys away from the bottle. He remained with the team long enough to launch them on an improbable 19-game winning streak that ended in Washington on August 25. Ban Johnson was in attendance, and as might be expected, he cheered lustily for the Senators.

It was during this time that the fans picked up on the "Hitless Wonder" designation—a newspaper invention probably coined by either Charles Dryden of the *Tribune* whose story of July 14 proclaimed: "Hitless Wonders Rally and Turn An Apparent New York Victory Into Defeat," or Hughie Fullerton, who also witnessed the White Sox saga unfold from the earliest days in Chicago right up through the bitter post-scandal years. Commenting in his *Tribune* game story of August 21, Fullerton noted that: "it is a wonder how they score so many runs on so few hits."

All eyes were on the Windy City that fall as the Cub juggernaut engaged the underdogs in the first (and last) cross-town World Series. It was war to the finish, only this time the battlefield was not a hotel room pitting one group of conniving magnates against another, but the playing fields and grandstands of two great rival teams.

The crush for tickets was on. Many unlucky fans unable to purchase seats were forced to do the next best thing; watch the plays as they were presented on a metallic board at the Auditorium Theatre and the First Regiment armory. A special telegraph transmitted the plays to a receiver standing by at each site.

Fielder Jones, concerned that the Chicago "Goliaths" had it all over his "Davids" at least on paper, tried to calm the jangled nerves of his players—and the owner who suffered through two sleepless nights during the World Series. "I figured that if our team lost its nerve, all would be lost," Jones told the *Saturday Evening Post* in the off-season.

The White Sox collected their wits and played with precision throughout the six-game series. Unheralded subs such as third baseman George Rohe, and the everyday heroes, Doc White, Ed Walsh, Frank Isbell, and Nick Altrock led the way. In the climactic final game, played at the 39th St. Grounds on October 14, swarms of fans scaled the nearby telegraph poles for a birds-eye view of the proceedings. Others tore their pants climbing the steeple of old St. George to witness Doc White shut down Frank Chance's Cubs by an 8-3 count.

The winning team's clubhouse was in bedlam. Souvenir-hunting fans pushed their way past the police officers and into the dressing room. They seized equipment, furnishings, even the discarded socks. Businessmen clipped the buttons off the players' jerseys with pocket knives. It was impossible for the Jonesmen to refuse the fans anything.

Eight hundred messages of congratulations poured in over the telegraph and cable lines. The White Sox surprise victory established this yearly post-season World Series as something unique within the lexicon of professional sports. Even today, no other championship round has a greater aura or mystique.

It was Charley Comiskey's moment of vindication. Shaken, and barely able to fight off the tears, the Old Roman summoned his manager to the team office. The crowds had at last departed the grounds for their local tap where the celebrations would continue.

"See here Jones," he stammered. "Come into the office, I want to give the boys a check." Commy's hand was trembling as he dipped the pen into the inkwell. He looked up at Jones. "I'm all in with the strain. You write it," he said.

The manager nervously attached the owner's name to the $15,000 bonus check. As he prepared to exit the office, Comiskey placed his beefy hand on Fielder's shoulder. "I am pleased with you for twice the amount of this check!"

* * *

In the spring, long after the novelty of the World Series triumph had worn off, the Old Roman reconsidered his surprising show of generosity. The 1907 contracts were in the mail minus a pay increase for most, if not all of the players. Comiskey had taken into account the $15,000 check and concluded the men would have to make due with their bonus. Anything over and above that would be foolish extravagance.

* * *

Fielder Jones on his status as player manager in 1906: *"I am practically a slave. So is every baseball player in the thirty-one leagues under the National Agreement. We are 'human chattels' in the sense that we cannot sell our ability—the only asset on which we can realize contracts of a satisfactory nature—in any market to which we must play ball within the pale of organized baseball or be listed as black sheep. The quotations on black sheep in the baseball world are very low—they are not at all attractive."*

Ed Walsh, the "Big Reel," was a pitching mainstay for the Sox in the early 1900s. In 1908 Walsh pitched a still-record 464 innings on his way to the last 40-win season in the Major Leagues. A few years after his playing career ended in 1917, he returned to the White Sox as a coach for most of the 1920s.

White Sox Rooters Association

WOODLAND BANQUET: MERCER, WIS.

WE CHATTER, CHATTER AS WE ROW
FROM BROOK TO LAKE TO RIVER
FOR MEN MAY COME AND MEN MAY GO
BUT WE GO ON FOREVER

THURSDAY, OCTOBER TWENTY-FOUR
NINETEEN HUNDRED AND SEVEN

Chapter
— Five —

When White Sox Fans Were Rooters

With a daring blend of rough-and-tumble no-holds-barred brand of baseball, the 1906 Hitless Wonder White Sox captured the imagination of the South Side sports fans. While it was true that the Cubs were performing a few miracles of their own on the West Side, Fielder Jones' scrappy, hustling ballclub endeared themselves to a large segment of the Bridgeport Irish community who identified with the sons of Eire' playing for Comiskey: rough-and-ready lads like Billy Sullivan, the scrap-iron backstop who patented the first air-compressed chest protector in 1909; the "Big Reel" Ed Walsh who came up from the Pennsylvania coal mines to become the preeminent spitball pitcher of the day; and Jimmy Callahan, the undisciplined prodigal son who managed the White Sox in two eras.

Comiskey made no apologies. Irish players populated the roster in the early years as he played to the sentiments of the neighborhood residents who revered the athletes as role models as much as the priests from nearby St. George's parish. Unlike the Chicago Cubs who changed ownership four times between 1898 and 1920, Charles Comiskey (the "Noblest Roman," or "Old Roman" because of his strong gladiatorial posturing), became one of the city's best known and revered sports figures. His decision to move the club to Chicago from St. Paul was a triumph against impossible odds.

The charisma, cunning, and personal magnitude of the Old Roman won many converts from the North and West Sides, especially after he embarrassed and humiliated the Cubs by stealing their original White Stocking nickname and signing their star-caliber players such as Clark Griffith and Jimmy Callahan to contracts.

In many ways, Charles Comiskey was a far more popular figure in his day than the flamboyant Bill Veeck 60 years later. For years, "Commy" was eulogized as a wise and benevolent owner, possessing humanity, style, and a crisp sense of humor. These opinions held up until the early 1960s when novelist Eliot Asinof and fellow historical revisionists isolated Comiskey's handling of the 1919 Black Sox Scandal as the only true and accurate reflection of his overall character.

Charles Comiskey owed his popularity to his skill in cultivating wealthy, powerful friends, and manipulating the press in ways that worked to his advantage. The Old Roman, like Veeck, understood that the loyalties of the media could be bought cheaply, much like the beer nuts and scorecards sold by the strolling vendors at the 39th Street Grounds.

Baseball writers for the major daily newspapers lived out of a suitcase and were rarely able to afford the amenities enjoyed by the athletes they were paid to cover. Unless they pontificated in a daily column like Ring Lardner's "Wake of the News" in the *Chicago Tribune*, the anonymous scribes of the Dead Ball era stayed in third-rate hotels and often toiled without a by-line. When rich and powerful sports magnate Charles Comiskey tipped his hat to the boys and provided sumptuous assortments of smoked salmon and fine wines as the White Sox train winged its way through the spring training camps or other American League cities, it was greatly appreciated.

By the same token, Comiskey lavished the same accommodations on the wealthy business merchants, captains of industry and politics, and the vaudeville entertainers invited through the portals of his South Side park.

Several years before Comiskey opened his "Baseball Palace of the World" on 35th Street, two of these well-heeled patrons drew considerable attention to themselves and the owner they ardently admired by whipping their fellow "cranks" (or fans), into a maddening cheering frenzy for the hometown team.

The two young men, one an established criminal lawyer who was the real-life inspiration for the fictional Charles Mallard (the "Beauty Steele") in Sir Gilbert Parker's best-selling turn-of-the-century novel *The Right of Way*; the other an ambitious song promoter and publicist who wrote the words and lyrics to 261 sentimental ballads familiar to the denizens of New York's "Gay White Way." The lawyer, Robert Emmet Cantwell, had little in common with the song huckster, Joseph Chesterfield Farrell, except their mutual respect and admiration for C.A. Comiskey.

Cantwell was a died-in-the-wool Chicagoan who was equally comfortable with the Prairie Avenue swells and the First Ward riff-raff he occasionally defended in criminal cases. He was a born actor and dazzling orator, but he had shunned the stage as inferior to the real-life drama of the courtroom. There he could write his own script.

Farrell was a celebrity in his own right, and was plugging the song *In the Good Ole' Summertime* when he made the acquaintance of Comiskey in the summer of 1903 through John McGraw. In July 1907, these two brilliant lights conceived the notion of organizing the boisterous grandstand fans into a cheering club, and thus was born the White Sox Rooter's Association.

Chartered on September 7 of that same year, Farrell was elected President, and Cantwell was designated to serve as Vice President and legal counsel. At first, Comiskey looked on with benign amusement at the doings in the grandstand, but when the little group enticed the *Chicago American,* flagship newspaper of the Hearst chain in the Midwest, to become the official news organ of the Rooter's Association, Comiskey realized he might be on to something here.

The *American* accepted its role, and much to the chagrin of the Cubs, faithfully promoted the antics of the Association. Such literary lions of the media as James Crusinberry and William Veeck Sr. (writing under the pen name of Bill Bailey), devoted valuable column space to the club. Comiskey reaped a gold mine in free advertising and publicity.

Each day the paper reprinted the words of Farrell's original fight songs that were handed out to ball fans on 3 x 7 index cards as they entered the grounds. The most popular ditty of the era was no doubt *Sullivan*, sung to the lyrics of George M. Cohan's *Harrigan*, a mainstay of the Broadway musicals of the era. It is

equally probable that the great George M. and Cantwell com-
posed the parody together during one of Cohan's visits to the
Chicago homestead of Thomas Cantwell (Bob's father), West
Town Assessor. Thomas Cantwell loved to tap dance with Cohan
on two marble slabs installed for his pleasure in the family parlor.

> *Sullivan*
> S-U-Double-L-I-V-A-N spells Sullivan
> Proud of all the Irish blood that's in him
> Divil's the man can steal a base agin' him -
> S-U-Double-L-I-V-A-N you see,
> It's a name that shame never
> Has been connected with;
> *Sullivan - that's he!*

Fans paid a dollar apiece to join the club. Portions of this
money were spent on monogrammed club sweaters, hats, and a
graphophone that Comiskey installed in the grandstand in back
of home plate to torment and annoy visiting players and managers. The night before Hughie Jennings and the Detroit Tigers
were scheduled to make their final 1907 appearance at 39th
Street, Cantwell, the silver-tongued orator, recorded a series of
cat calls and Bronx cheers on a disc. The graphophone was
cranked to its full capacity, and the off-key lyrics echoed through
the wooden stands.

> Tune: *When Johnny Comes Marching Home*
> The Sox'll start to climb in earnest now,
> EE-Yah! EE-Yah!
> And bury poor Jennings the human cow
> EE-Yah! EE-Yah!
> Oh Hughie is eating our grass so fast
> The way he is chewing it never will last
> But he'll never take the pennant off Charley Comiskey's mast
> *EE-Yah! EE-Yah!*

A different recording was made for each visiting American
League team. Just before Clark Griffith's Highlanders arrived in
town for a crucial series in the closing days of the 1907 season, the
American purchased ten $300 genuine Indian tom-toms for the

Rooters. The noise level was so distracting for Griffith's pitchers that he filed a formal protest to the league charging that the game was no longer being played on its merits. He demanded Johnson order the Rooters off the grounds for future games scheduled with New York.

The churlish Johnson advised the Rooters to "cut out a lot of rough noise," and exhibit gentlemanly conduct during the 1908 season. Tensions were already strained between the two league founders, and Ban's opinions on the Rooters only exasperated the situation. "I sell tickets!" Comiskey snapped. "I cannot be held responsible for the occupants of a box as long as they do not violate the laws!" Slamming his walking stick to the ground, Bob Cantwell vowed to keep on rooting by "means of an injunction" if necessary.

The league president reserved judgment on the matter until the following spring, at which time Cantwell, his wife, and three sons and several hundred rooters accompanied the White Sox to their training camp in Los Angeles. (The privately chartered White Sox train, stocked with free food and beverages for the press corps and camp followers was a continuing irritation to the players who were required to play a string of exhibition games in dozens of whistle-stop towns along the westward route. Despite the grumbling, the Spring Training express remained a yearly Comiskey tradition through the Depression years.)

The Rooters created quite a stir by their presence on the West Coast. They were viewed with curiosity and small measures of disdain by fans and the local press. One Los Angeles writer noted: "aside from Joe Farrell and Bob Cantwell, both of Chicago, no one showed any class."

In Los Angeles, Comiskey would lend encouragement to the local minor league team - he had the best interests of the game at heart - while Bob Cantwell held a clinic for the Angel fans as to the proper ways of cheering. The famed criminal attorney penned these recollections of the California junket:

> "When the Sox played the Los Angeles Angels, a minor league team, Comiskey played the role of genial host, the mentor, the baseball Zeus smiling down from his throne on the World Championship Olympus to encourage minor league development. When we went to Los Angeles, he'd go over to the Angel dugout halfway through the game so as not to

overwhelm the locals, to cheer them on against the demigods of his own aggregation. He always praised the White Sox as the greatest gang of players ever put together, and when he changed seats and apparent 'loyalties' during California games, his White Sox players understood this as noblesse oblige, although they couldn't have pronounced or defined it. The ballplayers knew their loyal owner could never be disloyal to them, and they honored him for encouraging the California home team. Charley got me to do it. I took all my jingles, parodies, cheers, and chants to Los Angeles to help organize the new Angel Rooters Association there. I showed them our White Sox printed programs, special hats, token white stockings, banners, mega-phones, and adapted White Sox songs to their local players' names."

* * *

During a time when the other owners did little in the way of promotional advertising and the game was sold to the public on its merits, Comiskey shrewdly encouraged Cantwell and Farrell to enlist the support of their influential downtown friends. The owner reciprocated the favor by doling out free passes to the honorary members of the club, among them Mayor Fred Busse, Police Chief George Shippy, Fire Marshal James Horan, and other public figures from city government, entertainment, and commerce.

The inner circle of Rooters—Cantwell, Farrell, building con-tractor John "Admiral" Agnew (one of the Comiskey Park build-ers); Edward Heeman and James McClean from the Board of Trade; State Senator Edward Redpath; restaurateur Johnny Burns; "Tip" O'Neill, a Western League official; and Alderman James Considine of the 29th Ward—became Comiskey's preferred traveling companions during what became a yearly fall expedi-tion to the wilds of northern Wisconsin.

Comiskey, a vain and proud man, enjoyed the fawning attention of these successful public figures who had constructed a hunting lodge at their own expense in a patch of woods outside Mercer, Wisconsin in 1907. The Home Plate, or Camp Jerome, as it was affectionately known, was the Rooters' clubhouse, built on 600 acres of fenced-in property that the Old Roman had acquired in 1903. Comiskey stocked the woods with 300 head of deer, a buffalo, a herd of elk, and the Camp Jerome mascot, "Big Bill" the moose.

Friends of the White Sox owner deified him in verse and song as the campers paddled happily up and down the Wisconsin streams in search of the elusive trout—or as Cantwell aptly put it—"the baseball bat as fishing rod."

"We chatter, chatter as we row—from brook to lake to river for men may come and men may go, but we go on forever."

At sunset the Rooters would gather around a roaring campfire to recite Shakespearian verse and the latest doggerel to spring forth from the nimble mind of Joe Farrell. Members unable to compose their own nonsensical rhyme, were court martialed (in good fun) or victimized by practical jokes.

Their love of good wine, impromptu light verse, and fresh venison roasted in these lush surroundings convinced Farrell and Comiskey sometime around 1912 to change the name of the organization to the more colloquial "Woodland Bards." Comiskey's private dining room forever became known as the "Bards' Room."

These were some happy carefree days on the South Side—the fading ember of the Victorian Age when men sought acceptance amongst their peers in the private club room and rugged outdoors. The quality of a man was often measured by the company he kept in the fraternal societies and prestigious private clubs listed in the social registers of the day. And as time passed, membership in the Woodland Bards was regarded as a symbol of attainment in the Chicago sporting world.

* * *

Whether it was the opening of the Three-Eye League in Dubuque in April, the annual Woodland Banquet in autumn, a small informal gathering of the old-timers at Quincy Number Nine, or Johnny Burns' bar and grill room, the Bardsmen packed the house to ensure that the loudest cheers were reserved for the Old Roman, their generous benefactor.

"Comiskey's generosity, generalship, friendship, and organization of a baseball club was unrivaled and marked the true greatness of the man." Cantwell's opinions of Comiskey came from the heart, and were universally held among his contemporaries of that era. These attitudes, of course, greatly contrast the interpretations of the latter-day historians.

At Tom Jones' barroom one night, Cantwell, Farrell, and Heeman touted Comiskey for mayor of Chicago, while Fred Busse, the Republican incumbent squirmed nervously in his chair.

"Commy there is no better/than you in this broad land/You're true blue to the letter/and all say that you are grand/Your friends they all follow you/that the whole world knows/As a man and a sportsman you are there/And some day you'll be Chicago's mayor/Commy, where art thou going?"

* * *

Wealthy, powerful men controlled the destiny of the Rooters' Association now commonly known as the Woodland Bards. The banquets and testimonials; the sale of megaphones, Sox rooting vests, and a lemonade concession at the ballpark helped foot the bills of the Association. It was inevitable that sooner or later a schism would develop among the self-appointed exponents of organized cheering.

The rift developed during the spring aldermanic campaign of 1908 when Jim Considine was scheduled to stand for re-election. Cantwell was a good friend of Considine, but fellow rooter Tim Gleason opposed his retention. Considine was defeated for alderman, and vicious rumors circulated that Gleason had diverted a portion of $2,000 in Rooter money from the proceeds at a recent ball to finance and win his opponent's campaign. In customary fashion, Cantwell threatened a court action to investigate the disposition of funds.

The charges were flying thick and fast as Cantwell and Farrell suddenly found themselves at loggerheads. "I furnished the brains, and Joe Farrell and Tim Gleason get most of the limelight!" Cantwell complained. On April 28, the finance committee exonerated Gleason of misdoings. The two men shook hands at Burns' restaurant and re-affirmed their commitment to rooting the Sox to the championship in 1909. The *Tribune*, however, cautioned the public to beware. "The lesson to the fan is to keep his hands in his pocket the next time he contributes for music and festivities which Comiskey is well able and willing to pay for himself."

Gradually Bob Cantwell distanced himself from the Rooters' Association. Problems continued in September 1908 when Cantwell vaulted a railing and raced on the field to slug a Boston umpire who ruled against the White Sox on a close play. Ban Johnson seized the opportunity and barred him from future American League ballgames. Cantwell appealed his assault conviction all the way to the Illinois Supreme Court, but the man who was so successful in winning not guilty verdicts for others could not gain a reprieve for himself.

This noted barrister continued a distinguished career at the bar and is remembered today as an early and strident foe of the unconstitutional extortion of confessions from criminal suspects by police in the notorious third-degree sweat box.

Joe Farrell, a tall, striking man with a resonant baritone voice, continued to provide the direction and leadership as the first and only president of the Woodland Bards. With the passing of the years the Bards abandoned the zany stunts and organized cheering sections that formed the original premise of the old Rooters' Association. No longer would Farrell and company challenge the West Side Cub Rooters to a long-distance walking marathon to Milwaukee to settle city bragging rights as they had in the innocent days of 1907. The members had become far too respectable for such nonsense.

The Woodland Bards of 1913-1914—the year Comiskey sponsored a baseball goodwill tour to introduce baseball to the four corners of the world—were older, wealthier, and more conservative in their thinking. The revelry was transferred from the grandstands of Comiskey Park to private dining rooms. There Farrell saluted his host in the Bards Room social club, which was adorned with the head of fallen deer and elk, along with souvenirs of happy, unforgettable hunting expeditions to Camp Jerome. Here in this masculine setting, the Bards sipped their sherry and smoked imported Cuban cigars with the owner, while the wives and lady friends socialized in the women's annex just down the hall. No doubt the Bardsmen considered themselves a logical extension of Comiskey's front office, even if the owner didn't see it in quite those same terms.

Joe Farrell's fondest memories of that period centered around the world tour he orchestrated with Ted Sullivan, Tip O'Neill and Ed Heeman. A baseball goodwill expedition had been on

Comiskey's mind for many years. He hoped to duplicate the success of Albert Spalding's 1888 journey, thereby carving a niche for himself alongside the names of the early pioneers of the game.

Financing such an enormous undertaking as this required substantial capital. But the Old Roman connived for John McGraw to put up large sums of money to bring his New York Giants along on the tour to play exhibition games against the Sox. McGraw's contributions were augmented by monies supplied by Heeman and his fellow Board of Trade men, who spent much of the trans-oceanic voyage playing games of chance in the stately club rooms below deck.

The five-month odyssey began in Seattle on November 19, 1913. The highlight was a command performance before His Majesty, King George V of England. Joe Farrell, who had earlier rescued Jim Thorpe during a bar-room altercation with some local toughs in Australia, was deputized to explain the finer points of baseball to the King, who was accustomed to the sport of cricket. His Majesty and the self-styled "bard" of Mercer, Wisconsin, sat together through an 11-inning game played in London's Wembley Stadium. The Sox bested McGraw's Giants 5-4.

The sojourning Sox returned home on board the *Lusitania* on March 6, 1914. After fending off a delegation of Federal League executives who stood dock side in New York harbor hoping to convince Comiskey and McGraw's star players to "jump" their contracts, the Old Roman and company returned to more pleasant surroundings in Chicago where the conquering heroes were greeted by 2,000 applauding fans at the LaSalle Street train station. The deafening cheers from his loyalists brought tears to Comiskey's eyes.

Assisted by two walking canes, the pale and sickly Sox owner, weakened by the rigorous journey, looked out on the throng and said, quite simply, "It was a good trip." The next night, the Bards staged a mammoth banquet in the grand ball-room of the Congress Hotel. In attendance were men and women from the social ranks; members of the judiciary, the clergy, business and industry, and the weary ballplayers about to begin another spring training. Charles Comiskey, the grandest Roman, had reached yet another pinnacle of his baseball career. Ahead lay the years of disgrace, the Black Sox Scandal.

* * *

The Woodland Bards hung together through World War I. They cheered the pennant-winning Sox in 1917, and again in 1919 when they won their fourth American League pennant. On the eve of the ill-fated '19 World Series, 240 of their most staunch supporters chartered a special train to Cincinnati for the opening game on October 1, only to find that the hotels around town were all booked. The Bards were provided emergency accommodations in a downtown hotel: beds were set up in the corridors. To a Chicago reporter, the arrangement smacked of a hospital ward, "which would not be an unfit spot for a few at that," he commented.

As the mood in the city that crisp fall afternoon was electric, the Bards proudly strutted into Redland Field sporting their prized numbered badges signifying membership in the club. The partisan Cincinnati fans jeered them, but to a man, the Bards remained supremely confident that the "greatest team of them all" would again prevail. By the fifth inning, their swagger and confidence had disappeared. The Redlegs turned the game into a Cincinnati rout. Returning to the Havlin Hotel, the Bards settled their wages with the oily gamblers who were deployed across the city looking for men such as these; men with the financial means to wager large sums of money. The disastrous outcome of Game I was enough to make a "Woodland Bard walk in his sleep," wrote George Phair, covering the game for the *Chicago Herald and Examiner*.

The Bards expected the White Sox to rebound in Game II, and their hopes were buoyed by the unexpected visit of an old friend, George M. Cohan, who had arrived from the East Coast to cheer on his favorite team. Cohan was anointed an honorary Bard during the 1917 World Series. He was cheered lustily by the Chicago delegation who broke into a beery rendition of *Sidewalks of New York*.

Did these loyal fans begin to suspect the fix was on? What could they have possibly been thinking as they helplessly watched Ed Cicotte serve up one fat, tantalizing pitch after another to the Redleg hitters? The answer was supplied on October 7, when the White Sox chugged out of the train station for a return engagement to the Queen City for Game VII. The mood in the club car was subdued. At Comiskey's side was his faithful retainer Joe Farrell and two other Bardsmen: Fire Battalion Chief Pecko Rogers and Pepper Hayes, the "sheriff" of Camp Jerome. The other 235 members, who had accepted less than their usual accommodations at the Havlin Hotel for the opening game stayed away, either by choice or design.

* * *

The Woodland Bards club certainly did not disband because of the Black Sox Scandal, but the spirit, fellowship, and good feelings of those early formative years evaporated when the revelations of wrongdoing surfaced in September 1920.

The Old Roman's wife passed away in 1922. His slowly deteriorating health, personal sorrow, and advancing age caused Comiskey to turn away from his friends and the companionship of the hearty fellows he once knew.

Joseph Farrell remained president of the Bards, or what was left of them, until 1926 when he accepted an invitation from Major Frederic McLaughlin and William Tobin to supervise public relations for the Chicago Blackhawks hockey team, recently transplanted from Portland. For the next 27 years, Farrell did his tub-thumping for the West Side hockey club. He wrote the words and lyrics to the famous Chicago Stadium fight song *Here Come the Hawks!*, which is still popular among hockey fans to this day. Farrell was unique: one of the best P.R. men in the sports business.

By the mid-1920s many of the older Bardsmen had passed on. Edward Gerhard Heeman died in 1924. Agnew was gone in 1922. When the enigmatic Cantwell expired in 1947, the *Chicago Daily News* had completely forgotten that he was once connected with the Woodland Bards. By then the Bards were an anachronism of a tired, forgotten age.

The 1917 World Champion Chicago White Sox.

CHARLES A. COMISKEY
"The Old Roman"

SEVENTEENTH ANNUAL

HUNTING AND FISHING TRIP

Charles A. Comiskey
AND PARTY

Jerome Fishing and Hunting Club
Trude Lake, Wis.

Leaving Chicago 6.00 p. m.
Wednesday, Oct. 11, 1916, via
CHICAGO & NORTH WESTERN
RAILWAY

MENU

DINNER

Blue Points on Half Shell

Celery   Olives   Salted Pecans

Clear Green Turtle, Amontillado

Individual Planked Jumbo Whitefish

Broiled Fresh Mushrooms

Broiled Butter Ball Duck

Currant Jelly

Lalla Rook Punch

Potatoes au Gratin   Baked Hubbard Squash

Prime Roast Beef

Grilled Sweet Potatoes   White Asparagus

Hearts of Head Lettuce Salad

Peach Tart

Caramel Ice Cream   Fruit Cake

Roquefort Cheese
Toasted Crackers

Coffee

Mullens Beer   Lanzon Cigars

Shortly after opening the Baseball Palace of the World in 1910, Comiskey brought in his only son, Lou (above) and Harry Grabiner (below) to help guide the Sox organization. Lou served as Sox president from 1931 until his death in 1939 and Grabiner devoted 44 of his 57 years to the Sox.

George Brace

Chapter
— Six —

Baseball Palace of
the World

"Ever notice the man who plays a second fiddle in the orchestra? What does he amount to? He is a little bald-headed galoot who makes the same motions for 25 years." — Fielder Jones, 1907

* * *

The restless and discontented White Sox manager led his unhappy troop of ballplayers into the Mexican interior for their Spring 1907 training sessions. Charley Comiskey had blazed a new trail as he helped introduce the American national game to the residents south of the border. The Mexicans, however, did not fancy baseball with their avidity of later years — bull fighting was still the preferred pastime. In fact, nobody in Mexico really paid much attention to Comiskey, whose singular ambition was to internationalize baseball. Comiskey was not to be outdone by his arch enemy Albert Spalding, who arranged baseball's first international goodwill tour back in 1888.

"Where is this Mexico?" inquired one of the grumbling athletes as the White Sox Express steamed out of the Polk Street Station in Chicago. Hugh Keogh, the press sage who hosted the "Wake of the News" column in the *Tribune* replied in verse:

"Its where the condor spreads its wings
The hot tamale rears its crest

The banderillio spares the quails—
And Senoritas do the rest!"

* * *

Individual accolades and international acclaim were less important to Fielder than the financial rewards coming from baseball. The Hitless Wonder era under Jones ingloriously ended when the pennant slipped away on the final day of the 1908 season and with it went the talented White Sox manager.

Fielder Jones, whose $10,000 income was the highest yearly salary paid to any one individual in Comiskey's employ up to that time, decided that money was far easier to come by in Portland, Oregon's forestry industry than toiling in the Old Roman's shadow. Jones' departure puzzled Comiskey, who believed that no player, however inconvenienced by salary differences with an owner, could simply walk away from the game —his life's calling. But Jones did exactly that. "My desire is to quit the game," he said. "Of course I should feel obliged to play if Comiskey meets my figures. I know he won't, and I'll be glad for it."

Jones was alluding to a significant front-office role for himself and a full partnership with Comiskey. The Old Roman, of course, had no partners, nor would he entertain any offers to that effect. Comiskey had amassed a minor fortune and joined Chicago's nouveau riche who recreated at the South Shore Country Club, the Edgewater Yacht Club, the Illinois Athletic Association, the Chicago Yacht Club, and the Elks. The acquisition of money entailed many societal obligations.

The owner closely guarded his financial position, and the accurate profit-loss picture of the White Sox at this time is not a matter of historical record. However, it is doubtful Comiskey finished in the red for any one of the 32 seasons he operated a club in Chicago.

The Comiskey family was interwoven into all administrative functions. One of Charley's nephews, one Charles Fredericks, served as the owner's personal secretary, attending to the ballclub's travel arrangements, spring training appointments, and club financials. At the start of each new season, young Fredericks purchased a 15¢ ledger book which he tucked away in his coat vest for the duration of the campaign. After recording the gate receipts into his notebook after each game, Fredericks rubber banded the bills and carefully placed them into a weather-beaten satchel. The monies were taken downtown and faithfully deposited in the First National Bank by Charley Fredericks that same afternoon. This is how the baseball families conducted their business affairs—along the lines of the ma and pa neighborhood candy store. And for many years it worked.

Charles Comiskey's only son was born in Dubuque in 1885. He was a shy, withdrawn young man, not quite the pioneering feudist his father had been. John Louis Comiskey was a kind and generous boy, beset with personal misfortune from his late teens onward. As a youngster, Lou showed great athletic ability as captain and tackle on the Christian Brothers School football team near 35th and Wentworth.

Whatever small hopes the boy may have had for a professional career on the playing fields were quickly dashed in 1900 when he contracted a malignant case of scarlet fever. Lou Comiskey never shook off the after effects of the terrible disease, and would spend his adult years in and out of St. Luke's hospital. His weight ballooned to over 400 pounds during this time. Specialists in Chicago and other cities were summoned to the young man's bedside to prescribe any number of fad diets, sanitarium treatments, and Turkish baths in the vain hope of bringing down his weight—with little success.

Lou Comiskey was brought into the organization about the same time as Harry Grabiner, a neighborhood waif whose pluck and determination to belong caught the Old Roman's fancy. Grabiner, who was destined to provide 40 years of dedicated and unbroken service to the family, began his career with the White Sox in 1905, removing discarded soda pop bottles from the grandstand with his brother Joe. When Charley Fredericks died in 1915, Grabiner stepped in as team secretary and Comiskey's closest aide-de-camp. However loyal and true, Harry was still the outsider by virtue of his birthright. There was no way for Grabiner to exceed . . . or succeed Louis in the organization.

Comiskey installed his son in the concessions end of the business after the new park opened in 1910, placing him in charge of the bottling plant under the grandstand. It was a task the prince in waiting happily accepted, for it provided him with a degree of blessed privacy he would not have enjoyed occupying the executive suite.

Lou Comiskey never paid much attention to his father's doings upstairs, and was probably just as happy to be spared the limelight that attended him. Worried that his son might feel slighted, Comiskey one day ordered Lou's desk transported into the owner's office. The arrangement lasted all of one week. When the son quietly moved back into the bowels of the stadium downstairs, his father asked what was the matter. In a revealing statement, Lou Comiskey replied: "You moved my desk upstairs and every time someone wanted to talk, you ran me out. So I decided to move back here where I can enjoy myself."

A fair and compassionate man, Lou Comiskey regularly fed an army of vagabonds and hungry tramps who lined up at the ballpark each morning for stale bread. During the hard times, an urn of coffee and free sandwiches awaited the nameless hoboes that lingered outside near the trash disposal area. Rained-out games in particular lured the homeless to Lou's doors. One morning, a commissary worker, uncertain of Lou's intentions for the room full of Kaiser rolls and sandwich meats from the previous day, asked if the entire lot of it should be sent to the hospital. "No!" Comiskey shot back. "The hospitals don't need it half as much as these people around the neighborhood do. See that they get it!" In quiet ways that often went unnoticed by the public, the Comiskeys lived up to their responsibilities as public people—bedrock values and social obligations handed down from John to Charley to Lou.

The notion of giving something back to the public was tragically intermingled with the Old Roman's burning ambitions to build monuments to his family name; be it an unfulfilled historic baseball legacy on foreign soil, or a pillar of concrete and steel for future generations to gape at in awe, that time was now at hand.

* * *

The American League was born in a climate of uncertainty and pessimism. Building a first-class baseball plant with grandeur, flair, and an appreciative eye for urban aesthetics was less of a concern to American League President Ban Johnson when measured against economic considerations. The tiny wooden parks that the American League teams began play in were constructed for the small sums of $3,000-$5,000 apiece on parcels of land made available to the owners — that is, locations offering favorable lease terms, or the already existing grounds of a defunct team.

Before the Washington Senators got going in 1901, the city was virtually barren of choice sites. The National League park was destroyed after the 1899 season, forcing Johnson to build well outside the center of the city. Similar circumstances existed in Philadelphia, where the Athletics were forced to play in Columbia Park, in the Brewerytown section of the city. Charles W. Somers, the "Daddy Warbucks" of the American League, financed construction of the tiny grandstand that did not provide for so much as a dugout for the players. Industrialist Ben Shibe held an option on the property, but was skeptical of the league's chances for sustained success, as everyone seemed to be in those days.

But when the Athletics welcomed 16,000 spectators on opening day 1901, with another 5,000 turned away at the door, Shibe uttered his famous phrase that was sweet music to old Ban's ears: "Count me in! Count me in!" he beamed.

Enthusiastic magnates like Shibe and Comiskey could do very little to accommodate the crush of fans who were turned away at the gates because there was simply not enough room in their wooden fire-trap enclosures. The A's and the White Sox were the top drawing cards in the first decade, and the flip side of their success was the lost gate revenues. The total receipts for the six-game, 1906 World Series between the Cubs and White Sox were $106,550. With larger parks on both sides of town, those figures would likely have been double the amount reported.

Comiskey had his first inkling that the 39th Street Grounds were wholly inadequate for professional baseball when 30,084 fans jammed into the park on October 2, 1904, to cheer on Doc White as he attempted to extend his scoreless-inning streak past forty-five. In its heyday, the South Side park comfortably seated no more than 7,000.

Overflow crowds were permitted to stand in roped-off sections of the outfield for the important games, or player testimonial days, of which there were many. Of course, this quickly proved to be an unsatisfactory arrangement all around, for it was common for fans to create disruptions with opposing players and umpires with whom they often came into intimate contact.

These were issues of grave concern, not only in Chicago, but elsewhere around the league. As Johnson's circuit gained increased stature and renewed confidence in its long-term success — bolstered by the strong showing of its teams in the head-to-head comparisons with National League teams in cities like Philadelphia and Chicago — the magnates were more willing to invest large amounts of private capital to finance new super structures. These new stadiums made use of an emerging steel-frame and concrete technology for large-scale projects like stadiums and skyscrapers.

The first wave of stadium building commenced in 1909 with the construction of Shibe Park, a Beaux-Arts masterpiece in Philadelphia, and it concluded with the unveiling of Yankee Stadium, the "House that Ruth Built," in 1923. In between, 13 similar structures arose within the neighborhood constraints of the urban core. They were to become the traditional baseball stadiums ceremonialized in modern literature.

Comiskey Park, Navin Field (Detroit), Fenway Park (Boston), Shibe, and Forbes Field (Pittsburgh) were privately constructed with little thought given by the architects to the future trends of suburbanization, the changing ethnic and racial composition of the inner cities, or the likely impact of the automobile on society.

The urban baseball parks from the "Golden Age," that the Baby Boomers longed for in the 1980s and 1990s, were built in the eager anticipation of a likely cash windfall awaiting the nineteenth century businessmen who owned the teams, nothing more. The fact that Fenway Park (1912), with its short left field wall has a charm and uniqueness all its own is one of those peculiarities of design the architects would likely have avoided were it in their power to do so. No doubt the zoning laws of the day made it impossible for them to claim Lansdowne Street in back of the left field wall for bleacher development. Shibe Park, by comparison, was built on an urban grid, and was more of a prototype of the kind of stadiums the magnates originally had in mind for their fans. The pleasant accoutrements that went with Shibe Park, were the architect's window dressing, that's all, and within the owner's budget.

In Chicago, Comiskey held an option on a West Side property bounded by Harrison, Loomis, Congress, and Throop Streets. The Old Roman allowed the option to quietly expire in early

1903; the site was deemed unsuitable in every respect. The Near West Side at the time was an Eastern European ghetto filling in with thousands of immigrant Italians, Russian Jews, Greeks, and Poles. They lived nearby in cold water flats along Maxwell Street and Roosevelt Road. They shared communal privies and had no money to spend on a leisure pastime they did not understand nor could attach much significance to when measured against the grim realities of poverty and crime confronting them everyday in the city streets.

The added presence of the Cubs at nearby Polk & Lincoln (now Wolcott Ave.), further discouraged Comiskey from building in this corner of the city. Plans for a concrete and steel edifice for the White Sox were already underway, but a project of such enormous undertaking could not begin until sufficient working capital could be raised. Seeking financial assistance from the state in the form of bond issues never entered into the debate. Construction costs were pegged between $500,000-$750,000—a far cry from the St. Paul days—but Comiskey would not begin until the money was firmly in his hand.

The twilight of the Comiskey dynasty began once the deal for a new stadium was struck, on December 22, 1908. The jubilant owner, who could not conceive of impending hardships, signed an agreement with Roxanna A. Bowen to purchase a tract of land due west from where the old Brotherhood Park once stood at 35th and Wentworth in the Canal Trustees Subdivision. Total purchase price: $100,000 plus the 1907 tax bill.

Mrs. Bowen was the daughter of "Long John" Wentworth, Chicago's intractable Civil War-era mayor, who fired the entire city police department one night in a moment of pique. To say that Wentworth was a rugged individualist would be flattering to his reputation. Mrs. Bowen signed over to Comiskey a piece of land that had suffered from benign neglect in the previous years. She was glad to be rid of it.

An Italian named Scavudo peddled vegetables from a truck farm on the corner of Portland Avenue (now Shields/Bill Veeck Drive) and 35th; wild alfalfa grew in what was to become centerfield. It would take many months before the Comiskey Park grounds keeper could rid the field of the unsightly weeds once the stadium opened. For years, Bridgeporters reserved the right to use the adjacent vacant land as a dumping ground for their accumulated garbage and had done so since at least the 1880s. Brotherhood Park, considered in its inception to be a first-rate baseball grandstand, had been razed long ago. It was now up to Comiskey to turn this sow's ear into a silk purse.

A north-south through street divided the easternmost portion of the property where the Brotherhood baseball park once stood from the location Comiskey had originally purchased from Mrs. Bowen. Owing to the sticky estate complications with the original deed holders and the city Torrens Department, the Old Roman was unable to secure the parcel of land he considered truly ideal for his "palace:" the corner of Wentworth and 35th. It wasn't until the final plans were made to build at 35th and Shields (two blocks west) that the disputed land finally freed up for purchase. Comiskey had to prevail upon a friendly alderman in the City Council to push through a zoning change that closed off Princeton Avenue to street traffic.

The plain truth of the matter is that Charles Comiskey had erred badly in his choice of a location. No longer inhibited by National Agreement restraints or the mandates coming from the irritating Mr. Hart, the enigmatic Sox owner was free to build his stadium anywhere in the city. The emerging North Side for example, offered many prime site locations in pleasant surroundings at affordable prices. Comiskey was not interested.

Charley Weeghman, founder of a local cafeteria chain that served upwards of 100,000 patrons a day, was the first one to recognize the coming importance of the North Side neighborhoods of Lakeview, Edgewater, Bowmanville, and Uptown as centers of commerce. "Lucky Charley" Weeghman had a clear vision of the future, but was laughed at by the local baseball establishment who still considered this side of town risky. The North Side was the last section of Chicago to be commercially developed. In fact, up until 1889, Lakeview was still a self-governed suburb.

Weeghman cleared the Northeast corner of Clark and Addison of its existing structures and built a superb new grandstand in less than two months' time for his Chicago Whales, the prima donnas of the ill-fated Federal League. The Feds were to be crushed by the National Commission monopolists after the 1915 season, but Weeghman Park would endure for many decades to come as Wrigley Field.

Partly out of stubbornness (Comiskey felt he had something more to prove to the National League—that he could continue to prosper along Hart's original boundary line), but mainly because of his moral certainty that the Wentworth Avenue streetcar line would continue to deliver to his doorstep thousands of Loop office workers and North Siders, to compliment his loyal South Side Irish following, Comiskey chose Bridgeport over all other locales for his new stadium.

He seems to have looked past the racial displacement already occurring in the neighborhoods south and east of Wentworth Avenue. Did he truly believe that the ever-dwindling numbers of "steam heat" Irish in these once solid ethnic enclaves, like James T. Farrell's Washington Park, would continue to anchor the fan base of his new park?

The White Sox doings held little interest to African-American baseball fans residing in the Black Belt east of Cottage Grove Avenue. The legendary Rube Foster was number one in the hearts and minds of the fans who followed the exploits of the great Negro League teams. Foster was a recognizable folk hero during those segregated times.

The schisms between white and black South Siders festered into an ugly and shameful race riot in July 1919. National Guard troops brought in by Governor Frank Lowden to restore peace to the stricken areas were bivouacked in Comiskey Park.

Racial tensions, predicated on fear and ignorance, only worsened in the ensuing decades. They presented an almost insurmountable problem to Sox owners in the late 1960s when fans stayed away from Comiskey Park in droves because of overexaggerated concerns about being mugged in the parking lot. Why hadn't Comiskey gazed into the crystal ball more closely?

* * *

Omens and portents of the evil days to come abounded in the months leading up to the grand opening of the "Baseball Palace of the World," an absurd, pompous designation given the park by the media, but it appealed to the owner.

With uplifting confidence in his own abilities, Comiskey supervised nearly every detail of construction. When one contractor was finished with whatever task he was assigned— Comiskey would direct his architect, Zachary Taylor Davis, to inspect the work area, and then pay in cash. Whatever private indignation Davis must have experienced having to be at the Old Roman's beck and call can only be surmised. An up-and-coming 38-year-old architect in the employ of Armour & Co., Davis had built a number of unassuming walk-up apartments in Chicago prior to receiving the first important commission of his career from Comiskey. The architect's preliminary design, submitted in October 1909, embodied the salient features of Daniel Burnham's City Beautiful concepts of spacious, tree-lined, baroque boulevards that offset the neo-classical structures of his own creation.

The Burnham-Davis vision was tragically impaired by Comiskey's opinion that a baseball park required an ample playing field in which a home run would be fully earned. The Old Roman subscribed to the "Dead Ball" style of play, and his stadium became a permanent shrine to pitching and defense. Comiskey envisioned a grandiose stadium; bigger and better than anything that had gone before, including Philadelphia's Shibe Park, the standard by which all others were judged.

Accompanied by Ed Walsh and Karl Vitzhum, a young architect on Burnham's staff, Davis toured existing stadiums in Cleveland, Pittsburgh, and St. Louis to study designs. In the end, the kite-shaped ballpark that emerged was a hybrid of Shibe Park's symmetry and Forbes Field's double-decked grandstands between first and third, with a detached outfield pavilion. Great emphasis has been attached over the years to Ed Walsh's role in selecting a design favoring his fellow Dead Ball-era pitchers, but it is doubtful that Comiskey would allow one of his players that much leeway in so weighty a matter as the construction of a stadium.

An inherently superstitious man, Charles Comiskey scheduled his ground-breaking for St. Patrick's Day, 1910, traditionally a lucky day for the Sons of Eire. Kneeling upon a piece of sod imported from the old country by catcher Billy Sullivan for the occasion, architect Davis laid in place the "magic brick" measuring 2 x 4 x 8. The solemn ceremony was witnessed by a proud gathering of Bridgeporters, and "Commodore" John Agnew, superintendent of construction. Restaurateur Johnny Burns marked the day by purchasing two flags—one bearing the image of President William Howard Taft and the other the insignia of Ireland. Together, they flapped in the breeze for all to see as Davis strutted over to the masonry to convene the celebration.

The lucky brick, painted a bright green hue according to legend, was quickly covered over by Davis who feared that the souvenir hunters and neighborhood scavengers would lay claim to it in the middle of the night. As it happened, the clump of Gaelic dirt was scooped up and carted away once the dignitaries had decamped.

The ground breaking was largely ceremonial—foundations of the stands were already in place. The entire construction schedule had clipped along at a break-neck pace. Still there had been disturbing omens and more than a few setbacks that made Comiskey apprehensive.

Opening day was scheduled for Friday, July 1. The Old Roman had attached great significance to the ancient superstitions of his forebearers who considered Fridays unlucky. Comiskey implored Ban Johnson to grant his belated request for an eleventh-hour schedule change. To juggle the schedule and move the opener back to Thursday when the team was spending its afternoon in the Motor City, would have been nice in the owner's estimation.

Ban Johnson said no.

* * *

Personal misfortunes were already mounting for those connected with the project, among them building contractor George W. Jackson.

A horrifying fire on board a wooden crib 400 feet off the Lake Michigan shore at 71st Street claimed the lives of 47 common laborers in a forgotten tragedy that revived memories of the 1903 Iroquois Theatre fire in downtown Chicago. The savage flames turned the platform into an inferno, and for the tunnel workers in Jackson's employ, it was sudden and inevitable death. The crib was called a firetrap, and the ordeal of the men an unnecessary tragedy. Contractor Jackson, whose firm was one of several retained by Comiskey to build the ill-situated ballpark, failed to provide the meager protection of a canoe, or a lifeboat moored to its walls for the stranded workers. Mr. Jackson purchased cemetery lots for the deceased, and turned his attentions to the Comiskey Park project.

* * *

George Jackson's troubles were a forgotten footnote to the "Comiskey curse," if indeed one believes in such things. There were other incidents, not all of them related to the team's misfortunes on the diamond, which lent support to Comiskey's age-old superstitions.

The day before the 1910 season got underway, a 46-year-old laborer named George McDermott tumbled off the stadium roof and died of internal injuries at Provident Hospital. Accidents such as this are an unpleasant, but not unexpected occurrence that management is always eager to downplay.

There is no accurate accounting of the precise number of tragedies that befell patrons at Comiskey Park over the years. The most famous incident occurred on May 17, 1913, when a section of temporary wooden seating 27 inches above the visitor's dugout collapsed. Three people were injured. The seating had been put in at the last minute to accommodate the crush of fans who came to pay their respects to Frank Chance, the ex-Cub manager, on his special day.

In the mid-1980s, a careless fan tumbled from the upper deck over third base and crashed into the cement walkway below. Little was said about the accident, either in the media or from the front office. In fact, one would have to speak with the people who were present at the game to learn anything more of it. Given the future marketing problems, the public's perception of the South Side neighborhood, and the sincerity of its various ownerships over the years, it is easy to see why such incidents were hushed up. Comiskey curse or tragic happenstance? Who can really say?

* * *

The first consignment of steel columns was delivered to the grounds on March 19, well ahead of schedule. But a strike of the structural steel workers delayed further construction for five weeks. Faced with a dilemma of great magnitude, Comiskey and Agnew greased the axle with "pluck and cold cash" as *Tribune* reporter Sy Sanborn reported. It appears that the Old Roman kept the tight schedule by importing scab workers whose efforts turned the wheel despite the strike.

The labor troubles, however, dealt a serious blow to Comiskey's budget and timetables. Because of the delays, the plant was not as aesthetically pleasing as Davis intended. Ornamental designs, classical cornices, and other embellishments that might have lent charm and grace to the imposing structure had to be sacrificed in order to complete the necessary essentials to make the park habitable by the July 1 timetable.

What emerged from all the years of careful planning was an uninspired "functional" ballpark that towered high above the landscape. The only exterior design to punctuate the tiresome red brick facade was the letter "C" set off in base relief at various intervals between first and third base. From the very beginning, Comiskey Park was a bland amalgamation of the kind of dull thinking that inspired any number of utilitarian factory buildings and warehouses arising in the neighborhood about this time. The "City Beautiful" vision of Daniel Burnham and his disciples was forever lost.

Aside from the mammoth proportions of the new stadium (363 feet down the foul lines, 420 feet to dead center), Comiskey Park featured a partially cantilevered grandstand that eliminated all but a single row of steel uprights between the bases. The support beams, which became an enduring source of controversy in later years because of the 2,000 or so obstructed-view seats, were not considered an impediment to the comfort and enjoyment of the fans. In fact, Comiskey was applauded by the baseball writers for building a park that was "fan friendly" in every regard.

The writers marveled at the many "innovations" afforded by the architect. The outdoor press area directly above home plate in the upper deck was considered to be the best in the circuit. The electronic scoreboard in centerfield was connected to the press box by a maze of wires, and it displayed the scores of all out-of-town games, save one . . . those of the Cubs and their opponents. The up-to-the-minute scorekeeping utilizing electricity was another 1910 innovation.

Fourteen turnstiles were installed along the main concourse at 35th and Shields, and they allowed management to keep an accurate count of the number of fans passing through the gates. The most expensive seats in the house were of course in back of home plate and between the bases. These fold-up chairs cost 75¢.

Pavilion tickets down the left and right field lines were sold for 50¢, but the grandstand patrons choosing these areas were hemmed in by cement barriers. There was an abundance of 25¢ bleacher seats for Comiskey's working class heroes, as one might expect. The outfield bleacher seats could be accessed from the turnstile at 34th and Shields, across the street from the Drexel Ice Cream factory. During rain delays, the Old Roman would open up the gates and allow his bleacher patrons to take seats under the roof of the pavilion.

The sportswriters who genuflected at the Comiskey altar were simply agape. So too were the other baseball magnates. The day before the gala opening, Comiskey proudly led John T. Brush and Ben Shibe on a private tour of the park. Shibe, who originated the movement toward steel and concrete ballparks found himself preaching to the choir when he remarked to the entourage: "They told me when I started that I was building 20 years ahead of my time. That was only three years ago and here is Comiskey building ten years ahead of me. I haven't anywhere near enough room for my fans, and Comiskey . . . ," his voice trailed off. "I have to start enlarging these stands next year!"

President William Howard Taft declined to attend the Friday curtain raiser, but dignitaries abounded. Baseball executives from the four corners joined in a chorus of praise for Comiskey, who had erected the eighth wonder of the world—the Roman Colosseum no less!—to their limited way of thinking. Twenty-eight thousand fans, which was the seating capacity of Comiskey Park until 1917 when the first "improvements" were made, assembled early in the morning and filled all available space in the grandstand. Pre-game entertainment was supplied by strolling musicians and vocalists whose songs echoed across the expansive stadium.

Umpire Tom Connolly stood before the crowd and in a clear, resonant voice, announced the starting batteries for Chicago "Walsh and Sullivan!" But no one heard. Connolly's voice was lost in the vastness of the arena, which meant that the umpire would have to be supplied with a megaphone from here on out. The opponent for this historic first game at Comiskey Park, appropriately, was the St. Louis Browns, who bore little resemblance to the great teams Comiskey captained nearly a quarter-century earlier. On this day, however, the Browns would prevail by a 2-0 score. The outcome of the game set the standard for all that was to follow. Davis had made good on his promise to build a pitcher's park glorifying the Dead Ball era.

The Baseball Palace of the World was open, and Comiskey was the proud papa. His statement to the press: "To be able to open to the baseball public of my native city the grandest ballpark in the world and to feel that no matter how large the crowd, it will be safe from fire and other accidents that are liable to occur in structures of less solidity is cause enough for a full crop of happiness today. To feel that the public is grateful to the fullest extent is added cause for my gratification."

Indeed, Charles Comiskey had eliminated the omnipresent fire threat and a potential insurance liability, which was another important consideration in deciding to lay it all on the line and build a concrete stadium. He had witnessed firsthand the tragedy that befell his friend, George Jackson, a year earlier.

The new park was rock solid, and could withstand a bomb. That much was proven 13 years later, when a trade union malcontent hurled a stick of dynamite at the main entrance at 35th and Shields. The only reported damage to the facility was several broken windows in the upper-level offices.

Rock solid, but unsatisfactory. The ballpark, with its bland, factory-like appearance became an anachronism of the changing times before it was a quarter-century old. The horse-and-buggy style of Dead Ball-play faded with the advent of the "rabbit" ball in 1920, and the coming of baseball's Supermen; Babe Ruth, Jimmy Foxx, Lou Gehrig, and Ken Williams, who stylized the three-run home run and the big inning in the decades to come. In Comiskey Park, of course, the traditional reliance on pitching and defense was mandated by the size of the place. Home runs were in short supply, and these spatial considerations greatly diminished the appeal of the home team to a larger cross-section of fans.

Even Charles Comiskey recognized that modifications to the original plan were in order. The trouble was, his enhancements only served to worsen the situation by making the park even more cavernous and imposing. Additional seating between the bases was installed in time for the 1917 World Series. It was the first in a long line of cosmetic changes and face lifts — some major, some of no consequence—put through by the ownerships over the course of eight decades.

The most significant improvements by far occurred over the winter of 1926-1927, when Comiskey pumped $600,000 into the plant, adding upper deck pavilions in right and left field. An elevated bleacher replaced the scoreboard in center field, and by the time the refurbished park was ready for its April 1927 unveiling total seating capacity topped 52,000.

There were 19 rows of seats in left field, 31 in right. This unusual discrepancy was due to the inability of the owner to have 34th Place in back of left field re-zoned to suit his purposes.

Zachary Taylor Davis was again called on to supply the design. His team of experts assured Comiskey that a capacity crowd could be emptied out of the park in six minutes via the concrete runways extending down from the left and right field upper deck.

The modernized Comiskey Park was indeed a symphony in concrete, built in anticipation of the many thousands of fans likely to pour through the gates to preview the great teams and legends of the game that made the 1920s baseball's true "Golden Age." The number of overflow crowds through the World War I years when the Sox were a decent ball club convinced Comiskey that these improvements were essential. However, the Sox filled their park to capacity only a dozen times between 1927 and 1951—mostly Sunday doubleheaders with the Yankees. The rest of the time the upper deck stood silent and forlornly empty as it cast a long, cold shadow across the playing field around the sixth or seventh inning. The swirling winds of early April and late September carried with them an unpleasant arctic chill, making the baseball idyll more of a test of endurance.

In retrospect, upper decking the Comiskey Park outfield was the *worst* possible decision the owner could have made. The added outfield tiers provided good viewing for Chicago Cardinal football games, but the expansion robbed the park of whatever degree of intimacy it retained in the early years, and it hastened the structural problems that were to occur in the 1980s.

Far from being the focus of community life in Bridgeport, old Comiskey Park had evolved into a "South Side Baseball Factory." So many acres of oozing, sweating concrete. The smoky haze from five thousand cigarettes wafting upward toward the light towers. The splintery, narrow wooden grandstand seats of World War II vintage, and a woebegone ballteam wearing baggy flannels cheered on by the plain people from the stockyards and steel plant. The enduring images of workman-like summers on the South Side.

But with the lure of a winning club, record numbers of fans returned in the 1950s. The fans will always return to the ballyard when the home team is going well. It is entirely another matter in those seminal years when a club is off kilter and out of contention by Flag Day. There has to be something more to offer the fans besides bad baseball. Wrigley Field, designed by the same architect, Zachary T. Davis, had that certain undefinable quality of character lacking in old Comiskey Park. That timeless, unique ingredient that gives a public building character is called charm.

Comiskey Park had stood for a long time, but ultimately it failed to withstand the most important test of all: the *test* of time. The brutal truth is, the crowned jewel of the stockyards district was an imperfect diamond and should never have been built . . . that way.

George Brace

Shortly before his death in 1939, Lou Comiskey declared "We're going to start carrying the mail this year!" Unfortunately, Lou died without getting the chance to see the Sox achieve his lofty dream.

Eight Fired by Comiskey; Wrecks Team

Before true bills against eight White Sox players for conspiracy to commit an illegal act were announced by the Cook county grand jury yesterday noon, President Comiskey of the south side club had prepared and issued notices suspending seven of them indefinitely, which means for the rest of the season. The eighth, Arnold Gandil, already was under suspension for failure to report last spring.

These notices, together with checks for their salaries to date, were served on three of the players before they were aware of their indictment, and the rest of them as soon as they could be located.

Notice of Suspensions.

The formal document, addressed to Charles Risberg, Fred McMullin, Joe Jackson, Oscar Felsch, George Weaver, C. P. Williams, and E. V. Cicotte, follows:

"You, and each.. of you, are hereby notified of your indefinite suspension as a member of the Chicago American league baseball club (the White Sox).

"Your suspension is brought about by information which has just come to me, directly involving you, and each of you, in the baseball scandal now being investigated by the grand jury of Cook county) resulting from the world's series of 1919.

"If you are innocent of any wrongdoing, you and each of you will be reinstated; if you are guilty you will be retired from organized baseball for the rest of your lives, if I can accomplish it.

"Until there is a finality to this investigation, it is due to the public that I take this action, even though it costs Chicago the pennant.

"Chicago American League Baseball Club,
"By CHARLES A. COMISKEY.
"President."

Kills Last Pennant Chance.

By this action the White Sox magnate wrecked the last chance of his team's winning a league pennant and possibly a world's championship this year, and perhaps for years to come.

Asked if he had taken this action suspending the suspected players before their indictment, he replied in the affirmative. Asked if he realized such action meant surrendering all chance for the world's pennant, he bowed his head.

Secretary Harry Grabiner of the White Sox later issued a formal statement on behalf of President Comiskey, conveying the presumption that the indictments issued were based on evidence furnished the grand jury by himself, through his attorney, Alfred S. Austrian, under whose direction the investigation has been conducted since last October, involving the expenditure of thousands of dollars.

Not Through Investigating.

The statement in part follows:

"Mr. Comiskey has been investigating for the past year, under the direction of Mr. Austrian, the reports implicating members of the White Sox team in the world's series of last fall, and the moment anything concrete or substantial in the way of evidence was procured, immediately conveyed it to the grand jury and to the chief justice.

"We presume it was this evidence that caused the indictments to follow. We do not propose to discontinue the investigation, and will use every effort to put baseball on the plane it deserves, to which it belongs, and to keep it there."

"WE THREW WORLD SERIES." CICOTTE, JACKSON, ADMIT

To Indict Gamblers Today Is Plan.

Following the indictment of eight White Sox players on a charge of conspiracy to commit an unlawful act, in relation to the throwing of the 1919 world's series games with Cincinnati, and the confessions of two of them, Eddie Cicotte and Joe Jackson, the grand jury got ready last night for more indictments today.

The jurors intend today to find the missing link—the man who was the go-between—the man who gave the gamblers' money to the ball players. This man is said to be Abe Attell, a former prizefighter.

Those Indicted.

The eight indicted men are:

EDDIE CICOTTE, pitcher, admitted he received $10,000 from the agents of a gambling syndicate.

JOE JACKSON, outfielder, confessed $5,000 was paid to him.

FRED McMULLIN, utility man.

OSCAR (HAPPY) FELSCH, center fielder.

CHARLES (SWEDE) RISBERG, shortstop.

CLAUDE WILLIAMS, pitcher.

GEORGE (BUCK) WEAVER, third baseman.

ARNOLD (CHICK) GANDIL, former first baseman, who quit major league baseball at the beginning of the present season.

Williams on Grill Today.

Jackson said he was promised $20,000, the price he asked, and was given only $5,000.

Claude ("Lefty") Williams, the man who handed Jackson the $5,000, will be the central figure in the investigation today.

Williams will be asked who gave him the money. He may also be questioned as to his career in the Coast league, and he may be asked as to his knowledge of a scandal regarding fixed games that occurred shortly after Salt Lake City entered the league. Williams, questioned as to his part in the conspiracy, was noncommittal last night.

Raps Jackson's War Record.

After comment on the shipyards record of Joe Jackson during the war, Williams said:

ADMIT GUILT

EDDIE CICOTTE left for his home in Detroit yesterday immediately after confessing to the grand jury his part in the throwing of the 1919 world's series. "I was a fool," was his sobbing comment as he came from the jury room.

JOE JACKSON confessed and moaned as photographers before making his confession yesterday. But when he came out he was erect and smiling. "I got a big load off my chest," he said, as he posed for the photograph shown here.

His head hung in shame, sobbing, willingly, hanging his head, now and then wiping his streaming eyes.

Tells of Tempters.

"Risberg and Gandil and McMullin were at me for a week before the world's series started," he said. "They wanted me to go

Chapter
— Seven —

Champagne and Ashes: The Black Sox Scandal and its Tragic Aftermath

A tired, broken-down pitcher ambled into Comiskey's office on the eve of the 1917 World Series to convey his warm wishes. The strain of pitching 2,245 innings over six consecutive South Side seasons had cost Edward Augustine Walsh his career. His powerful right arm was weak and tired; the deadly spitball that had baffled so many batters was flat and eminently hitable.

Just three years earlier when the Federal League promoters began offering signing bonuses to players willing to jump their contracts, Walsh's arm gave out and the chance for financial reward that had eluded him for much of his years in the Comiskey stable, disappeared. Walsh was offered $75,000 from the Baltimore Terrapins if his arm was sound. In his heart of hearts, Big Ed knew that he could not live up to his end of the bargain and sign a three-year Federal League contract. He graciously declined the Feds' offer and resumed his yearly salary wrangles with Comiskey, the gruff and tightfisted owner, who had given Walsh every indication that his loyalty would be rewarded with a managerial offer someday.

But someday never came, and arm-dead Ed Walsh was released by Comiskey in 1916 when he was of no further use to the ballclub. He attempted a comeback with the Boston Braves a year later, but it fizzled after only 18 innings.

Now, at the hour of Comiskey's latest triumph Walsh had dropped by to wish him luck. The owner arose from his roll top desk, festooned with a bronze statue depicting Comiskey in his playing days, and grasped his former employee's hand affectionately. It was an emotional moment for the two of them—differences aside.

"No one deserved a pennant more than you Commy," the Moose stammered. "And I guess I was as happy as you when the boys clinched it. I only wish I were right once more to help beat the Giants for the World's title." With that, Ed Walsh shuffled out of the office.

Tears welled in Comiskey's eyes after hearing these words. Turning to Grabiner, Comiskey whispered: "There goes the greatest pitcher that ever lived!"

* * *

Comiskey's offer to have Walsh pilot the White Sox was never tendered, and the testimonial day for the greatest pitcher to don the Pale Hose had to wait . . . until 1958, when the grandson, Chuck Comiskey, summoned the old man to Chicago for his long overdue "day." The big Irishman was a ghostly image of his former self. Unable to walk, an Andy Frain usher pushed the wheel-chair ridden Walsh to the pitcher's mound for a last hurrah before dying. Who among them remembered what a potent figure he had been in his youthful days? Who among them still cared?

* * *

It was 1917, and a new White Sox team stood on the threshold of another world championship. The Old Roman had meticulously rebuilt his ballclub with a generous infusion of cash to pay the salary of Eddie Collins, the stellar second baseman from Connie Macks' A's who had arrived in Chicago on December 8, 1914. Collins received a $15,000 signing bonus and a five-year guaranteed contract from Comiskey valued at $75,000. Eddie was a Columbia University man, and nobody's fool when it came to securing the money up front.

The arrival of Joseph Jefferson Jackson from the Cleveland Indians on August 20, 1915, cemented the White Sox position in the upper tier of the American League. Harry Grabiner, the bright, young genius now in his mid-twenties had outbid three other teams for "Shoeless" Joe. Harry paid the Indians $31,500 and chipped in three indistinguishable non-entities for the privilege.

Ed Cicotte (pronounced SY-cot-ee), a luckless second-rate pitcher with the Boston Red Sox was sold to Chicago in 1912 for the waiver price. In the next five years, Cicotte tinkered with an experimental knuckle ball pitch with varying degrees of success. Then in 1917, further refinements produced Cicotte's deadly "shine ball." Ed Cicotte seemed destined to become a perennial 20-game winner, and the full measure of an Ed Walsh if the scandal had not intervened.

Add to the veteran mix a bumper crop of maturing youngsters such as Joe Benz, Urban "Red" Faber, George "Buck" Weaver, and "Reb" Russell, and Comiskey found himself in the enviable position of riding herd over an emerging American League juggernaut. It was to become a ballclub of legend—a fearsome baseball team acknowledged to be among the finest in history; Babe Ruth's 1927 Yankees being no exception. It was a team that captured top honors in 1917. Their 100 victories remain a benchmark of success for South Side teams yet to come.

The Black Sox scandal is a sordid, but defining moment in sport history that has captured the fancy of poets, chroniclers, and idealists. But few writers have penetrated the deeper significance of the period than Dr. Harold Seymour in his book *Baseball in the Golden Age*. Eliot Asinof's scintillating *Eight Men Out* is a distant second in the genre. It is the consequences of this affair and the tragedy befalling the White Sox ballclub that form the subject of this discussion. The Black Sox scandal became a national event with devastating local repercussions. The Black Sox; bitterly, bitterly, once more.

* * *

"Hey Pants, show us your knickers!" He was the "Iowa Busher," manager of the Chicago White Sox. The unfortunate sobriquet haunted Clarence "Pants" Rowland, throughout his baseball career—ever since he had shown up at a semi-pro game one ignominious day, wearing a pair of his brother's hand-me-down knickers.

Manager Rowland's task was a difficult one. Few of the veteran players listened or took him seriously. His youth and inexperience kept getting in the way. Instructions to players took the form of a well-meaning suggestion, or sage piece of advice. Sometimes they listened, but most of the time the athletes paid no mind. He was after all, just a "busher." Behind-the-scenes leadership was provided by Comiskey, of course, and a sturdy little man summoned out of retirement when it became evident that Rowland needed help bringing the thoroughbreds across the finish line.

The leader on and off the field was "Kid" Gleason, the fifty-something coach, who developed a great rapport with the youngsters like Lefty Williams and Swede Risberg. When Rowland and Comiskey parted the waves after the shortened wartime season of 1918, Gleason stepped in.

By previous standards, Charles Comiskey's profits during the Black Sox era were enormous. As his team gained new respect for its diamond exploits, the owner's reputation only continued to soar. Comiskey was Chicago's "first man of sport," and in 1917 he siphoned 10% of his gross receipts—$17,113.00—to the Chicago Chapter of the American Red Cross to aid the relief effort in war-torn France. During the pennant season, he encouraged grandstand patrons to donate their spare change to the "Clark Griffith Ball and Bat Fund," to purchase athletic equipment for the Doughboys fighting the good fight overseas.

Baseball, the national pastime, garnered favorable publicity on the surface, but the seeds of scandal and disunity were already being planted. There were many disturbing sidelights to the team's merry romp through the '17 season. It was later alleged that the White Sox players were "schooled" in corruption by club officials—Comiskey, Grabiner, and Travelling Secretary Joseph O'Neill presumably—to convince players from the Detroit Tigers to "throw" key September games when the outcome of the pennant race remained doubtful.

Back-to-back doubleheaders played in Comiskey Park on September 2-3, 1917, resulted in four successive Chicago victories that virtually tucked away the league championship. Tiger stalwarts including Ty Cobb, "Hooks" Dauss, Bobby Veach, Howard Ehmke, and Donie Bush allegedly received a cut of Comiskey's reward money for "rolling over" on command.

These allegations came out much later, in the Black Sox trial of 1921. But little notice was taken of these charges.

The 1917 World Series was a marvelous showing, pitting the seasoned John McGraw against the "Busher" Rowland; Gotham and its many attractions versus the Second City; a re-match of the two teams that traversed the globe three years earlier, and for the time being, relief from the grim war news.

The hoopla of a Giants-White Sox World Series sparked renewed activity among the gambling fraternity. It was estimated that one New York broker logged $100,000 in wagers on Game One. The National Commission, baseball's governing body and "purifying" sentinel, did nothing to enjoin the players from betting on the outcome of *their own game.*

New York Giant outfielder Benny Kauff bet $200 against $2,000 that his team would knock off the White Sox in four straight games. After Chicago captured the first two contests in Chicago, the determined Mr. Kauff wagered $600 against $5,000 that the Giants would prevail in Gotham. Inspired by the hometown cranks, McGraw's Giants pitched back-to-back shutouts in their home park. A curbside betting frenzy followed. In every Broadway poolroom, cigar stand, and saloon, New York "sports" were betting big time on the Giants to sweep the remaining games. Benny Kauff, the dwarf-like centerfielder who was drummed out of organized baseball in 1920 for complicity in a stolen car ring, raised the stakes. So sure was he of victory, that he wagered $1,200 against $1,000 on the Giants.

Kauff's gambling habits were small time compared to the activities of New York's biggest bookmaker, Arnold Rothstein, whose winning share of any venture was always 90%. Rothstein was a flashy, but dangerous gangster from the New York slums who bankrolled underworld entrepreneurs like Waxey Gordon, Owney Madden, and Jack "Legs" Diamond. "A.R." was a rich and resourceful man who allowed others to do the dirty work— like fixing a World Series if necessary.

In Game Five, A.R. bet $25,000 on the cuff, and came up a winner when the Giants pulled their fat out of the fire with an 8-5 victory. The next day, the odds makers listed New York as a 7-5 favorite. However, Eddie Collins scurried across an unguarded home plate to seal the World Championship for Chicago.

After the battle, Manager Rowland raced to the Astor Hotel to receive from John Brush, secretary of the National Commission, a check for $91,733.15, representing the winners' share of the proceeds. As soon as the money was distributed among the boys, a gang of happy White Sox including Joe Benz, Eddie Cicotte, and Lefty Williams, marched down to 44th Street where they laid out a wad of greenbacks to "Diamond Joe," their favorite Broadway character famous for his wholesale gems.

The conquering heroes and their wives boarded a fast train to Chicago shortly afterward—outfitted in new diamond rings and stickpins. At the LaSalle Street Station, a riotous celebration, and thousands of Chicagoans awaited the clean and alabaster White Sox. Champagne, diamonds, and caviar. It was a grand and glorious time to be alive.

* * *

Back in New York, "A. R." stewed over his misfortunes. All his life he played the odds like a champ. Rothstein was a mathematical genius; few doubted his capacity to pick the winning nag at Saratoga, or the outcome of a prize fight. The Jewish gangster had not come this far in life by being a sap. Nothing in this life could be left to chance. He knew that now.

* * *

Bookmaking on baseball had been an unfortunate byproduct of the professional game. Since the early 1870s, pool sellers traded openly on the field and in the grandstands. Members of the fraternity visited ballplayers in the hotel lobbies where the team was staying on the road, and the saloons nearby afforded them a rich opportunity to cultivate new friendships over free beers, hours after the game had ended.

In the antiquarian days prior to the formation of the National League, the president of the National Association instigated a small riot one day by attacking a bookie he had accused of trying to bribe star players of the New York Mutuals. It was often whispered that certain star players could be "handled."

"In the vernacular of the period," the *Literary Digest* commented in 1912, "baseball was rotten." The symbiotic ties between player and gambler continued long after William Hulbert and his cronies supposedly restored order and stability to the game in 1876.

Bookmaking at the nation's racetracks by agents of the highly organized syndicates (John Morrissey, Herman "Beansie" Rosenthal, and Arnold Rothstein ruled New York; Mont Tennes, James O'Leary, John Condon in Chicago), resulted in numerous state-wide prohibitions against thoroughbred racing that closed down 289 of America's premier racing ovals by 1908.

Professional baseball games provided the handbook men with a new means to continue their livelihood and an inexhaustible market. Matching wits with a sidewalk bookie and the promise of a quick payout provided the competitive stimulus by which an average fan could live vicariously through his favorite ball team, or athlete. The Black Sox Scandal was not only a predictable occurrence, but an inevitable one. One can only wonder why it didn't happen sooner, or to another team.

* * *

Acting on a newspaper man's tip, detective sergeants William McCarthy and Joseph Hughes of the Stockyards District Station waded through the Comiskey Park bleachers in search of gamblers. It was a mild, late summer afternoon, the thirteenth of September, 1920. On the field, the incumbent champions were toying with the Washington Senators, the way the great teams sometimes do. Allow the visitors an early lead, instill in them a measure of false hope, before burying the opponent in a late-inning avalanche of runs. The technique was perfected by the White Sox, and elevated to an art form by the Yankees in the next decade.

Kid Gleason's team had played disappointing baseball much of the year, however, and now found themselves in third place, but only a game-and-a-half behind the Cleveland Indians who occupied the top rung.

In the box seats, where the businessmen congregated, the bookmaker named his odds and recorded: $380 - $300. Since no money was passed and all bets were accepted on credit, no arrests were possible. Meanwhile, the "nickel pikers" in the cheap seats were nabbed and hauled away. The mild distraction was barely noted, as Oscar "Happy" Felsch stepped up and jerked the ball into the distant left field pavilion. The fans were delirious with joy. Who cared about a bunch of pikers anyway?

The town was rife with rumor. There had been whisperings for some time now that the 1919 World Series, the second appearance of the White Sox in three years, had not been on the square. The Sox had laid down before the unconvincing Cincinnati Redlegs in an eight-game series loss. Until now, there had only been rumors and suspicion.

A gale-force storm broke just five days later when a Cook County grand jury pried a confession out of Ed Cicotte who admitted to conspiring to throw games with eight other teammates and a consortium of shadowy gamblers allied with Rothstein — the only man in America outlandish enough to try to "fix" the World Series.

"The eight of us got together in my room three or four days before the games started," Cicotte stated for the record. "Chick Gandil was the M.C. We talked about throwing the series. Decided we could get away with it. We agreed to do it. I was thinking of the wife and kids and how I needed the money. I told them I had to have the cash in advance. I didn't want any checks. I didn't want any promises, as I wanted the money in bills."

The day before the series began, Cicotte continued: "I found the money under my pillow. There was $10,000. I counted it. I didn't know who put it there, but it was there. It was my price. I had sold out Commy. I had sold out the other boys; sold them for $10,000 to pay off a mortgage on a farm."

The confessions of Cicotte and "Shoeless" Joe Jackson speak for themselves and the arguments for their guilt are manifold. The crestfallen Jackson recalled his grand jury testimony during trial deliberations in 1921. He said he was "threatened" by his more complicitous teammates: "Before we broke up, I climbed (sic) Gandil and McMullin and Risberg about it. They said to me, 'You poor simp, go ahead and squawk. Where do you get off if you do? We'll all say you're a liar and every honest baseball player in the world will say you're a liar. You're out of luck. Some of the boys were promised a lot more than you and got a lot less.' That's why I went down and told Judge McDonald and told the grand jury what I knew about this frame up. But the World Series averages of some of the Black Sox players suggest otherwise. Jackson batted a robust .375. George "Buck" Weaver, the least culpable of the eight, chipped in with .324. Both players were flawless in the field. Oscar Felsch, "Swede" Risberg, and "Chick"

Gandil, if individual guilt can indeed be proven, played poorly and must bear full responsibility for what happened.

The exposure of the fix was precipitated by the *Chicago Herald & Examiner* in a copyrighted story that told of a gambler's attempt to influence the outcome of a Cubs-Phillies game played August 31, 1920. The charge was substantiated by William Veeck, Sr., of the Chicago National League ballclub, who had ordered his star pitcher, Grover Cleveland Alexander, to be bumped ahead in the rotation in order to thwart the conspiracy. Alexander was promised a $500 bonus if he came up a winner in this game. But even with the "Mighty Aleck" on the slab, the Cubs still lost 3-0.

Veeck went public with the story after receiving five anonymous communiques from Detroit gamblers, tipping off the North Side boss of unusually heavy wagers being placed on the Philadelphia team. The brazen gamblers hoped to maneuver Veeck into pitching Alexander out of turn, thereby flattening the steep odds against Chicago that day.

A few days later, Chief Justice Charles A. McDonald of the Criminal Court ordered a broader-based grand jury investigation. With the crookedness now out in the open, the question was on everyone's mind: what terrible evil had befallen baseball?

In 1920, the average fan believed he was sold out by avaricious ballplayers who betrayed the great father figure Comiskey. With the passage of time and the modernist spin of the historians applied, the owner emerges as the tight-fisted overseer, and his corrupted players as the underpaid field hands suffering under the overseer's whip.

The truth, inevitably, lies somewhere in the middle.

The Old Roman paid his players what the market would bear. His salaries were in line with what the other owners were paying, less in some cases, more in others. At times Comiskey could be surprisingly generous; bench-warming substitutes and slump-ridden ballplayers were occasionally rewarded with extra coin as an inducement to play harder. Closer research bears this point out. Others, like Walsh, fought with Comiskey year in, year out, and left Chicago with rancid feelings toward the city and the family. The notoriety of an Ed Walsh, as opposed to a "Ping" Bodie for example, who was satisfied with the White Sox salary system, resulted in greater media criticism directed toward Comiskey.

Representative Yearly Salaries of the Chicago White Sox, 1919-1920

Honest Players	Base Salary	Incentive
Dickie Kerr	$3,600	($100 signing bonus)
Eddie Collins	$15,000	(multi-year)
Ray Schalk	$12,000	($340 monthly renewal bonus)
Red Faber	$6,600	($211 monthly renewal bonus)
John Collins	$4,800	($1,200 renewal bonus)
Nemo Leibold	$4,800	($1,200 renewal bonus)
Eddie Murphy	$4,800	($1,200 renewal bonus)
Roy Wilkinson	$4,800	($600 renewal bonus)
Harvey McClellan	$2,400	($600 renewal bonus)

Manager		
Kid Gleason	$7, 250	

Black Sox	Base Salary	Incentives
Ed Cicotte	$9,075	($3,285 bonus)
Buck Weaver	$7,644	N/A
Oscar Felsch	$7,400	N/A
Joe Jackson	$6,299 (1919)	N/A
	$8,000 (1920)	N/A
Lefty Williams	$5,524 (1919)	N/A
	$6,000 (1920)	N/A
Chick Gandil	$4,500	N/A
Swede Risberg	$3,435	N/A
Fred McMullin	$6,000	N/A

If the Sox owner erred badly in his judgments, it was his underestimation of his star players' resolve to capitalize on the moral ambiguity of the era in which they lived. What was the difference, say, between Benny Kauff placing bets on his own team, and Chick Gandil tanking games at World Series time? Is Kauff less guilty, because the National Commission saw nothing wrong with contracted players making bets, as long as they were made on behalf of the team they played for?

There is an interesting correlation between the presumed guilt of the conspirators and the amount of money Comiskey was paying them. Jackson, Weaver, and Cicotte played well in the 1919 series. Their actual planning and participation in the scheme is a matter of interpretation. The dollars that were passed from the gamblers to the players is the proof of the fix. Gandil, a ten-year veteran possessing average to above-average skills was paid slightly less than Claude Williams, who did not become a member of the starting rotation until 1916. The owner was stingy with respect to Gandil and Risberg, but with these exceptions, the salaries of the 1919-1920 White Sox team were not out of line with the league averages of the day, and some players, notably McMullin and Faber, were on the high end of the scale, given their length of service in the Majors and respective abilities. Then there is the question of the bonus monies allegedly due Cicotte for his brilliant work during the two championship seasons.

Eliot Asinof states in his nonfiction novel *Eight Men Out*, that Comiskey promised to award his star hurler a $10,000 bonus if he won 30 games. Asinof writes: "When the great pitcher threatened to reach that figure, it was said that Comiskey had him benched." If Asinof dug deeper into the records for 1917, he would have discovered that Cicotte was afforded ample opportunity to win 30 and was not held back or benched. Eddie started five games between September 14 and September 29, 1917, just prior to the close of the season. He won four and lost one.

In the 1988 cinematic adaptation of Asinof's book, Director John Sayles revives this dubious allegation, only this time he places it in the waning days of the 1919 pennant chase. If Comiskey reneged on his promises, it was not due to a deliberate intrigue that would compromise or delay the pennant clinching. That much seems certain.

By early September 1919, Cicotte's arm was tired from over-work, and his control suffered as a result. As the Sox pennant became more of a certainty, Kid Gleason decided to rest both Cicotte and Lefty Williams during a six-day stretch between September 11-17, in order to test the effectiveness of two reserves, Erskine Mayer and Bill James. The two star pitchers missed no more than one scheduled turn in the rotation. The next day, September 17, the knuckle-balling ace was granted permission to visit his family in Michigan before the season wound down. Cicotte was back on the mound on the 19th, hurling a complete game victory. He would start two more games before the curtain fell on the season, on September 28.

During the Black Sox trial, defense counsel brought up the point that Comiskey required his players to launder their uniforms. If that was a good indication the owner was a cheapskate, then the entire league stood guilty as charged. For it was standard procedure in those days for the players to assume responsibility for the care and upkeep of their equipment. Comiskey was a man of his times; a Victorian-era magnate who believed in thrift and self-reliance. One has to be careful about applying modern day standards of conduct to a nineteenth century figure. If so, then Connie Mack, Clark Griffith, and the other owners must also be condemned for their miserly transgressions. Griffith, the canny "Old Fox" who purchased the Washington Senators in 1919-1920, was as vociferous in his opinions against management as Comiskey during the various player revolts back in the 1890s. Griffith, like Comiskey, became everything he eschewed. Magnate Griffith was a notorious skinflint who required his ballpark ushers to shove aside the hometown Washington fans, so that a foul ball or a home run that had sailed into the stands might be retrieved for future use.

* * *

During the 1919 World Series, Charley Comiskey had relayed Kid Gleason's concerns that some of the players were not playing up to their abilities to John Heydler, the president of the National League. Comiskey could not bring himself to directly confront Ban Johnson, now his mortal enemy, so Heydler had to intervene. It was a perfunctory move on the owner's part. Had he not done so, Comiskey's league charter would have been placed in jeopardy if his foes could prove that he had deliberately engaged in a coverup. Comiskey gambled that Ban Johnson, out of sheer obstinacy, might want to push the entire matter under the carpet rather than attach significance to Comiskey's opinions. On the contrary, Johnson jumped zealously into the fray and launched a costly investigation of his own.

The league president personally located Bill Burns, a rogue gambler, and ex-Sox pitcher, in a fishing village bordering the Rio Grande River in Texas, and brought him back to Chicago as the state's star witness.

Burns' testimony proved to be devastating to Comiskey and the operations of professional baseball. Since the State of Illinois had no statute covering sports bribery, it was doubly hard for the prosecution to draw up a bill of particulars against the conspirators.

The prosecution, represented by former Illinois Congressman George Gorman, tried to prove that a weak and nebulous conspiracy existed to injure the business of Comiskey; that the players had perpetrated a confidence game on one Charles K. Nims, a White Sox fan who had lost $250 betting on his favorite team; and that by doing so the Black Sox had breached their contract. Comiskey had provided Jackson and Cicotte with the services of his highly qualified private attorney, Alfred Austrian, senior partner in the firm of Mayer, Myer, Austrian, & Platt (now Mayer, Brown & Platt). The smooth-as-they-come Mr. Austrian advised Comiskey of his options following the 1919 World Series, and appears to have sanctioned a plan to sacrifice Jackson and Cicotte to the grand jury in order to save the Old Roman possible embarrassment and a likely scandal.

The players waived immunity and thus allowed the state to enter the confessions into the record when opening arguments were heard on June 27, 1921. Four months before the trial began, the grand jury records and the confessions inexplicably disappeared. Who stole the confessions, and for what purpose? Suspicion was leveled at Comiskey and Austrian. Ban Johnson accused Arnold Rothstein of paying $10,000 for the theft of the properties. The New York gangster, who appeared as a friendly witness during the grand jury hearings, issued a terse statement: "My name was dragged into this by men who thought they might evade trouble for themselves or get some advantage by bringing me into it. Ban Johnson needs to watch his step; the most peaceful men can be driven too far." It was baseball's sorriest moment.

* * *

Charles Comiskey was through with the eight players long before the ordeal of a trial began. In March, as the team began its spring training rigors in Waxahachie, Texas, Comiskey formally notified the eight of their unconditional release. This contradicts the widely held opinion of the younger Veeck, and others, who believed that Comiskey would have brought the players back, had he the power to do so.

A broken and dispirited Comiskey, showing the visible signs of age, was summoned to the courtroom of Judge Hugo Friend as the state's first witness on July 18, 1921. Appearing ill at ease in the presence of a packed courtroom that included many down-cast looking little boys, Comiskey was reminded by Counsellor Benedict Short, one of 12 defense attorneys, that he too had been guilty of breaching a contract back in 1892, when Comiskey jumped to the National League. "I didn't break any contract!" shouted Comiskey, as he defiantly rose to his feet, wagging an accusing finger at Short.

"Well you jumped from one league to another," the lawyer interjected. "I didn't break any contract, nor did I jump." Comiskey leaned back in his chair. "You can't belittle me!" "You're trying to belittle these ballplayers," admonished Short. The courtroom was thrown into an uproar as Short and Comiskey angrily gesticulated over minor technicalities. Judge Friend banged his gavel, and warned the spectators that he would have to clear the room if order was not restored. Until this moment in his life, Comiskey was seen by all as a mythic and heroic figure of the Irish working class. Now an attorney had made him look vain, petty, and foolish. Every inquiry elicited in Comiskey an irrational outburst.

Evidence was introduced showing that the receipts of the team had jumped from $521,175.76 in 1919 to $910,206.59 in 1920. How had these players injured Comiskey's business? The owner's unceremonious firing of Clarence Rowland after the 1918 season was recalled, and a three-year-old lawsuit filed against Comiskey in the Federal court seeking the dissolution of his team as a trust was also brought up. The lawsuit undoubtedly played in the back of Commy's mind the very night he awakened Heydler from bed to confide his suspicions. At that moment Charles Comiskey was painted into a dark corner he was never to escape from. The courtroom fell silent. The historians would pen the epitaph.

* * *

Without a preponderance of evidence to show that the Black Sox intended to throw games *as well* as defraud the public, the jury had no choice but to exonerate the offending ballplayers. The verdict was handed down on August 2, 1921.

The very next day, Commissioner Kenesaw Mountain Landis reiterated that the players would remain on the ineligible list regardless of the verdict. There were no winners in this case, except perhaps the attorneys. Baseball was forever impugned. The players had to live with the consequences of their deeds for the rest of their sad, unhappy lives, and the days of the Chicago White Sox as the cornerstone franchise of the American League were gone for good. The torch had been passed to the team from New York.

* * *

The cruel betrayal of his players was a bitter, personal blow to Charles Comiskey. The press corps maintained a respectful vigil to the owner during the post-trial era, and reasonably expected Comiskey to rebuild with a veteran nucleus of Collins, Kerr, and Schalk, and an infusion of talented new players. In a year's time, perhaps, they would be the same exciting White Sox ballclub.

The indefatigable greatness of the great man is to rise above adversity . . . thrive on it, if necessary. The Black Sox disgrace provided Comiskey the window of opportunity to do so.

Long before Landis handed down his decision, Comiskey's agents were already beating the bushes in search of replacement talent. Some of the names were submitted by Manager Gleason. The Southwestern University alums, who played pick-up games with the Sox during the 1920 spring training paces, were invited back for a closer look. A number of other players were recommended by veteran players Ray Schalk and Harvey McClellan who had themselves a busy winter scouting the sandlots. A bewildering array of eager-eyed, but inexperienced recruits vied for berths on the White Sox team when the spring camp convened in Texas.

They had stepped off the train from the minor leagues, the college campuses, and local sandlots to answer the desperate call.

From the Salt Lake City club of the Pacific Coast League, came three-quarters of an infield. Comiskey had easily outbid Charles Ebbets of the Brooklyn Dodgers for the services of shortstop Ernie Johnson, whose abilities were grossly overestimated; third sacker Eddie Mulligan, a Cub castoff of recent years; and the slow-afoot first baseman Earl Sheely, the only one of the trio to live up to advance press clippings.

* * *

The Replacement Sox: 1921 Spring Training Invitees

Player	Position	1920 Affiliation
Ernie Johnson	IF	Salt Lake City, P.C.L.
Eddie Mulligan	IF	" "
Earl Sheely	IF	" "
Joubert W. Davenport	P	University of Arizona
Jack Tesar	P	Cedar Rapids, Three-I League
Bib Falk	OF	Southwestern University
Dominic Mulrennan	P	Columbus, American Association
Douglas McWeeney	P	Milwaukee, American Association
Victor Olson	P	Yellowstone League, semi-pro
Joe ("Bugs" Bennett) Morris	P	Western League
Howard Fenner	P	Kalamazoo, MI, semi-pro
Russell Pence	P	Litchfield, IL, semi-pro
Ed Franks	P	Utica, New York State League
Everett Yaryan	C	Wichita, Western League
Guy McWhorter	P	Richmond, Virginia State League
Harold Bubser	IF	Oak Park, IL, sandlotter
Pete Turgeson	IF	Aberdeen, South Dakota State League
John Mostil	OF	Milwaukee, American Association
Bob Ostergard	IF	Southwestern University, Texas
Clarence Hodge	P	Nashville, American Association
Jeff Stafford	P	Southwestern University, Texas
Pete Jorgenson	P	High School Principal, Guttenberg, Iowa
Bobby Beauchamp	P	U.S. Navy
Chick Reinhardt	C	Racine, Wisconsin semi-pro

Every one of these fellows was labeled "can't miss!" by his respective promoter, and Comiskey wanted desperately to believe them. But only Falk, Sheely, and Mostil were to be of any lasting importance to the White Sox in the coming decade. Some never played a day of Major League baseball.

Within the next few years it became apparent that Comiskey no longer was capable of building a team overnight, as he had in 1914-1915, when the blank check strategies lured Eddie Collins and Joe Jackson to the South Side. The disappointing seventh-place finish in 1921 was not wholly unexpected by Comiskey. After all, these things *do* take time. The .500 break-even season of 1922 was even more encouraging. But a year later the bottom fell out again . . . and the team tumbled back down to seventh place. Acting on the good advice of Grabiner and an army of advance men scattered throughout the nation, Comiskey continued to spend beyond his means. The owner startled the baseball world on May 28, 1923, with the news that he had purchased infielder Willie Kamm of the San Francisco Seals Pacific Coast League club. The acquisition of Kamm for the astronomical sum of $100,000 had only one modern parallel from a dollars and cents standpoint. That involved the $125,000 sale of the immortal Babe Ruth from the Boston Red Sox to the New York Yankees in 1920.

"In clinching this deal, I had to guarantee the sum of $100,000 and in addition, two pitchers," Comiskey beamed. He was back in the news again, generating positive headlines for a change. "As far as I know, and I have been in the game as long as any of them, this consideration overshadows any that has ever passed from a big league club for the services of a minor league player."

Baseball's free-spending era was already underway, but as usual, the generosity of the owner toward outside interests did not equate into real dollars for the rostered veterans. Kamm proved to be an excellent acquisition; undoubtedly the finest third baseman to grace a Comiskey diamond up through the Robin Ventura era. But he was a reluctant warrior. Kamm believed that he was entitled to a cut of the $100,000 purchase price, but was quietly rebuffed by Comiskey and the owner of the Seals. That was a private affair between the owners. Willie was a lengthy holdout in 1930 after Comiskey's current manager Donie Bush refused to appoint him team captain, a ceremonial title that carried with it an additional $3,600 in salary money. Listless and unhappy, Kamm stirred dissension in the dugout and was traded to Cleveland a year later. He was another casualty of Comiskey's ill-advised fiscal policies.

New Comiskey phenoms were paraded before the Chicago press corps each and every spring. Maurice Archdeacon, a $50,000 prospect from the Rochester club of the International League batted .402 as a late season callup in 1923. A year later, he was off the roster. Nineteen-twenty-six brought to camp a fresh-faced 19-year-old sandlotter from San Antonio, Texas, named Art Veltman who surely seemed destined for greatness. "Why, he's faster than Ty Cobb!" Grabiner gushed. Veltman came to the plate exactly four times that season.

Where the money was coming from was anybody's guess. But there was gold in that front office, apparently. And in 1928 another $123,000 of Comiskey money enriched the Pacific Coast League; this time the Portland club was the happy beneficiary. In return, the Sox received Chalmer "Bill" Cissell, a hard-drinking ex-cavalry man from the Missouri Ozarks. Ed Burns of the *Tribune* estimated that "Spider Bill" cost the Comiskeys $768.75 a pound. "He's a *swell* punk," Burns satirized.

The unsolicited opinions of outsiders, and the jealousy of teammates placed this sensitive "rook" in a tough, pressure-packed situation. "My advice to youngsters is: don't get signed to a Major League club for $123,000," Cissell said, looking back on it. "The ballyhoo I got was the greatest burden any ballplayer ever carried into the majors. I couldn't help figuring all the time how many good cavalry horses you could buy for $123,000." Bill Cissell never put up the box car numbers to satisfy his employers—or his own expectations. He completed a modest ten-year American League career in 1938, and spiraled downward thereafter.

On a grim January morning in 1947, the alcoholic ex-ballplayer was removed from a dingy South Side rooming house, unable to walk and suffering from malnutrition. After Cissell passed on to a better world than this, his funeral expenses were paid for by 23-year-old Chuck Comiskey when surviving family members back in Missouri were unable to come up with burial money.

Maurice Archdeacon; Art Veltman; Bill Cissell; outfielder Mel Simons (purchased in 1931 for $50,000); and pitcher Leo Mangum ($65,000 in 1924) were the noteworthy failures of the Comiskey youth movement that served no other useful purpose than lining the pockets of the minor league hucksters. In those days the White Sox had no formal working agreement with minor league teams, nor did they have their own farm system.

Therefore, each cash transaction was a buyer-beware proposition. The money lavished on expensive rookies belied the shabby treatment of veteran ballplayers who remained among the lowest paid men in the game. Comiskey's heartless treatment of World Series hero Dickie Kerr, for example, who signed up with an outlaw semi-pro team in 1922 to protest past salary injustices, discouraged many of the South Side faithful who stood by the owner in the post-scandal period. Kerr was one of the most popular players of his era, and a sentimental reminder of the glory days.

To restore fan confidence and shore up his own sagging popularity, Comiskey reinstated Kerr to the active roster in 1925. When he took the mound for the first time on August 15, a contingency of fans presented him with a floral horseshoe amid thunderous applause from a large crowd. It was a tearful, emotional reunion for Kerr and his legions of admirers, but the hero of the 1919 World Series was ineffective in a dozen appearances and he never played Major League baseball after 1925.

Desperation measures failed to slow the attendance slide. A second world tour commenced in 1924, but Comiskey's dogged attempt to internationalize baseball went largely unnoticed by the public. Chicago fandom, which Comiskey had seduced and courted for better than a quarter-century turned fickle. The White Sox were unlovable losers, playing in their palatial, vacant factory in the grimy part of town, as the numbers show.

Cub-Sox Attendance, 1921-1932

Year	Sox	Cubs
1921	543,650	410,110
1922	602,860	541,993
1923	573,778	705,049
1924	606,658	720,962
1925	823,231	623,630
1926	710,339	886,925
1927	614,423	1,163,347
1928	494,152	1,148,053
1929	426,795	1,485,166
1930	406,123	1,467,881
1931	403,550	1,089,449
1932	233,198	976,449

Failure compounded disappointment. Increasingly, the Old Roman distanced himself from the day-to-day operation of the ballclub, leaving Grabiner, son Louis, and secretary Lou Barbour to attend to the business of baseball. Beset by ill health and painful memories, Comiskey went to live with Lou, Lou's wife Grace, and the three grandkids. In the summertime, Commy retreated to the solitude of his Northern Wisconsin retreat. The Old Roman contented himself with the knowledge that Ban Johnson was just as bitter as he, now that Judge Landis and the ruling triumvirate had stripped the League President of much of his power.

The Black Sox players suffered for their sins against baseball, and were ruthlessly hounded by the commissioner every time they dared set foot on a diamond within Landis' sphere of influence. And Arnold Rothstein was moldering in the grave — shot dead in a Manhattan poker game.

Comiskey, a man of unparalleled contradictions, was alone with his thoughts most of the time. The Woodland Bards social club had long since disbanded, and the Camp Jerome property in Mercer was acquired by Wisconsin officials who converted the North Woods sanctuary into a dam. The family purchased a dairy farm further away in Oneida County, and it was there that "Citizen Comiskey" reposed in self-exile. The arrival of his bouncing grandson Charley provided small measures of solace and comfort. He naively believed that the baseball team he founded in Chicago would remain in the family for decades to come; the future almost secure.

Near the shores of Sand Lake, small boys bobbed and weaved on a makeshift diamond. They chased the flight of the baseball in the good ole' summertime. Mr. Comiskey would have dearly loved to demonstrate first base technique, but the old bones were aching and unwilling. Brittle and sorrowful, Comiskey reclined in a comfortable chair on the back porch of the North Woods cottage. Days and days of pessimism—the pessimism of disillusion—had taken their toll. Away from the cheering multitudes, away from the bungalows and taverns of Bridgeport, Comiskey lapsed into a coma and died peacefully in his sleep on October 25, 1931. He had outlived Ban Johnson, and that was reward enough.

* * *

An inventory of Comiskey's assets placed the value of the estate at $1,529,707. In this bitter Depression era, when attendance had slipped to dangerously low levels, Austrian's announcement that the estate showed no indebtedness was all the more remarkable. For years, Comiskey was rumored to possess more available cash than most successful men in Chicago. Old suspicions seemed to be confirmed. Control of the ballclub passed to J. Louis Comiskey. Despite two flattering purchase offers from a pair of local wheelhorses in Republican politics: coal magnate George Getz, and Albert D. Lasker, the architect of the 1920 reorganization that recruited Judge Landis, Lou made it abundantly clear that he was in charge henceforth. The absence of a will made it possible for Lou to do what he pleased with the club, but against his better nature, he fulfilled his father's wishes and took on the duties of president and vowed to restore the Sox to past greatness. But it would be another two decades before the team would attain a semblance of respectability on the field.

In the last decade of the Old Roman's regime, the White Sox spent $1 million on unproductive minor league recruits. White Sox talent scouts did more damage than good. Their sorry record of non-accomplishment was reflected in the yearly rosters populated by slow-footed, one-dimensional players; pitchers that couldn't pitch, and fielders who often mistook their gloves for hand warmers. In his terse farewell statement to the press on October 9, 1931, outgoing manager Donie Bush left little room for doubt as to where he believed the White Sox stood in the grand scheme of things. "I don't mind losing ballgames if there is a prospect of better days ahead, but I feel that whatever reputation I possess as a manager would be jeopardized by remaining another year." The salty-tongued, hard-driven Donie Bush was given one more crack at managing in the show. He guided the Cincinnati Reds to an eighth-place finish in 1933 and never piloted a big league team again. So, maybe it wasn't just a personnel problem.

* * *

As to the White Sox, Lou and Harry formulated their own secret plan to reverse the trends. For the first time in memory, a Comiskey, and not Grabiner, personally negotiated the salary contracts with the men. Lou Comiskey signed every player on the

1932 roster in an effort to inspire confidence among the players in his regime. Ted Lyons, one of the few Roaring 20s collegians of lasting importance, was rewarded with a $15,000 fair-market-value contract. For the future Comiskey promised: (1) no more six-figure giveaways to minor league owners; (2) an attempt would be made to earmark this money toward proven Major League stars; (3) the future acquisition of a minor league club of high classification with their own man in charge of player procurement; (4) the hiring of two experienced scouts to canvass the nation. This agenda for change bore fruit by decade's end.

Point two, an item of great interest to Sox fans, was accomplished on the eve of the 1932 World Series as the Cubs prepared to square off against the Yankees. "Uncle Lou," as his associates called him, stunned the baseball world with the perfectly timed announcement that a straight cash purchase had just been finalized with Connie Mack.

Three of the biggest stars in the American League were to join the White Sox pantheon in 1933. The linchpin of the chart-busting $150,000 deal was the slugging $30,000-a-year outfielder Al Simmons. With drama and flair, the Comiskey publicity mill tantalized fans with this additional Simmons caveat: home plate would be moved 14 feet closer to the outfield walls in 1933 in eager anticipation of the sorely needed home run thunder to compliment the singles hitters who filled out this incomplete roster.

The White Sox also gained an experienced outfielder in George "Mule" Haas, who was an excellent motivator and coach for the younger players, along with Jimmy Dykes, firebrand third baseman and future manager. Simmons' contributions were negligible—a colossal disappointment if the truth be told—but he was good box office.

However, the moribund Sox increased their attendance in 1933 by nearly two-fold. J. Lou correctly called the shot on Dykes—he recognized a leader among men, and awarded him with the manager's chair in May 1934. Dykes became the "eminence grise" of the umpire baiting fraternity, eminently quotable, and up to the task of whaling on the Cubs in the annual postseason city championship.

The fabled City Series was played for pride in its heyday of the 1920s and 1930s. The players wanted to win as badly as the fans — maybe even more so. And Dykes took personal delight in sticking the needle into the side of the North Siders following fresh White Sox victories. Today the so-called "Windy City Classic" is a dreaded event, hated and scorned by the players and media alike who make no secret of the fact that their off-day could be better spent on the golf course, or at home. The malingering veterans and minor league callups whose names are penciled into the lineup card go through the paces woodenly and the fans sense it. They swing at the first pitch and pray for rain. "Get the damned thing over with! I don't live in Chicago, what do I care about what these fans think? I'm not a fan, I only play the game!" is an attitude reflected in their play.

Jimmy Dykes was a Chicago original. Few Sox managers since then, with the possible exception of Eddie Stanky in the 1960s, provided as much local color. In Detroit one afternoon, the field boss apprehended the owner's son munching on a sandwich in the clubhouse. Young Chuck Comiskey, a spirited lad who donned the White Sox flannels when the mood suited him, smiled mischievously. He knew that he had broken training rules. Dykes slapped the 12-year-old with a rather stiff $10 fine.

Dykes was ideally attuned to the times in which he played. He provided added direction to a bumper crop of young players when the minors finally began to yield a harvest in the mid to late 1930s. Rip Radcliff, Luke Appling, Monty Stratton, and "Iron" Mike Kreevich, were players to be counted on; scrapping, hustling boys out to prove their point. They were developed with the greatest of care, and nurtured by "Professor" Dykes and his lab assistants, pitching coach Muddy Ruel, and hitting instructor "Mule" Haas. "I got the best manager in baseball, didn't I?" Lou exulted. "You can't pick guys like Dykes on street corners."

Lou Comiskey, when his shaky health did not stand in the way, roared like a lion. He pushed the right buttons, and the Sox climbed into the first division in 1936. Uncle Lou shrewdly recognized that night baseball was the wave of the future, and to showcase his young stars before larger audiences, he ordered light towers to be installed in July 1939. He was both innovator and traditionalist. When it came to the small details, or some sentimental matter that was near and dear to his dad's heart, like the color of the hosiery, Lou refused to break with the past. Each year the uniform salesmen came calling on the ballclubs, and since there were no regulations guiding the selection of styles, it was common for the Sox and other clubs to change the color schemes every few years. But when it was suggested that the Sox change to multi-colored stirrups, Lou had this to say: "My dad founded this organization and it was known as the White Sox for the very reason that the players wore white stockings. They'll continue to wear them because that is one tradition I'll keep as long as I live!" (Note: The white stockings were discarded by Chuck Comiskey in 1949, 10 years after his father died).

Breaking with the past litany of failure, Comiskey committed his financial resources toward a farm *system*, and not just one or two high-priced farm *hands*. Thanks to Uncle Lou's money and Dykes' recommendations, the tree had already begun to bear its fruit, even before the first 81 minor leaguers reported to Longview, Texas, in the spring of 1939.

These young men comprised the first wave of ballplayers who were destined for assignment on the four new White Sox Class D Affiliates of the South Western League. Lou Comiskey hired Bob Tarleton, the former business manager of the Dallas Steers to set the machinery in motion with coach Billy Webb. With new working agreements launched between the minor league teams in Dallas, Longview, Kansas City, Milwaukee, Rayne Louisiana, Lubbock, Texas, and Chicago, the Sox were headed in the right direction, to the point where they had to be considered a serious factor in the A.L. race.

June, 1939: "We're getting better. Give Dykes a few more players that he needs and we'll be fighting the Yankees for that pennant in two or three years." A month after this cheerful appraisal, Lou Comiskey succumbed to heart failure brought on by complications of the disease that sapped him of his youthful vitality, and adult productivity. He was only 54 years old. Harry Grabiner issued no formal statements—the ballclub was in the midst of an afternoon doubleheader with Boston when word was sent down from the Eagle River, Wisconsin, summer home where Lou died. In typical Grabiner fashion, the Comiskey Park grounds crew was dispatched to the center field flag pole where they slowly lowered the American flag to half mast. No one except Harry grasped the significance of the moment.

* * *

Lou Comiskey's will designated the First National Bank of Chicago as trustee, and further charged the institution with complete supervision of the assets. All but fifty shares (which belonged to Harry), of the 7,500 shares of Comiskey stock were placed in separate trusts for the widowed Grace, and her three children, who were to receive their inheritance when they attained the legal age.

The will was a curious muddle that granted the bank absolute power over the estate. Lou Comiskey's language was deliberately vague and misleading, and it opened the door for a vicious ownership fight in the years to come. It was Comiskey's desire that the bank hold on to the stock until his only son reach "... his age of majority." The legal loophole that ultimately split apart the family allowed the bank or the surviving heirs to sell the team "... if circumstances arise after my death, which in the opinion of the trustees would render a sale prudent and desirable."

There is little doubt that Lou Comiskey intended for Charley to run the White Sox as soon as he was old enough to do so. But he did not state this clearly, or with any great conviction. Therein lies the real tragedy of the White Sox in the second half of the twentieth century. Bank President Edward Eagle Brown said that he would respect the decedent's wishes, but scarcely six months later, the bank resigned from its duties as trustee, and filed petitions to seek "outside bids" to sell the team after deciding somewhat belatedly, one would think, that baseball was a "hazardous enterprise."

The Comiskeys were one of the last of the "founding families" of baseball still actively involved in the game in 1939. Their continuous 40-year ownership was imperiled at the eleventh hour due to the vagueries of the will, which Lou had drafted back in 1932. It was the first time, but certainly not the last time, that grave concerns were expressed about the future of the White Sox in Chicago.

In a dramatic counter-move, Grace Reidy Comiskey renounced her dower rights to one-third of the estate, and asked for the one-third immediately and without condition. The testy legal showdown with the powerful downtown bank who had helped finance the 39th Street Grounds back in 1900, was resolved to the family's satisfaction on February 29, 1940, when Probate Judge

John F. O'Connell denied the bank's petitions following a heated two-hour "debate" between rival attorneys. "I'm elated, the fact is we all are!" beamed Grace, the aloof, but iron-willed dowager. "We're satisfied that the Sox are going to stay in the Comiskey family, right where they belong!"

"Shoeless" Joe Jackson. To this day, Jackson's participation in the Black Sox scandal is still being debated.

Ed Cicotte confessed to Charles Comiskey: "I don't know what you'll think of me but I got to tell you how I double crossed you. I'm a crook. I got $10,000 for being a crook." "Don't tell it to me," Comiskey growled. "Tell it to the Grand Jury."

Grace Reidy Comiskey (above), wife of Lou Comiskey, supervised the affairs of the ballclub from 1939 until 1956.

At her death, Grace bequeathed her majority interst in the White Sox to her surviving daughter Dorothy (left), bringing about a lengthy court battle between Dorothy and her brother, Charles A. Comiskey II, (right), over control of the White Sox. Young Charley was the grandson of the Old Roman and the only son of Lou Comiskey. Charley served as Sox vice-president for much of the 1950s.

Chapter
— Eight —

Family Business to Corporation, 1940-1970

And through it all, Harry Grabiner never gave up. Faithful in spirit and true of heart, Harry envisioned better days than these for his beloved Chicago White Sox. Lou's passing sounded a death knell to the family business, ushering in a quiet, but unsettling decade of White Sox history. One by one, the star calibre players who had been nurtured in the farm system by Uncle Lou marched off to war. "Boys," the cheerleading Harry would exult on opening day, "this is the year we'll win the pennant!" The roster of war time replacements was paper thin after 1941. But from the owner's box on a bright and shining opening day when Harry was surrounded by old friends and returning Bardsmen from the glory years who had come back to pay their respects, all was right with the world.

From a point of service in the American League, only Connie Mack and Clark Griffith logged more time with one organization than Harry Grabiner. He was the quiet man of Chicago baseball; well respected, but uncomfortable, and sometimes aloof with the press. Curiously, Grabiner was more at home in Hollywood where he mingled among the movie celebrities in their cafe haunts. Harry's daughter was June Travis, the Hollywood motion picture actress who appeared in a number of Warner Brothers B-grade films like "The Big Game" and "The Star" during the 1940s and early 1950s. With Lou Comiskey gone, Harry Grabiner made all the necessary player moves and supervised the finances as he saw fit. Nothing escaped his watchful eye; there would be no more exorbitant outlays of cash for vaunted rookie prospects or over-the-hill stars, as there had been in the twenties and thirties.

The White Sox reported a $55,141 loss in 1942, but would turn a profit every year thereafter through 1957. Fiscal conservatism was the watchword of the day—winning was secondary to financial survival. Typical of Grabiner's approach to running baseball operations was a 1944 player move that brought the slick-fielding third baseman Floyd "the Blotter" Baker to Chicago. Harry acquired Baker by first selling catcher Tom Turner to St. Louis for $12,500 with an option to purchase a Brownie utility player at the end of the season for $2,500. The player who came later was Baker, who became a mainstay at third base for several more years—vintage Grabiner. The Sox plugged a hole at third base, but more importantly Harry had enriched the coffers by $10,000.

Harry's frugality and unwillingness to spend money on anything less than a sure winner was a management philosophy long upheld by the matriarch Grace Comiskey and her slavishly devoted daughter, Dorothy, who assumed a position of prominence in the decision-making process as team secretary following her dad's passing. Grace, Dorothy, Dorothy's sister Grace-Lucille, Harry, and the two family attorneys, Roy Egan and Tom Sheehan, presented a cheerful, unified front to the media during these rigid, conservative times.

But there was an undercurrent of suspicion and mistrust leveled at Harry; still very much the outsider. Grace long suspected that Grabiner sparked the palace revolt that nearly resulted in the First National Bank snatching the ball club away from the Comiskey family in 1940. Grace Comiskey's fears were grounded in old antagonisms dating back to the time when the Old Roman was alive. But Harry, now without the founder or Lou around to protect him, was vulnerable—out on a limb for the first time in 40 years.

Young Charley Comiskey, away at school for much of the time, was only beginning to grasp the significance of the future role he was destined to play in the family business. The sadly disillusioned Grabiner pulled the young man aside one day, and said: "It's a shame you're not ten years older." Harry's voice was filled with more than a trace of melancholy. Charley Comiskey remembers: "He told me: 'I really need you. I've been around a long time, and I only wish I could be training you as your grandfather once trained me.'" That day would come, but Harry Grabiner would not be present to lend moral support and provide direction for Charley's apprenticeship.

As the Comiskey ship floundered haphazardly through the war years, the gulf continued to widen between Harry and the two "nervous aunts" who were running the organization to the best of their abilities. The vision, the direction, and imagination were lacking. Harry had a legion of admirers in the sports world, not the least of whom was William Louis Veeck, Jr., who had known and respected Grabiner since he was in knee pants, and the young White Sox executive was attempting to rebuild the franchise after the Black Sox Scandal.

During the war years when "Barnum Bill" was quartered in the Far East, and Harry was in command at "Fort Comiskey," the two men corresponded by mail. Mostly they talked about buying a baseball club—the White Sox was one team that came to mind. However, Grace refused to entertain any sale offers, prompting the restless and dissatisfied Grabiner to announce his retirement from the organization in December 1945.

Scarcely five months later, Harry and several of his monied Chicago friends, including Arthur Allyn, Sr., Newton P. Frye, Les Armour, and Sidney Schiff, formed a syndicate with Bill Veeck, Jr. and purchased the Cleveland Indians. Grabiner, the faithful steward of the White Sox was given a new lease on life as vice-president of the talented Indians ballclub. He would live long enough to sample one more taste of pennant fruit, in 1948, when the Tribe won the World Series behind the leadership of Chicagoan Lou Boudreau. Harry was followed out the White Sox door by Jimmy Dykes, who resigned as manager on May 24, 1946 after 12 years and 13 days at the helm. The long-running Dykes-Comiskey soap opera ended in a bitter "take it or leave it" salary dispute between Grace and Jimmy. It happened every two years or so when the manager's contract came up for negotiation, but this time Grace refused to bend to the demands. She accepted Dykes' resignation without reservation. The Comiskeys kept the story under wraps—until a gossip columnist caught up with Dykes in a Hollywood drug store and scooped the Chicago media.

Grace replaced Dykes with perennial fan favorite Teddy Lyons, but the old "Baylor Bearcat" as Lyons was known, was not cut from the same managerial timber. Lyons' credentials as a bonafide Hall of Famer and the winningest pitcher in Sox history did not necessarily equate into effective leadership of a ballclub, and in 1948 the Sox lost 102 games.

Grace Comiskey intended to surround herself with baseball men rich in experience to issue recommendations, proffer advice, and insulate her from hyper-critical fans and the press. And this is what she expected from Lyons. The Sox president kept current with the game through the local sporting pages and baseball periodicals as best she could, but Grace lacked the requisite skills for building a well-respected organization—one that top college and amateur players would gravitate towards. Her choice for General Manager ran along these same lines.

Leslie O'Connor was a former Chicago criminal attorney, who, like Grabiner, toiled in the shadow of a powerful baseball man for much of his career, in this case, Judge Kenesaw Mountain Landis. O'Connor logged 24 years in Landis' office as his aide-de-camp. But he was to be bypassed for promotion by an owner's faction led by Lee McPhail, which chose A.B. "Happy" Chandler as the new Commissioner when Landis died in 1945.

Chandler was a smiling Kentuckian who was about to shepherd baseball out of the racial dark ages and into the modern era. Whatever goals Chandler hoped to accomplish were not shared by the seething O'Connor, who quit after his new boss signalled his intentions to shift the Commissioner's office to Cincinnati. When the White Sox offer came through, O'Connor eagerly accepted—on the rebound. "Les tried to hold it together the best he could," Chuck Comiskey recalls. "But he did not really *want* to run a ballclub. He was a lawyer, and lawyers aren't necessarily the best businessmen in the world."

An embarrassing low for the Sox franchise was achieved in October 1947, when O'Connor attempted to sign a 17-year-old prep pitcher named George Zoeterman from Chicago Christian High School, in violation of existing Major League drafting rules. A rule had been passed prohibiting *any* Major League ballclub from signing high school students belonging to the National Federation of State Athletic Associations (NFSAA). Commissioner Chandler slapped O'Connor with a $500 fine, which the Sox G.M. adamantly refused to pay. Then Chandler barred the White Sox from conducting further contract negotiations and normal league business until they swallowed their medicine. In effect, the team found itself evicted from the American League!

The fine was paid of course, but the team had become a laughing-stock—a baseball joke that no one could take seriously.

"There was a negative thinking in the ballpark," Charley Comiskey states, as he reflected back on those days, "everyone was used to just going along . . . do a job . . . collect a paycheck. The ballpark people knew they weren't going to get a pay increase because the money just wasn't there."

In 1949 the White Sox were forced to take out a loan to finance the team's spring training junket to Pasadena, California. "We struggled. As the tickets were sold, we were spending the money. We did that through 1949 and 1950. And then we could start to see the daylight," Comiskey recalled.

* * *

The Old Roman's grandson remembered driving to the ballpark in a chauffeur-driven limousine on Sunday afternoons, with his grandad sitting beside him, tall and erect and wearing a white Hamburg hat. Comiskey remembered the aroma of burning cigars in the Bards Room, and his father's friends and grandfather's friends playing card games and telling stories of the famous Woodland hunts of years past. He remembered the only time in his life he saw his father cry—that afternoon the phone call came in from Texas and the doctors advised Harry Grabiner that Monty Stratton would never pitch again; his left leg had been shattered by a misfired bullet in a hunting accident. Most of all, he remembered the heartaches, the triumphs, and the tradition.

And now in the fall of 1948, when White Sox fortunes had sunk to a low ebb, Charles Albert Comiskey II was summoned to Chicago to restore pride to the name. A handsome six-footer with an athletic bearing, Chuck Comiskey cut his baseball eyeteeth in the White Sox farm system at Wisconsin Rapids and then later as the president of the Waterloo club of the Three-Eye League.

Charley understood the gravity of the situation and what was required of him. But it did not make his rendezvous with destiny any easier. "I was not ready to take over a big league club—it was force fed to me," he said. "I will say this, the older people in the game; Mr. (Branch) Rickey, and Mr. (Clark) Griffith would talk to me till three a.m. teaching me theory, how the game operates, and the fine traditions to uphold."

As a brash young executive just coming into the league, Chuck Comiskey had a few ideas of his own about building winning traditions, while the Macks, Tom Yawkeys, and Clark Griffiths grumbled about the need to "break up" the Yankee dynasty. This struck the 24-year-old Comiskey as faulty logic. "Somewhere down the line I told them that the Yankees were an asset to us all, and what we've got to do is build our own organizations up to where the Yankees are. I copied the Yankees. I *stole* from the Yankees, and I'm not ashamed of it." The great awakening was at hand.

* * *

Chicago White Sox fans savor the memories of the 1950s renaissance, but ironically, they often look past Chuck Comiskey's accomplishments as the principal architect, builder, and interior decorator of the House of Comiskey during the Sox "Go-Going" glory years. In the early "Go-Going," Grace and Dorothy stepped back and allowed Chuck a free hand to wheel and deal as he saw fit.

As his first order of business, Comiskey decided to ask waivers on the *entire team*. Only one player was claimed by the other A.L. clubs, and that was catcher Aaron Robinson, who the Sox promptly sent to the Detroit Tigers for 21-year-old left handed pitcher Billy Pierce and $10,000 in cash. The Sox coveted the forkballing Michigan sandlotter Ted Gray, but had to "settle" for Pierce instead. "Our strategy was to get rid of the old heads and come in with youth," Comiskey said. "After all, this is a business, and if we gave [the fans] something better to look at, at least they'd have to buy a scorecard."

Then, in the Fall of '48 a human hurricane hit Chicago in the presence of "Frantic" Frank Lane, former director of the Yankee farm club in Kansas City, and later the capable president of the American Association. Comiskey said, "I knew I was young and there was an awful lot of practical baseball operations I knew I would not be able to handle, so the thing I decided to do was get a good general manager. The first man I thought of was Frank Lane."

Ironically, it was Les O'Connor who introduced the free-wheeling Lane to young Comiskey at the 1948 All Star Game in St. Louis. "Chuck, this is a guy I think you ought to meet," O'Connor said. Four months later, Lane had O'Connor's job. The deal was cut at the Barn Restaurant on 79th Street, not far from Midway Airport. Lane had a few hours to kill, and was waiting to catch a flight to Minneapolis. The younger man and the older seasoned executive developed an immediate, (but short-lived) rapport.

Lane endorsed Comiskey's plan to bring in new blood, and was eager to climb aboard. "So then I had to go back and convince my mother and the attorneys that I needed someone of that caliber who had been around the farm systems. The main thing the White Sox needed were players." Comiskey's inexhaustible drive—he worked 14-hour days and attended roughly 500 civic booster luncheons during that first year—and Lane's willingness to gamble paid immediate dividends. Between October 1948 and February 1953, Lane completed 155 player transactions (trades, waiver deals, cash purchases), involving 220 players.

Frank Lane was a super-charged personality and was unafraid of sticking his neck out. Days of quiet complacency on the South Side . . . and the feeling that just getting by was good enough . . . were over with. "When I was offered the job," Frank Lane said in 1953, "people told me, 'don't take it! That's a graveyard! The Comiskeys won't let you spend any money! You'll never be able to get anywhere up there.' But it hasn't been that way at all. The Comiskeys have given me all the cooperation and support a man could ask for, and they've let me keep plowing much of our profits back into the ballclub."

Key acquisitions fueled the comeback: Pierce in '48; Chico Carrasquel and Nellie Fox after the 1949 season; Luis Aloma and Saul Rogovin a year later; then the historic arrival of the first black player in Chicago, Minnie Minoso, the "Cuban Comet," to properly inaugurate the "Go-Go" era in May of 1951. Seventeen consecutive first-division finishes were to follow for this team, an achievement paralleled in modern times only by the New York Yankees and Baltimore Orioles. Frank Charles Lane introduced these young, largely unproven ballplayers to Chicago at the rate of one or two per year. Add to the mixture an astute judge of pitching talent in manager Paul Richards, and the moribund White Sox franchise suddenly found itself breathing first-division air for the first time since the late 1930s.

The daring, crowd-pleasing ballclub, whose hit and run, base-stealing heroics were ideally tailored to the contours of Comiskey Park drew a million paying customers for the first time in its history in 1951. In recognition of the team's memorable 14-game winning streak that year, Mayor Martin Kennelly presented Chuck Comiskey with the key to the city. Happy smiles all around.

Under the stewardship of Lane and Comiskey, the value of the franchise nearly doubled to $6,000,000 in those pre-inflationary times. The profits were immediately funneled back into the farm system and the maintenance of Comiskey Park, now approaching uncomfortable middle age. In the early 1950s, the family was budgeting $500,000 per year to satisfy mounting renovation costs. "It was money better spent in player development," Comiskey sighed, "But when we looked at the park, we realized we had a lot of work to do. We painted the railings, the fascias, the seats, exterior walls, and completed various upgrades." A new press box for the football Cardinals went up; elevators connecting the ground level to the upper-tier press areas were installed; additional flood lighting in the parking areas mitigated safety concerns for the time being; leaky plumbing in the upper deck restrooms, which contributed to flooding problems downstairs, was replaced; the front offices were enlarged; a ticket office fronting 35th Street was built to keep up with the unexpected public demand for White Sox tickets; and the electronic "Chesterfield" centerfield scoreboard comprised the second major wave of Comiskey Park renovation completed between 1949-1952. But, the expenditures on the old ball park during this period were a cause of growing concern to the ownership.

* * *

All things considered, it was a remarkable turnaround. From outhouse to penthouse in just three short years, the "Go-Go" White Sox had supplanted the Cubs as Chicago's premier baseball attraction for the time being. The fortunes of the North Side ballclub had dwindled since their last pennant in 1945, but Cub owner Phil Wrigley applauded each new White Sox success. In fact, he thrived on the competition, and neither the Comiskey family nor the Wrigleys viewed the other as a mortal threat to their operation. Phil Wrigley, a millionaire sportsman in the tradition of Boston's Tom Yawkey, was viewed by Charley as a respected elder of the tribe. He solicited the advice and opinions of the chewing gum magnate, because both gentlemen optimistically believed that Chicago was a big enough pond for all to swim in. Baseball. . . . "was too much of a business to be a sport and too much of a sport to be a business," the soft-spoken Wrigley liked to say.

Sox victories kindled baseball interest in the city. That was Phil Wrigley's heartfelt belief, and he encouraged the Comiskeys to scale the heights. "The Chicago Cubs of that era could have easily become the four-ton gorilla of Chicago sports had Phil Wrigley possessed the same passion and charisma for baseball as his late father, William Wrigley," comments George Castle, a correspondent for *Sport* Magazine. "With the dawn of the television era in the late forties, and a willingness to loosen the purse strings, Phil Wrigley might have succeeded in driving the White Sox out of Chicago—the way George Halas drove the Chicago Cardinals football team out of the city in 1960."

Above all else, Mr. Wrigley was a man who believed in fair play . . . and upholding the two-team traditions. The 1950s were to be baseball's last golden age. The family ownerships were firmly in command. The quality of the talent on the field was not yet diluted by expansion; and integration of the leagues was achieved with minimal devisiveness. The fans gradually accepted and welcomed black athletes as civil rights took hold within the spheres of the national pastime. To boys and girls growing up in that happy, bygone era, the players loomed larger than life. An 11-year-old boy could recite the name of the 25th man on the roster of the eighth-place team without hesitation. The summers seemed longer; each game was an affirmation of America's bucolic roots—our passion. Baseball was at peace with itself. In the house of Comiskey, however, a serious family rift cast a pall over the wonderful success of the "Go-Go" White Sox.

* * *

". . . Tragedy," as Aristotle defined it, "is an imitation, not of men, but of action and life."

The unfolding tragedy of the Comiskey family, and for that matter the fortunes of the White Sox in the second half of the twentieth century, were grounded in pointless warfare between the two surviving siblings, Dorothy and Charley. Neither Dorothy Comiskey Rigney, nor the family attorney Roy Egan, nor to a lesser extent Chuck, could heed the warnings, accept personal criticisms, or admit the errors of their ways until it was too late. The headstrong young executive antagonized his sister and mother in early 1952 when he petitioned them for a modest increase to his $8,000-a-year salary. Chuck justifiably believed that he deserved more money to support his growing family. In Chuck's own words: "My sister wasn't putting in an hour at the park and we were drawing the same amount of pay. She was really drawing two salaries because her husband (John Rigney) as the farm director, was also bringing home a Sox paycheck."

Monetary differences aside, Comiskey was frequently at loggerheads with Roy Egan, the bookish, gnome-like co-counsel who was brought into the front office with fellow attorney Tom Sheehan on the advice of Alice Reidy, Grace's sister. Egan, as one of the four voting board members, widened the breach between Chuck and his mother and sister after Comiskey stormed out of the January 18, 1952 meeting. Grace had promised to bring the issue of Chuck's pay raise to the table for discussion, but broke her word. "She assured me that I would receive my increase, then all of a sudden nothing was mentioned at the meeting," Chuck recalls. Sometime after that I went to her apartment and she said to me, 'You're making good money for your age!' I told her that I just wanted equality, that's all." Roy Egan told reporters that young Comiskey was the victim of "some bad advice." Egan, according to L. Yager Cantwell, who litigated on behalf of Chuck Comiskey, was "a miserable lawyer. His thing was mismanaging the White Sox. He couldn't talk and he couldn't write."

Chuck resigned as the Sox's Vice-president and Secretary, and accepted an executive position with Gordon McLendon's Liberty Broadcasting System in Texas, which broadcast baseball games across the South and Southwest from ticker tape. McLendon had launched the Liberty network in 1949, and was well on his way to upending an exclusive trade monopoly between baseball and the Mutual Broadcast Company, when Commissioner Ford Frick took decisive steps to thwart McLendon's ambitions. Frick ordered McLendon to suspend operations because Major League Baseball was concerned that Liberty's broadcasts were hurting the local networks. After Chuck's career move was unexpectedly nipped in the bud, Grace restored both salary and title to her jobless son the following June, but the front office rift remained irreconcilable. Neither Grace, Dorothy, nor the attorney Roy Egan could forgive Chuck for his breach of protocol. The defection of Frank Lane after the 1955 season compounded the difficulties. Over the years, Chuck had differed with Lane on a number of important matters. But for the most part, their disagreements were a matter of personal style.

The Sox general manager completed a number of astute trades that bolstered the fortunes of the ballclub during this era of Yankee hegemony—trades that kept the Sox in the hunt, albeit, a distant third place when all was said and done. But there had been a number of costly mistakes also. The departures of first baseman Eddie Robinson, a bonafide home run threat, and speed merchant Jim Busby for over-the-hill Ferris Fain and Sam Mele, were among the notable failures of the 241 trades completed during the Lane regime. Lane was a bear for efficiency, but irascible and reckless in some of his dealings.

Late in the '55 campaign—a season when expectations for that elusive pennant ran high on the South Side—Lane engaged in a verbal sparring match with umpire Larry Napp over a particularly close call that went against Sox catcher Sherman Lollar in a game with the Boston Red Sox. As per his usual custom, Lane bench-jockeyed the umpire from his vantage point in the box seats in back of the Sox dugout. This time however, he crossed the boundaries of good common sense when he cursed a blue streak at American League president Will Harridge, and the supervisor of umpires, Cal Hubbard, who was seated nearby. The next day Commissioner Ford Frick slapped a $500 fine on Lane and ordered him to apologize to Harridge.

Comiskey believed that Frank was dead wrong in this instance, and publicly berated Lane for his gutter language, and unbecoming conduct. Lane, miffed at Chuck's failure to stand up to the league on his behalf, submitted his resignation on September 21. Shortly afterward he went to work for the August Busch family in St. Louis as the new Cardinal General Manager.

Lane's departure from the Chicago scene, however, was not such a tragic loss, as history would later demonstrate. Frank Lane would be fired in St. Louis after just two years, and later forced to resign from his next job in Cleveland when it became apparent that he had all but scalped the Tribe in a series of questionable trades. Lane could be accused of turning the lights out on the Indian franchise—for the next 35 years—by dealing away an exciting array of younger players.

Such was the flawed genius of Frank C. Lane. He was brilliant when he had nothing to work with but seemed to be incapable of turning a good ballclub into a champion. Contrary to Lane's gloomy predictions in the spring of 1956, the White Sox did not wither and die in the standings, but in fact got better once Chuck was elevated to the dual vice-presidency with John Rigney. However, Grace and Dorothy continued to fluster and fume over Lane's decampment.

"Although in large measure, the White Sox are the team they are today because of Frank," Dorothy would whine to the court in 1958, "it is public knowledge that he left the Sox because Charley made Lane's job impossible. I am firmly convinced that if Frank Lane had stayed on and not quit in disgust over Charley, we would have had a pennant flying over the park today." So too, did Grace buy into this faulty logic, overlooking the undeniable achievements of her son, later *hired* Lane, and who had convinced Cleveland manager Al Lopez to come to Chicago in 1957 when Marty Marion (Paul Richards' successor) was found wanting.

White Sox success in the early to mid-1950s was measured by the market value of the team, which had spiraled upward from $2,325 in 1952 to $6,000 net worth just four years later. Both mother and daughter thought they knew what was best for the White Sox and that was to put the brakes on Chuck's burning ambition to single-handedly run the team as his father and granddad. As it turned out, they didn't know what was best.

Grace Reidy Comiskey suffered a fatal heart attack at her Lake Shore Drive apartment on December 10, 1956. She was 63 years old, reputed to suffer a serious drinking problem, and in frail health since her initial heart attack in March 1950. Though seldom seen around the Comiskey environs in her declining years, she had ruled with an iron hand and was guided by cold-blooded malice. And her malice told her that Dorothy—not Chuck—was the mature, sensible one. Grace controlled 4,000 of the 7,540 shares of White Sox stock. In her probated will she vested control of the ballclub to Dorothy by granting Dorothy 500 more shares of stock than Charles.

This set in motion a vicious court fight that would drag on for the next two years and would ultimately cost the family control of its cherished institution. As executrix of her mother's will, which included a controlling interest of 54%, Dorothy was empowered to elect three of the five board members under the cumulative voting law in Illinois. Through the advice of Roy Egan she permitted the board to reduce its size from five to four. Later her attorneys tried to rectify another one of Egan's legal blunders by seeking a reversal through the courts.

Unshakeable in the belief that his destiny was woven around the ballclub, Chuck Comiskey initiated litigation in November

1957 to force his sister to distribute the 2,582 shares of stock held by their late mother. Chuck Comiskey, refusing to back down or negotiate, succeeded in attaining a court decree to limit the board members to four.

His legal victory guaranteed him equal voice on the club's board of directors and in the club's operation—a stalemate ensued with Dorothy and Roy Egan on one side, Chuck and his father-in-law, Frank Curran, on the other. It was to become a lengthy and all together unnecessary legal action pitting the singular-minded young Comiskey against a condescending older sister. Dorothy believed it was her mission in life to uphold Grace Comiskey's wishes for the Sox at all costs, and to "resist Charles' ambitions to become White Sox czar," as Dorothy derisively referred to Chuck. She called her brother "impetuous" and characterized his legal actions as "harassment."

Nevertheless, it soon became quite clear that Dorothy harbored no personal ambitions to operate the White Sox and was perfectly willing to recede into the background in order to raise her two young daughters and devote her spare time to her great hobby in life, her horses. It was also clear that she would not step aside and allow continuity of family ownership now that Chuck's "rite of passage" was complete. In baseball parlance, Dorothy wanted to play the role of "spoiler," and this she did quite well.

The fight for control of the club was a very serious legal matter and it was regrettable at this juncture that Mrs. Dorothy Rigney could not come to terms with the fact that Charles was no longer the 14-year-old adolescent who, as she described him, "almost always has had everything he has wanted."

Throughout this entire mess, it was appropriate that Chuck was represented by the heirs of Robert Emmet Cantwell, President of the White Sox Rooter's association in 1906-1908, and co-founder of the Woodland Bards social group, and one of the Old Roman's closest friends. Robert E. Cantwell, Jr., Robert Cantwell III, and Louis Yager Cantwell scored important victories in 11 out of 13 court battles for their client.

In April 1958, nearly six months into the battle, Judge Robert Dunne released 1,041 shares of stock to Chuck that were to be held in trust for him until his thirty-fifth birthday. In an effort to cease hostilities, Dorothy offered Chuck a pale compromise. If he agreed to allow her to elect three members to the board, and drop the suit, she would appoint him president. This was unacceptable to Charles. The title would be an honorary one under these conditions.

At this point, in June 1958, Dorothy commenced secret negotiations to sell her stock to outside interests. First there was John Jachym, who in 1949 had briefly owned stock in the Washington Senators. Then and far more significantly, Bill Veeck and his entourage breezed into town to open preliminary discussions. Leo Fischer of the *Chicago American* broke the story on July 2, sending shock waves through the baseball world.

Veeck had been out of baseball since 1954, when he transferred the St. Louis Browns to Baltimore. The eastern establishment was against him and all the carnival antics that came with him, but he continued to shop the market for new ballclubs. Veeck had gone to the well twice before in the 1950s before hitting paydirt with the White Sox. First he was outfoxed by John E. Fetzer, an astute radio-TV executive from Kalamazoo, Michigan. Fetzer headed one of seven investment groups submitting a sealed bid to purchase the Detroit Tigers in 1956 from the Briggs family who had owned the ballclub for 21 years.

Fetzer succeeded in gaining control of the Tigers after sniffing out Bill Veeck's original bid and upping the ante by $300,000. The source of Fetzer's information was H.G. Salsinger, an aging baseball writer from the *Detroit News* who opposed Veeck on principal. But Fetzer had simply played a better hand and came away the winner.

After failing to re-acquire the Cleveland Indians the next year, Veeck and company set their sights on Dorothy's stock. And for Veeck, if not the White Sox this year, then sooner or later another ballclub ripe for the picking would emerge. The predatory nature of the baseball business in the late 1950s in some ways foreshadowed the take-over frenzy that gripped Wall Street in the 1980s. Baseball teams had become interchangeable parts— speculative commodities. This year you own Club A, the next year Club B—and then out. The emotional attachment and personal identification between a team and a city can only come when an owner purchases a team and remains true to the fans over the long haul.

Not to be outdone in all this, Chicago insurance magnate Charles O. Finley became a runner-up in the Tigers-White Sox sweepstakes. Finley's office happened to be in the same building as Will Harridge's, the third president of the American League, and Charley was a frequent guest at Harridge's yearly Christmas party. Charley seemed to enjoy hobnobbing with the movers and shakers of the baseball world. While still the "great unknown" in 1958, Finley wanted to join the lodge in the very worst way. After losing out to Fetzer for the Tigers, Finley signed an agreement to pick up Veeck's 60-day option on the White Sox stock if Veeck's grace period expired. Finley's original offer in the range of $3.2 million exceeded Veeck's price for the stock by $500,000. However, various clauses and contingencies in each of these agreements reduced the sale price substantially. In this ungentlemanly game of high stakes finance, Chuck faced two formidable adversaries.

Before it was all over, he outbid them both with the full backing of the American National Bank, but still didn't get the club. Dorothy would have realized an additional profit of $148,000 over the Finley bid, and $500,000 more than Veeck (which required that Veeck control 80% of the total stock in order for Dorothy to receive the sum in total). Chuck refused to budge, especially now that outsiders were involved. Hedging on the matter, and tantalized by Finley's offer of an additional $500,000, Dorothy tried to buy back Veeck's option in order to reap a greater profit from Finley.

How quickly Dorothy's early public pronouncements belied her ultimate actions: "My family is a baseball family, and from the time I can first remember, baseball was our whole life; first my grandfather, then my father J. Louis Comiskey, and my mother were all dedicated to making the White Sox champions. . . .

After my dad's death my mother and I fought to keep control of the club for the Comiskeys."

But in the end, she did not fight hard enough. One of Chuck Comiskey's attorneys, L. Yager Cantwell argued to the court:

"Dorothy wants money, and doesn't want the White Sox. Charley wants the White Sox and doesn't want money. Dorothy has proven by everything she has done that she is only interested in getting money for her stock. Charley has proven by everything he has done that he wants to own and manage the White Sox. He hired Frank Lane—and trade by trade, year by year—has built the most exciting "Go-Go" ballclub in Chicago history, a team which has yet to fulfill its destiny, which can still bring a World Championship to Chicago.

"What should this Court do with these two heirs? They have compatible needs, compatible wants, and desires—with a perfect split of money and ballclub.

"All the law books, all the decision, all the logic in this universe cries out to this Court—'Give Charley what he wants—the White Sox: Give Dorothy what she wants—the money.'

"But now we come to a strange problem: Dorothy wants to take *less* money from Bill Veeck than what she has been offered by Charles Finley, and less money than what she has been offered by her own brother.

"Why? Greed cannot be the answer. If it were, she'd accept Charley's offer. She will not turn down Veeck, and she will turn down her own brother.

"It is rumored that on some of our darker, stormy and rain-swept nights, the ghost of the Old Roman walks the halls and upper decks of the Baseball Palace of the World, and like Hamlet's father, mourns over what has happened to his kingdom."

* * *

On March 5, 1959, Probate Court Judge Dunne threw out Chuck's petition to rule the Veeck sale null and void. Judge Dunne added a few gratuitous words to his opinion: "All too often children who have inherited property are willing to pub-licly quarrel about their inheritance and in so doing, drag into the litigation the good names of their deceased parents or grandpar-ents from whom they received their inheritance," the judge seemed to be directing them towards Dorothy rather than to Charley—who had done everything in his power to prove his good will and desire to manage the cherished family business. The appeals would drag on for another year. Chuck Comiskey went to court with copies of the first of three wills to support his contention that the ball club was to be his some day. But it was only a collection of meaningless words written long ago.

Words that counted for very little when all was said and done.

* * *

Looking back on the Summer of '59, "Bill Veeck romanced us," states John Kuenster, publisher of *Baseball Digest*, and one of the *Daily News* beat reporters who covered the Sox in the heat of the pennant drive. "I was one of several reporters—Jerome Holtzman, Dick Dozer in Chicago; in Cleveland it was Harry Jones—Veeck had a way with words. No doubt about that." The

charm, the wit, and the flamboyance of "sport shirt" Bill capti-
vated the media and energized Chicago fandom. On and off the
field there was something magical about the Veeck-led White
Sox. Even the big four-game series with the New York Yankees
that traditionally broke the bank for the Comiskeys—and the
hearts of White Sox fans come Monday morning—took on added
meaning in '59. For the first time in memory the Sox were actually
winning the big showdowns with the American League elite. The
solidarity, the esprit de corps of the aging Sox led by the fiery
moundsman Early Wynn, the silent star Billy Pierce, and the pint-
sized infield magicians Nellie Fox and Louie Aparicio, cata-
pulted the team to a first-place lead they never relinquished after
July 22. In many respects this was a surprise pennant. Only
manager Al Lopez possessed the confidence in spring training
that this team had the necessary firepower to beat out the
Yankees and Indians after years of second- and third-place
frustrations.

Meanwhile, Veeck romanced the press corps at home and on
the road in the long-forgotten traditions of the Old Roman. "He
would spend all night with the writers at Miller's Pub in Chicago's
Loop and all the other places they would go to drink, and Bill
would pick up the tab," recalls commentator Bruce Levine, of
WMVP in Chicago, and contributor to the *Sporting News* and
other baseball publications. "He was a bright and brilliant guy
who could speak with authority on any subject. If he were alive
today he would have his own talk show in all likelihood. I see Bill
Veeck as a cross between Oprah Winfrey and the John McLaughlin
group."

A record advance sale, great promotional stunts—"Mar-
tians" landing in the outfield during one game, cow milking
contests, and the unforgettable "I'm a Smith and I'm For Al!"
Night (to lend moral support for struggling White Sox outfielder
Al Smith)—made every game seem more like a carnival midway
than a baseball contest. "The way he is operating, Veeck probably
will break the Comiskey Park telephone records, both local and
long distance that were established by former General Manager
Frank Lane," Bill Gleason glowingly reported in the pages of the
Chicago American. With the convictions of a Madison Avenue
pitchman, Gleason added: "Bill talks to everybody who asks for
him and seems to enjoy it too. He has a knack of making every
caller feel that he has been waiting to hear from them." A

headline from the *Chicago American*: April 1, 1959: "Chuck? Who
He? Busy Bill Running Show!"

As for Charley Comiskey, the minority stockholder was
unable to come to terms with the volatile mixture of anger,
malice, and disappointment, the heroics of the team that he had
built must have come as a bittersweet triumph. Chuck had
refused to sell his stock to Veeck, which cost the new ownership
group an estimated $1,300,000 in taxes. "I'm patriotic!" Chuck
grinned as Veeck only seethed. Comiskey was not averse to
reaping tax advantages. His accountant Max Auerbach advised:
"You know Chuck, you could stick a million in your pocket,
remain in baseball, and have the option to buy back in someday."
Comiskey decided it was not worth the gamble, but far more
important to hang on to the stock. He was simply not sure he
could buy it back as easily as Auerbach suggested once it was in
the hands of the Veeck group. Chuck Comiskey had been given
the title of executive vice-president, his salary increased, and he
was awarded a liberal expense account. Conciliatory gestures, to
be sure, but they did not placate Comiskey.

Angered by Comiskey's unwillingness to sell him the stock,
Bill Veeck refused to publicly criticize Chuck—he waited until
the publication of his 1962 memoir *Veeck—As In Wreck* to take his
punches at the Old Roman's grandson and the other "baseball
Crown Princess" in waiting. In Veeck's way of thinking, Chuck
Comiskey, Walter "Spike" Briggs, Jr., (who inherited the Detroit
Tigers when his father passed away in 1952), and Connie Mack's
sons in Philadelphia were wealthy, spoiled, and arrogant; their
reasoning faulty if they believed daddy's holdings were theirs by
divine right. "It is never easy for the Crown Prince to find, upon
reaching the accession that Francois Villon and his beggars have
taken over the palace," Veeck wrote.

Yet, there were only two American League ownerships stand-
ing squarely in the Bill Veeck camp when Veeck went before the
American League potentates with a request to relocate his St.
Louis Browns to Baltimore for the 1954 season: Spike Briggs and
Charley Comiskey. Amid the ambitious plans Veeck had to
vacate St. Louis, an air of intrigue and duplicity hung in the air,
all of which is covered in detail in his book, *Veeck—As In Wreck*.
Chuck Comiskey recalls a midnight conversation he had in an
East Coast hotel with Newton Frye, a Chicago lawyer who was
one of Veeck's important backers through several baseball ventures. "Only one man in the American League told me the truth

during these last few days, and that was Charley Comiskey," Frye told Chuck. "I never saw so many liars and connivers in all my days."

* * *

The 1959 pennant was won on the tried and true formula of pitching, speed, and composite team defense. It was an enterprising ballclub, perhaps not as strong as Marty Marion's 1955 edition, or as well balanced as the 1957 team, but it had a lot of heart, and the club took the full measure of the Los Angeles Dodgers in the World Series before succumbing in six games. The "Go-Go" White Sox of 1959 vintage were an inspired team who interrupted a string of New York Yankee pennants. Could they have done so without Bill Veeck? Doubtless to say the colorful showman livened up the proceedings and the renewed fan interest spilled over to the ballclub. Perhaps there would have been no pennant under the Comiskeys in 1959. Certainly it could not happen again under Veeck, and it didn't.

* * *

A successful baseball organization is predicated on one governing principle: you build from within. The bedrock foundation of continuing success—not just one or two winning seasons woven around a ten- or twenty-year litany of failure—is the quality of talent developed in the minor leagues. It begins with the scouting system, and in the early to mid-1950s before Veeck arrived, Dorothy Comiskey's husband John Rigney rebuilt the entire system from scratch and hired some of the shrewdest judges of talent in the land. The impressive list of scouts included among others: Dario Lodigiani (Pacific Northwest); Harry Postove (Supervisor, Eastern Region); Ted Lyons (Southeast); Hugh Mulcahy (Central States); Mel Preibisch (Southwest); Johnny Mostil (Midwest); Fred Shaffer (Alleghenies); Jack Sheehan (Central States Supervisor); and Hollis Thurston (Far West Supervisor).

There existed a healthy competition to see who among them could deliver the most bonafide prospects to the big-league level. Comparisons of their results inevitably followed at the organizational meeting each year in Chicago. By the late 1950s, a future first-string lineup was maturing in the high minors through the efforts of these men.

From the Class AAA Indianapolis team: outfielder John Callison, pitcher Barry Latman, and first baseman Norman Cash; Dubuque, Midwest League: catcher John Romano; Colorado Springs, Western League: catcher Earl Battey; Davenport, Three-I League: first baseman, Don Mincher; Memphis, Southern Association: pitcher Ken McBride. All these promising youngsters (who achieved varying degrees of success with other teams) were traded away by Veeck and Hank Greenberg after the 1959 season for a collection of fading veterans acquired in the mistaken belief that they could lead the White Sox to a repeat pennant in 1960.

John Callison and Earl Battey were destined for greatness... but not in Chicago. Earl Battey was originally scouted by Hollis Thurston, a notable Sox pitcher from the 1920s, then personally signed to a White Sox contract by Chuck Comiskey in 1953. A star athlete at Jordan high school in Los Angeles, Battey was a shy, sensitive youth. He had no father, and his mother worked as a hotel maid. "I said: 'Mrs. Battey, I couldn't give you any more than $6,000 (league limitations on signing bonuses were then in effect), but you have to believe in Charley Comiskey. I want you to know I will be his father, and I'm sure to take care of him.' And I felt that," Comiskey added. There was little doubt that the strapping black athlete from L.A. was going to make the big time. The only question was when.

Earl was a disappointing late season call-up in 1955-1956. He would caddy for Sherm Lollar each of the next three seasons but failed to demonstrate the defensive acumen that would win him three Gold Glove awards in the 1960s. Impatient with Battey's progress and confident that the brittle Lollar had a few more good seasons in his 37-year-old legs, Hank Greenberg traded Battey, Don Mincher, and $150,000 in cash to the Washington Senators on April 5, 1960. In return, the Sox received a one-dimensional slugger in first baseman Roy Sievers, fast approaching the twilight of his career.

The deal was consummated with Veeck's blessing, while Chuck Comiskey was flying to Miami from Puerto Rico. Nobody bothered to consult with Chuck beforehand, or inform him of the development later. He found out from the teary-eyed Battey in Miami as he stepped off the plane. "I told Earl that the whole organization is starting to change. All I can say is you did everything I've asked. You're going to be a great Major League player some day." And he was.

The spoiled rich boy—"Crown Prince Charley"—might have told Greenberg and Veeck if they had cared to listen. But relations between Chuck Comiskey and Hank Greenberg were hard and edgy. "He was the guy who really screwed up the deal between Comiskey working with the Veeck group, and Comiskey not working with the Veeck group," Chuck explained. "Bill and I could have worked something out, but Bill turned negotiations over to Greenberg who was very untruthful to me." Veeck and Comiskey had originally agreed to divide responsibilities down the middle. "Bill and I sat in the Bards Room one day, and he said to me, 'Chuck, you know the player end of it. I'll stick to the promotions.'" Relations soured when: ". . . Hank [Greenberg] was trying to control the baseball operation. He was just not a guy you could sit down and talk with. We couldn't communicate on anything." What happens to a team after the ripe cherries are picked from the tree? Or to put it another way: "How does a Fred Shaffer or a Mel Preibisch feel when one of his kids finally makes it in the big time? And now all of a sudden he's not going to be with the organization," Comiskey said. "The result is, you start losing the good scouts because they have no direction."

Bill Veeck made those deals with the expectation of winning the 1960 pennant when the Yankees appeared most vulnerable. Bruce Levine explains: "After 1959 Veeck knew he was going to sell the team. He knew it all along—and wanted one more good year to cement his place in history." The consequences of those trades, however, haunted the franchise well into the 1970s. Unbeknownst to Veeck who was about to decamp to the Eastern Shore of Maryland, the die was already cast and another sundown loomed on the horizon for this ballclub.

* * *

The Bill Veeck ownership quietly expired on June 10, 1961. His health, which otherwise had been robust—despite a debilitating wartime injury that ultimately cost him the use of his right leg—was not a concern until the complications of pneumonia and a more serious undiagnosed illness forced him to seek treatment at the Mayo Clinic in Minnesota. Forced to interrupt a busy schedule of appearances before church, fraternal, and civic groups, not to mention the day-to-day operation of a ballclub that was floundering in ninth place at the moment, Veeck, Arthur Allyn, Jr., and other partners in the CBC Corporation decided to put their 54% up for sale.

While Veeck was undergoing tests at the Mayo Clinic, Greenberg stepped in to supervise the affairs of the club. The ex-Detroit Tiger slugging star had been an integral part of the Veeck operation since 1947 when his playing days ended. During Veeck's Cleveland adventure back in the 1940s, Greenberg functioned as the general manager. After the White Sox sale was consummated, Greenberg sold his stock in the Indians for $400 a share and in turn became a major stockholder in the White Sox.

Control of the White Sox might have reverted back to Chuck Comiskey eventually. Hank Greenberg, however, vetoed a proposed sale to an investment group. The group was headed by 39-year-old La Salle Street attorney Bernard Epton and the television comedian Danny Thomas, who entertained in Chicago during his nightclub career, and had a fondness for the city and its sports teams. The popular Lebanese entertainer had strong Chicago ties to Father Patrick McPolin, a South Side priest affiliated with the St. Jude's Children's Hospital that Thomas generously supported.

Epton was the brother of Judge Saul Epton of the boys court and a comer in local Republican politics. Epton held out hopes of someday winning a Congressional seat, but was thwarted by the powerful Democratic organization forged by Mayor Daley. Virtually every major piece of consumer protection law related to the insurance industry in the coming decades resulted from Epton's work. In 1983 he fulfilled his political ambitions by running against Harold Washington for mayor of Chicago—but he lost an emotionally charged election remembered today as one of the most divisive campaigns in city history. When Washington became Chicago's first black mayor, Epton was slandered as a racist by his opponents; a bitter personal stigma he would carry with him to the grave.

Bernard Epton knew Chuck Comiskey from his early days in the Hyde Park community on Chicago's South Side, and they were on friendly terms. When Dorothy first voiced her intentions to put the stock up for sale, Bernie was an interested third party who indicated that he would entertain a notion of buying Mrs. Rigney out and joining forces with Chuck. However, because of the presence of Veeck and Finley, the idea of Epton purchasing controlling interest in the Sox had to be shelved for another three years.

In 1961, when Epton and Danny Thomas were in a two-horse race for the White Sox stock, some of the CBC partners voiced suspicions about the rival group's financial wherewithal. Lurking in the background was Epton's ally Chuck Comiskey, and that was enough to "queer the deal" from Greenberg's perspective. "Hank was against the deal right from the start," Veeck told the press at the time, "because he felt that if we gave them the option, then they would go out and try to peddle the club." To Charley Comiskey, presumably.

Bernie Epton put up a $1,000 option—ten times the amount given to Mrs. Rigney by the CBC partners in 1959. It was not acceptable to Greenberg, who explained that: "It's customary to put up five to ten percent of the sale price to get an option." Epton's purchase offer of $4.8 million was formally presented to Allyn on June 4. The strength of his financial position, however, was of some concern to the Veeck group, which preferred to deal with the people they knew from inside.

After stalling Bernie Epton for a few more days, the agreement with Allyn was leaked to the press on the tenth. The price: an estimated $3.25 million. Chuck made immediate overtures to Arthur, Jr., but was firmly rebuffed. "I did not buy out Bill Veeck and Hank Greenberg to sell to anyone else," Allyn said. And he meant it.

* * *

Until he purchased Bill Veeck's 54%, Arthur Cecil Allyn, Jr. had attended only two baseball games in his life. Allyn, like Chuck Comiskey Jr., was the heir of a family fortune, in this case a La Salle Street securities and investment firm founded by his father. Arthur C. Allyn was a jovial entrepreneur who had converted a small family hardware business into a diversified portfolio that included a Georgia chicken ranch, oil wells in Texas, and a Chicago garment concern. Art Sr. was a towering figure in the La Salle Street brokerage business in the 1940s and 1950s; a sportsman from Evanston, Illinois, who was much admired for his business savvy and personable nature. He had arranged the financing for Bill Veeck in his previous baseball ventures in Cleveland and St. Louis and continued to remain active in White Sox affairs.

After a heart attack claimed his life in October 1960, the elder Allyn's holdings were split evenly between the two sons, Arthur Jr. and John. Art involved himself with the ballclub, and John took over the investment end of the business. Oddly enough, the professional sports world was less appealing to the bookish Art Jr. than to his brother John who was an avid golfer, outdoorsman, and every inch his father's son. "People in baseball are not very interesting," the new owner candidly remarked, a revealing statement in and of itself.

High finance, scientific research, and collecting rare butterfly specimens were more to his liking than intermingling amongst the jock culture. Art cherished his butterflies and housed them in the Allyn Museum of Entomology, which he was to build near the Sox training camp in Sarasota, Florida in due time.

The Chicago White Sox were an important addition to the Artnell Corporation (a hybrid of the first names of Art Sr. and his wife Nellie). The team was acquired for its long-term capital gains potential, and not because of a magnanimous gesture on Arthur's part or because of his altruistic love of sport. Chicago at the time was on the upswing. The city was vibrant and sure of its future. There was potential ahead for men of vision. Urban renewal was uprooting many deteriorating South Side neighborhoods in the 1950s. Massive slum clearance had commenced during the regimes of Mayor Richard J. Daley and his two predecessors.

Beginning in early 1959, blighted areas of substandard frame housing, vacated storefronts, and empty lots east of the ballpark along Wentworth Avenue were razed in order to make way for Interstate Highway 94, a link between Northwest Indiana and the south suburbs to downtown Chicago. The condemnation proceedings raised mild levels of protest from South Side residents, but nary a whimper from Veeck, Allyn, and company who believed that the new expressway would be a tremendous boon to White Sox attendance.

The ease and convenience of the Dan Ryan Expressway (I-94)—ball park exits in each direction—guaranteed that suburban commuters would no longer have to risk life and limb driving through the high-crime neighborhoods to the east in order to reach the ballpark. The Dan Ryan whisked them from the distant suburbs or central city directly into White Sox parking lots and out again with minimal inconvenience.

For a moment at least, Comiskey Park enjoyed a second life. Record gate attendance (1,644,460 in 1960), significant neighborhood improvements, and a reasonably competitive team convinced Allyn that the White Sox were on the rise and were a sound financial investment. Since Lou Comiskey's day, the strategy of each new management group was tied to improving the stadium first, and then giving proper attention to the baseball organization. As previously noted, the founder's son tinkered with the outfield dimensions, installed light towers, an electronic public address system, and added various front office amenities. Son Charles built the Cardinal pressbox, installed permanent riser seating in the upper and lower concourses, added the centerfield scoreboard, and a street-level ticket office. When Veeck came in, he whitewashed the red brick facade, swept clean the interior, built the enclosed baseball pressbox, created the left field "picnic area," and added exploding fireworks to the scoreboard.

Now it was Arthur's turn. First he spent $116,000 to replace the 51-year-old clubhouses where the players dressed, along the first and third base lines. The problem of flooding dugouts following a heavy rainstorm was momentarily alleviated by new submersible pumps. The existing players' clubhouses were among the worst in baseball in terms of comfort, player safety, and maintenance. The 1962 renovation project provided 7,554 square feet of air-conditioned clubhouse for the umpires, the Sox players, and the visiting team. The improvements were ready for the 1962 season and were praised by the visiting American Leaguers. By 1986, the player facilities were nearly as antiquated as the ones Arthur had replaced a quarter-century earlier. The cost of maintaining old Comiskey Park was too much . . . for *any* ownership, and the deep-seeded problems were apparent long before Jerry Reinsdorf staked his claim for the White Sox.

* * *

Art Allyn was a drawing board visionary whose ideas rarely went beyond the conception stage. To his credit, he anticipated some future marketing trends in baseball and was among the first professional sports moguls to lay the ground work for a private stadium club. Eager to cater to his influential downtown customers, Allyn announced plans to build the "Coach and Nine," a private dining club and cocktail lounge for the season ticket holders. Allyn hoped to accommodate up to 600 patrons directly across the street from the main entrance of the ballpark on a site formerly occupied by the Central Screw Company. The "nuts and bolts" of the matter: the factory was knocked down and the vacant property yielded greater revenue as a parking lot.

Allyn, a latter day "Don Quixote" in horn-rimmed glasses and a butch crewcut jousted with the politicians and tantalized Chicago sports fans for nearly two years (1967-1969) with the intriguing promise that a privately financed multi-purpose stadium would one day arise south of the Loop for the White Sox. For the American Football League franchise he promised to relocate to the city after A.F.L. moguls turned down Allyn's $4.5 million bid to purchase the struggling Denver Broncos in 1964. But again, Allyn was unable to deliver the private club, the football team, or a new stadium during his eight-year ownership. Art tinkered with less costly measures in the mid-1960s, including a Wisconsin summer camp for boys that opened in 1964 and a private jet airplane to ferry his ballclub around the country. But after a few years, the overhead cost grounded the Sox jet and dwindling public interest eventually cancelled the Artnell-owned summer camp.

Try as he might, there was very little of substance that Art Allyn could accomplish during his eight years at the Sox helm. The other owners found him abrasive and difficult to work with. Consequently, many of his ideas and opinions were ignored by the baseball fraternity. A substantive revenue-sharing proposal tendered by Allyn's emissaries at the 1964 winter meetings was immediately shot down by fellow American League owners as socialistic.

Minnesota Twins owner Calvin Griffith snorted: "Who the hell was helping me when I was poor?" Griffith became rich and successful in the Twin Cities after transferring his Uncle Clark's ballclub from Washington following the 1960 season. Minnesota was the top drawing team in the A.L. in the 1960s and Cal reaffirmed baseball's governing principal: every man for himself, and screw you if you don't like it.

* * *

Chuck Comiskey left baseball for good after he sold his stock to a group of 11 local business entrepreneurs on December 14, 1961. The syndicate of wealthy Chicagoans, all under the age of fifty, was headed by Thomas A. Reynolds, Jr., a young attorney at Winston & Strawn who would one day take over the firm that employed him. In the 1980s, Reynolds spearheaded efforts by the Illinois Sports Facilities Authority to build the new Comiskey Park.

Reynolds and his group had earlier tried to buy the club directly from Veeck, but were turned away. Next they solicited Art Allyn with a generous purchase offer for his 54%. Had they succeeded, in all likelihood, they would have returned control of the organization back to Comiskey, were it in their power to do so. But the Reynolds syndicate underestimated the resolve of Allyn and his CBC conglomerate. Allyn fended off all sales offers which prompted Reynolds RBR Corporation (Tom Reynolds, his boyhood friend William Bartholomay, and Bryan S. Reid), to sell their stock to Arthur in May, 1962. It marked the first time since 1939 that the White Sox were under single ownership.

The long battle to gain control of the family business thus ended on an anti-climactic note for "crown prince" Charley, who refused to harbor a grudge, or to speak ill of Bill Veeck, or the book Veeck was soon to publish.

* * *

Art Allyn soon realized important tax breaks from his purchase of the stock that had been denied Veeck. These tax breaks lasted about six years, by which time the ballclub had fallen flat on its face due to internal and external forces, bad planning, and the aftermath of Veeck's trades. The talent in the minor league organization was bankrupted, and the parent club was on a collision course with the second division through no real fault of Arthur's. The inevitable fall from grace was delayed until 1968, because the few good prospects remaining in the organization played up to their capabilities. Pitchers Joel Horlen and Gary Peters achieved stardom by 1963, and some smart trades by general manager Edwin Short kept the Sox in the thick of things, generally speaking.

Short, a former sports director at WJJD radio in Chicago and publicity guru who wrote scripts for long-time Sox broadcaster Bob Elson in his younger days, was hired by Comiskey in 1950. He would succeed Greenberg in August 1961 and commit the Sox to a youth movement, which coldly shoved aside pitcher Early Wynn on the eve of his 300th career victory. Short also sent a crushed and disheartened Billy Pierce to the San Francisco Giants after 12 years on the South Side; and most disheartening of all, he sent Nelson Fox to the Houston Colt .45s for two undistinguished minor leaguers.

None of these players, who had contributed so much to the success of the organization over the years, were honored by management for their achievements. Short demurred: "We can't afford to let this team grow too old and fall apart completely."

The younger pitchers who came along—Gary Peters, Juan Pizarro, Joel Horlen—and a fine bullpen anchored by Eddie Fisher, Hoyt Wilhelm, and Bob Locker, compensated for a wobbly, weak-kneed offense that conjured up distant memories of the Hitless Wonder era.

The talent-shorn White Sox nearly stole pennants in 1964 and 1967 (finishing in second and fourth respectively), because Veeck and Greenberg had managed to at least preserve the pitching talent on the minor league levels. The White Sox of the early to mid-1960s were an overachieving ballclub—due to the genius of the men in the dugout. Al Lopez and his successor Eddie Stanky kept these players on their toes despite the woeful show of offense.

Ed Short made some great trades in the early going. The acquisition of rookie pitcher Tommy John from the Cleveland Indians in 1965 was an inspired coup. But as the decade wore on, Short abandoned his youth movement and exchanged promising youngsters for aging post-1950s veterans such as Gary Bell, Woodie Held, Russ Snyder, Don Pavletich, Bobby Knoop, Rocky Colavito, Ken Boyer, and Bob Priddy. They only dragged the team further down after 1967.

The memorable '67 season was a watershed year in White Sox history. The team battled the power-laden Detroit Tigers, Boston Red Sox, and Minnesota Twins for the A.L. pennant right down to the last week of the season, but could not muster the proper levels of enthusiasm among apathetic White Sox fans.

Unbelievably, the fans boycotted the park during the heat of a pennant race when Art Allyn entered into preliminary discussions with a Milwaukee syndicate headed by Judge Robert Cannon, the former counsel for the Major League Baseball Player's Association, and Allan H. "Bud" Selig. Both men were committed to returning big league baseball to beertown following the defection of the Braves to Atlanta.

The truth of the matter was that all along, Art Allyn viewed baseball as a business, nothing more. It was never in his blood, and Bill Veeck should have intuitively sensed that fact before he shunted aside the Epton-Thomas group in 1961. The butterfly collector and his nattily attired general manager who favored butterscotch shirts and magenta slacks as his preferred ballpark garb, were one of the main reasons why the Sox were not drawing fans to the park—neighborhood safety concerns notwithstanding.

Ed Short was surly and uncommunicative; Allyn lackluster and tough to penetrate. With the exception of an occasional "Old-Timer's Day," a "Teen Night," or an S & H Green Stamp give-away, marketing and promotions were virtually non-existent. And, in any event, the fans mistrusted the motives of the front office. A banner paraded around the grandstand one day in 1969 summarized the prevailing attitude: "Short Stinks!"

The Art and Ed show had worn thin with the fans. That much was obvious. Their credibility sunk even lower when Arthur sprung his little surprise on Chicago baseball fans late in the 1967 campaign. Henceforth, the White Sox would play one "home game" against each A.L. opponent in Milwaukee beginning in 1968.

Their philanthropic mission, as Art explained, was to "help" Selig's Teams, Inc., investment group land a new tenant for County Stadium. It was an elaborate smoke screen designed to bolster sagging gate revenues and leverage Mayor Daley and the city to help Allyn secure land for the South Loop stadium. In actuality, the only team the Milwaukeeans coveted were the White Sox, and Art would have undoubtedly moved the Sox once efforts for a new stadium were exhausted. However, A.L. President Joe Cronin was dead set against it, and despite Selig's hard sell tactics (which included a flying junket to the A.L. cities to meet with the owners face to face) only the Kansas City Royals, New York Yankees, and Minnesota Twins indicated any degree of support for the move.

Nineteen-sixty-nine marked the first year of divisional play in baseball. Exiled to the Western Division alongside the two new expansion clubs, Seattle and Kansas City, the foundering Sox drew only 392,762 fans to the silent and empty Comiskey Park. Excluding the attendance at the 11 Milwaukee games, it was the lowest turnout on the South Side since 1944. The book loss was in excess of $500,000.

Across town, the Cub renaissance had bloomed. The Wrigleys had emerged from their two-decade slumber and had charmed the TV generation who had grown up with daytime baseball aired on WGN. Television exposure complimented an exciting and colorful aggregate of ballplayers whose images adorned pizza boxes, grocery store giveaway items, books, magazines, and pin-on buttons in the Summer of '69. The secret of their success was marketing . . . marketing . . . and marketing. Overnight they had become Chicago's team; the Cinderella "Cubbies" of the swinging sixties—Ron Santo, Ernie Banks, Billy Williams, and company. Where were the White Sox? Hiding in fifth place of the American League West and nowhere to be found.

The success of the Cubs during this era, and the wholesome family atmosphere of charming Wrigley Field contrasted with the indifferent ownership, the lackadaisical team play, and the austere ballpark on the South Side. For all of the cosmetic improvements implemented for the fan's convenience by the Comiskeys, Veecks, and Allyns over the years, the dull white baseball factory at 35th and Shields failed to conjure up warm, fuzzy memories of the past among the ticket holders.

Sox Attendance	Cub Attendance
1967 - 985,634	1967 - 977,226
* 1968 - 803,775	1968 - 1,043,409
**1969 - 589,546	1969 - 1,674,993
1970 - 495,355	1970 - 1,642,705

* Includes 265,552 Milwaukee patrons. ** Includes 196,784 Milwaukee patrons.

Baseball feeds on its nostalgia. It's what keeps the game strong amid lockouts, strikes, and salary disputes. Nostalgia for a time and place far removed is what the National Pastime is all about in the final analysis. But when Sox fans recall their good old days, their memories are linked to specific boyhood heroes: Minnie, Nellie, "Little Louie" Aparicio, and the games these men played . . . not the look and feel of a mottled old ballpark, the smell of grilled hotdogs, or the visual aesthetics of an infield covered in 1969 with garish-looking, lime green astro-turf, which Arthur Allyn installed in the vain hope of livening up the offense.

A family affair. Grace Comiskey (wearing veil), her daughter Grace Lucille (to her right), and son Charles (front row, right) are flanked by well wishers and cousins.

Joe Barry, Grace Comiskey's brother-in-law, and the White Sox travelling secretary in the 1930s and '40s, offered young Charley Comiskey some friendly advice—"it's a lot of heartache kid!"

For a brief time in the early 1970s, Dick Allen brought fans and victories back to Comiskey Park. In 1972, Allen led the American League with 37 home runs and 113 RBIs.

Chapter
— Nine —

A Struggle Just to Survive
(1970-1981)

"The irony was all too clear," wrote *New York Daily News* columnist Dick Young, "Milwaukee was making it possible for [Art] Allyn to afford Chicago." The gate revenues coming out of the Wisconsin city during the Cub awakening of 1968-1969 kept the Allyns out of the poor house. But Arthur didn't want Chicago. In fact he didn't even want to have anything more to do with *baseball* at all. In 1969, the White Sox were run by his second in command, Leo Breen, and five Artnell vice-presidents. Art officially divorced himself from the operation that year in order to pay more attention to other Artnell businesses that held a far greater appeal for him.

Bud Selig truly believed he had a ballclub in hand as his group hammered out the final picky details of the package: a five-year television contract, leasing of the 16-year-old County Stadium, and a final sale price pegged at between $10 million and $13 million. Arrangements were nearly complete . . . in Selig's mind. Two areas of disagreement, and stiff league opposition held up the deal, though. Allyn was unwavering in his demand for $14.7 million. Arthur also had his problems with his younger brother, John, who had remained publicly silent on policy matters over the years, but was a 50% owner, nevertheless.

John Allyn was better suited to running a ballclub than his brother, but had chosen to maintain a lower profile much of the time—and that was regrettable. The White Sox might have profited from his wisdom and insights before the unfortunate set of circumstances they found themselves in unfolded.

An outdoorsman with a yen for golf and hunting, John Allyn grew up a Cub fan while living in Evanston. He shared his father's belief that ownership of a sports franchise entailed obligations; obligations to the fans and the stockholders. Baseball represented more than just an entry on a ledger sheet. But at the same time, it was also a business and had to be cautiously maintained.

When it came to Milwaukee, the younger Allyn drew his line in the sand. It was ridiculous to think that a city dwarfed in size by Chicago and suffering a massive civic inferiority complex at the hands of its neighbor to the south could pirate away the Comiskey Park franchise. John proposed a 50-50 split of the Artnell divisions. He would take over the White Sox from Arthur, assume the current liability, and split off the corporation. The older brother said fine, take it if you want, and retired to Florida with what was left of his holding.

Amid a great deal of family bitterness, John went ahead with the deal with his eyes wide open. He predicted that 1970 would "Be the poorest we can envision—worse than this year." And it was . . . "We took a very cold, calculated look at the thing."

John Allyn was a very courageous man, and White Sox fans who still thrive on the ballclub—its past, its present, and its uncharted future—owe this man a great debt of gratitude because he saved the team from possible oblivion, not once, but twice. In between crises he had to deal with the "cult of personality" evolving around the enormous unfed egos of broadcaster Harry Caray and prima donna superstar Dick Allen, who some people mistakenly identify as the "savior" of the franchise.

The only savior when all the votes are counted is John Allyn.

* * *

Mr. Allyn weathered the 1970 storm admirably. Record-setting losses on the field (106), and dangerously low attendance in the stands (495,355), did not discourage him from going forward with rebuilding.

To be successful, John knew that an owner must sell the total baseball experience — the game on the field, the promotions, and the ambience of the park. But John Allyn also knew that he had three strikes against him going in. There was much candor in his words when he admitted: "The entire Sox operation has lost its public image."

Proving that rebuilding need not traumatize the fans for five years, John Allyn retooled the organization in a manner reminiscent of Chuck Comiskey two decades earlier. The axe fell on Ed Short and his manager, Don Gutteridge, within a 24-hour period in September 1970. Stu Holcomb, the former athletic director at Northwestern University, was Allyn's first choice for executive vice-president. He quietly dipped into the California Angels farm system to procure a new manager in 42-year-old Chuck Tanner, and a director of player personnel in Roland Hemond, a soft-spoken New Englander who came up through the Milwaukee Braves organization. These men were counted on to work a miracle or two.

For a time it appeared that Hemond was Frank Lane reincarnate, and Tanner was another Paul Richards. Roland's whirlwind trades during the off-season altered the complexion of the team. While stopping well short of Lane's strategy of placing the entire team on waivers, Hemond travelled a more conventional trade route to acquire a quartet of players from the Angels' farm system who fueled the 1971 comeback: outfielders Jay Johnstone and Rick Reichardt, pitcher Tom Bradley, and catcher Tom Egan. It was these moves that helped elevate the Sox to a far more respectable third place finish.

Chuck Tanner was a player's manager. He was their pal, their disciplinarian when necessary, and their father protector who shielded them from the reporters when the chips were down, as they so often were after Dick Allen's one big year on the South Side.

With Tanner's encouragement, Hemond had aggressively pursued the power-hitting Allen in trade talks for over a year. The deal sending left-handed starter Tommy John to the Los Angeles Dodgers for Allen was a *fait accompli* in December 1971 amid great rejoicing in Chicago. The savior had been delivered to rescue the mere mortals.

Richard Anthony Allen was a star of the 1960s with an eggshell-thin temperament and non-conformist reputation. During his six years in the City of Brotherly Love, the Philadelphia boo-birds threw rocks at him, fired BBs at his automobile, and heckled him unmercifully every time he stepped onto the field. On one occasion a group of ornery fans chased his wife down the street. No player since the late, great Ty Cobb inspired so much enmity from the fans as did Richie Allen.

He was a bad actor—an unreliable, sullen, lazy player who couldn't get along with anyone. That was the rap that his manager Bob Skinner and others in the Phillies organization hung on him over the years. Some of the complaints against Allen may have been racially motivated. Others, way off base. But at the same time, the fans were perceptive enough to recognize that their star player was merely going through the paces at times.

It took a generous infusion of White Sox cash and massive ego massaging to convince Allen to join the White Sox in 1972. Just ten hours after 600 major leaguers vacated the spring training camps in baseball's first-ever player strike, Allen signed a $130,000-per year contract with the White Sox and proceeded to Sarasota to begin his workout. Richie ("Call me Dick") Allen hated spring training (he didn't care much for batting practice either), and his decision to hold out was a smoke screen designed to prolong the off-season. Thoroughbred horses were his real interest in life, and every spare moment was given over to the pursuit of his hobby.

Dick Allen won two-thirds of the Triple Crown in 1972, leading the American League in home runs with 37, and RBIs with 113. It was a dream season for the fans, who idolized their aloof, anti-establishment hero in mutton chop sideburns. No boo-birds. No rock throwing. Nineteen-seventy-two was the season of Dick's content.

Allen was gracious and humble in that first year. "In Philadelphia I did some things that were written about, but I did them because all I wanted was to get out," he told New York sportswriter Murray Chass. "Hell, I wouldn't think of doing those things here. I've known Chuck Tanner for a long time. If I did anything bad, it would reflect on him, and I'd have to live with it."

It was the tailend of the peace and love era and Chuck Tanner seemed to be the self-appointed White Sox yoga when it came to dealing with his silent star. Speaking of Allen, the 1972 American League Most Valuable Player, Tanner cooed: "He's Babe Ruth, Rogers Hornsby, and Ty Cobb all put together!" The low octane

Hemond, who was not usually prone to wild exaggeration, summarized Allen's achievements thusly: "He's the savior of the franchise."

Unfortunately for Sox fans, the salvation was short lived. Allen's arrival proved to be good box office. The turnstiles clicked off 1,186,018 paid admissions in 1972, proving once again that the Sox were still a viable attraction in Comiskey Park. As long as the winning ways continued, and management could trot out All-Star caliber players each night. Anything less than that and White Sox attendance would go south.

But even with Allen supplying breathtaking long-distance home runs and with colorful Harry Caray spouting irascible commentary in between the times he touted the sponsor's beer, WFLD-TV chose not to extend its five-year, $1 million contract with the White Sox. In fact, the team had to pay another low-voltage UHF outlet, WSNS-TV, to air their telecasts beginning in 1973.

Mr. Allyn and the marketing department believed that they could easily recoup these losses by hiring broadcast maven Marshall Black to sell local sponsor time. Marshall Black's success or failure was predicated on a happy and content Dick Allen. For that matter, the entire organization walked on eggshells every time Richie sneezed. Was he happy? What can we do to make him *more* happy?

* * *

It was the Michael Jordan approach to running a sports team. You mortgage the franchise on one marquee attraction and hope that the athlete possesses the maturity, confidence, and strength of character to remain focused. But unfortunately for Mr. John Allyn, who deserved a far better fate, his superstar was no Michael Jordan. "Dick Allen leads by example. Dick Allen marches to his own drummer," alibied teammate Bill Melton and others in the organization in a puzzling attempt to justify the two sets of clubhouse rules that Tanner imposed.

Management went out of its way to accommodate Allen. His special status was confirmed in 1973 when Hemond, a kind and decent man, added Richie's 32-year-old brother Hank to the roster in order for him to complete his pension eligibility in the big leagues. Hank Allen was a washed-up utility infielder who had logged a few years with the Washington Senators in the 1960s. In the White Sox scheme of things, he was a useless addition who occupied a roster spot that might have otherwise gone to a deserving minor leaguer or a veteran from another team. But as long as Richie was happy. . . .

Dick Allen played only half a season in 1973. A freakish collision with Angels first baseman Mike Epstein in late June shelved the "Big Bopper" for the balance of the year. The White Sox, with one of the highest payrolls in baseball after signing Allen to a new three-year, $250,000 per-annum contract, tumbled into fifth place.

With a healthy squad and renewed optimism, Chuck Tanner bragged that his 1974 edition was the strongest in team history by far. The farm system was still extremely dry. Nyls Nyman, Stan Perzanowksi, Jim Geddes, Lee "Bee Bee" Richard, Jack Kucek, Buddy Bradford, Kevin Bell, Jim Otten; one right after another, on and on . . ., and the starting pitching was a leaky sieve after Wilbur Wood and Jim Kaat took their turns on the mound.

By virtue of winning the last two games of the '74 campaign, the Sox pulled up even with the league at 80-80. It was an empty achievement. After mid-September when Dick Allen walked out on his teammates, the ballclub was finished, as John Allyn's pennant illusions turned to dust. The slugging first baseman called his teammates together and explained that he was not leaving the ballclub—just baseball. He took off his glasses and went into Tanner's office to weep.

Dick Allen, who provided so many thrills in 1972, had betrayed the ownership, Roland Hemond, his teammates, and the fans for no other reason than boredom. The Sox were languishing in fourth place, far behind the pack. Allen could not foresee his club winning anytime soon. And he didn't seem to care very much for Chuck Tanner's recent decision to stiffen the training rules either.

None of this augured very well for the ownership, who had very little left in the marketing arsenal besides Harry Caray to offer Sox fans looking ahead to the 75th anniversary season.

In all of the years John Allyn was associated with the ballclub, he exuded enthusiasm for the game. He liked to speak of the democratic values associated with baseball; the attributes of

Jimmy Dykes, the "Little Napoleon" of Comiskey Park stares intently at his ballclub. Dykes piloted the Sox for 13 seasons, 1934-46.

Despite his brilliant play, Sox great Luke Appling performed before many empty seats in cavernous Comiskey Park in the 1930s and 1940s.

Bill Cissell was an expensive $123,000 acquisition who died penniless in a Chicago rooming house in March 1949.

Luis Aparicio broke in with the Sox in 1956 and became one of the greatest shortstops to ever play the game.

Minnie Minoso, the first black ballplayer in Chicago, hit a home run in his first White Sox appearance. Minoso's exciting play made him a fan favorite, and he still is today in his sixth decade in professional baseball.

The Spirit of the "Go-Go" White Sox was typified by Nelson Fox — but the Veterans Committee has thus far excluded him from the Hall of Fame.

Harold Baines (top) and Carlton Fisk (bottom) led the Sox through the 1980s and to the team's first division championship in 1983.

1993 American League MVP Frank Thomas (top) and Cy Young winner Jack McDowell (bottom) anchor a Sox team that many predict will dominate in the 1990s.

team spirit, individual initiative, and sportsmanship over greed. Mr. Allyn was no cheapskate. Even with his depleted resources and the reported $8 million Artnell losses sustained between 1970-1975, he always managed to reward the players whose performance measured up to the standards he had set.

There was grumbling to be sure—Mike Andrews and Rick Reichardt were let go because of major salary differences—but John Allyn's sincere desire was to win and to keep everyone happy.

John's problems with announcer Harry Caray had been simmering on the burner for some time; almost from the moment the colorful but crass play-by-play man and his travelling six-pack sauntered up the I-55 freeway from St. Louis in 1971. Harry's contributions to the White Sox success in the early 1970s were undeniable. He replaced the aging Bob Elson who had broadcast White Sox games since the early years of the Depression.

Elson's laid back, bland descriptions of the game were perfect in the 1940s and 1950s, but no longer viable with a younger audience that demanded fast-paced action and stinging commentary from their announcers each night. The popularity of Howard Cosell and slam-bang Monday Night Football mirrored the societal changes that had overtaken professional sports by the early 1970s. The grand old game was taking its lumps from the N.F.L. during the Richard Nixon-Vietnam era. It was no longer the national pastime, and Cosell seemed eager to pronounce the last rites: "Baseball is a sport that is popular with little boys and *very* old men."

Harry Caray was a part of that trailblazing cadre of announcers—outspoken, witty, and satirical in his observations. In fact, he pioneered the style years before Cosell came to the attention of a national audience. Caray was instrumental in the Sox resurgence of 1971-1972, during which he cultivated an enormous fan following. His dealings with the individual players in the line of fire was an entirely different matter however. Chuck Tanner, the players, and their families didn't appreciate Caray's blunt sarcasm, and they complained to management on more than one occasion. Slow-footed third baseman Bill Melton and outfielder Ken Henderson were the favored whipping boys. Caray and Melton nearly came to blows one night in 1975 at the Marc Plaza

Hotel in Milwaukee, a situation that undoubtedly convinced Allyn that a change had to be made.

How much of Harry's tell-it-like-it-is on-air negativity contributed to a breakdown in team morale when the losing ways returned in 1973, 1974, and 1975, can only be surmised. "Harry Caray became bigger than the organization," John Allyn Jr. said. "My dad thought Harry was doing his job to promote Harry. And that seemed more important to him than objectively announcing ballgames. He showed the Sox in an ambivalent light. He picked on his favorite targets, and his goals were not in sync with the organization, and at that point something had to be done."

WMAQ radio, the flagship station of the Chicago White Sox from the late 1960s onward, had its own concerns about Harry's style. They put him on a seven-second tape delay in 1974 in order to edit out objectionable material before it hit the air. John Allyn was forced to walk a dangerous tightrope. On the one hand he had to contend with his resentful athletes and on the other, an announcer who commanded listener loyalty, the undying gratitude of a dozen or so famous Chicago restaurateurs, and Harry's sports cronies who patronized Eli's, Gene & Georgetti's, and other watering holes along the boulevard. Harry touted them (ad nauseam) each night, and pretty soon they became as well known to TV viewers as the ballplayers on the field.

But in the end, John Allyn came down on the side of the players. The news of Harry's firing was delivered over the air by the owner on October 1, 1975. Allyn made his startling announcement during a Johnny Morris evening sports segment on WBBM-TV. Caray was at home at the time and had not been properly informed by club officials of what was to transpire. But then John Allyn had more pressing matters on his mind, like finding a way to come up with the cash to meet his last payroll of the 1975 season.

John Allyn did not have to wait long to absorb a Caray broadside: "I can't believe any man can own a ballclub and be as dumb as Allyn," Harry retorted. "Did he make enough to own it, or did he inherit it?" There was nothing he could say or do to defend the controversial firing in such a way that Sox fans could begin to understand the difficult position Allyn found himself in at the moment.

* * *

"If you talk to Jerome Holtzman, he will say that one of my dad's bigger flaws was that he was too nice, and the result—he wasn't as tough as he needed to be at times. Other people would say he was the eternal optimist," comments the younger Allyn. As to the other Allen, the reticent Sox owner bore his sulky star attraction no personal malice. But in hindsight it is easy to see that the loss of Dick Allen, the meal ticket, severed the fragile cord of solvency that held together the various divisions of Artnell still controlled by John Allyn.

Sox Attendance in the Dick Allen Years		Post-Allen Year	
1972	1,186,018	1975	770,800
1973	1,316,527		
1974	1,163,596		

Days before firing Caray on TV, John Allyn had sent word of his predicament to Bill Veeck, who had been itching to get back into the game for some years. Failing to pay the athletes meant that every player on the roster was a potential free agent. Veeck had been speaking informally with Allyn about a sale since early July. Now, the team was his for the taking. As the 1975 season wore on, John Allyn found it increasingly difficult to pay gate receipts to the visiting teams. The checks were almost always sent out late.

Sox Vice President Leo Breen, who had been closer to the embattled Allyns than anyone in the organization at that point in time, outlined the particulars to Veeck. The money had to come now. It couldn't wait. Allyn received the $550,000 loan—which Veeck had arranged through the Continental Bank after a new syndicate of White Sox investors had been assembled. Allyn's asking price came down to $10 million from the original $13.5 million figure he bandied about in mid-summer when his position was more tenable—and what the Seattle syndicate was prepared to pay to secure the White Sox. By early October, the situation had reached a crisis point in the house of Allyn. The banks wouldn't increase loans to cover the cash flow deficit, and the I.R.S. demanded $400,000 in back taxes, stemming from a business reversal that nearly bankrupted Du Pont Glore Forgan,

Allyn's brokerage house during the 1973 recession. At this most inopportune moment, Arthur Allyn Jr.—the litigious older brother who tried to peddle the Sox to Milwaukee interests in 1969, emerged from retirement brandishing a lawsuit at John. He sought an additional $500,000—money his kid brother simply didn't have.

"When Artnell got split up in 1969, there were some questions raised by Arthur about the allocation of monies," John Jr. explained. "Uncle Arthur always thought that some numbers were played with, and his allocation was not what it should have been. Of course my dad, Leo Breen, Arthur Andersen & Company, and everyone else involved felt quite the opposite."

Veeck's loan forestalled an impending calamity. But John's available Artnell cash from his business equipment company, a candy manufacturer and a Florida motel he owned, amounted to only $9,600. "The I.R.S. problems were personal in nature, and had nothing to do with Artnell. They were not the reason for selling the Sox," John Jr. revealed, "But my dad had this black cloud hanging over his head, which dragged him down. He had to sell. There was simply no other choice." Personality differences and old antagonisms between the two brothers, which had very little to do with baseball, drove a wedge in the Artnell enterprises. The corporation as it existed at the time of the senior Allyn's death in 1960 was dissolved shortly after the White Sox sale was consummated. The feuding Allyn brothers rarely spoke to each other in the twilight years of their lives.

* * *

The ballyhooed second coming of Bill Veeck after a 15-year hiatus was one of those rare moments in life when fate and the luck of the draw spelled yet another new beginning for the White Sox franchise and their fans. The team has withstood so many eleventh-hour crises in its history that it is remarkable it is still intact and playing baseball on the ancestral grounds of Bridgeport. The Allyn-Veeck sale underscored the fragility of the franchise. Bill Veeck had come to Chicago to work a little magic, reunite with a few old friends in the Comiskey press box, and celebrate the last hurrah that every public man who has basked in the limelight at one time or another is entitled to.

"Sometime, somewhere, there will be a club no one really wants. And then ole Will will come wandering along to laugh some more. Look for me under the arc lights boys, I'll be back." - Veeck—As In Wreck.

It was a self-fulfilling prophecy, but just barely. The American League took a dim view of Bill Veeck—always had. It didn't appreciate his style, his *joie-de-vivre*, and it didn't like his promotions, which it considered an affront to baseball. And most of all, these arbiters of decorum didn't appreciate the sarcasm directed toward their institution.

Hoping to keep Veeck out of the league and head off a potentially ruinous lawsuit at the same time, the league magnates offered John Allyn what they considered to be a generous solution to his dilemma. At an emergency meeting held in Kansas City, the owners floated Allyn a payroll loan in return for a 90-day option to shift the White Sox to the Pacific Northwest. The city of Seattle had filed a $32.5 million lawsuit against baseball after their expansion Pilots fled to Milwaukee on the eve of the 1970 season. They wanted a replacement team right away.

The White Sox situation offered the proverbial quick-fix solution, which had guided the decision-making process since the days of Ban Johnson. The answers were deceptively simple. Send the Sox to Seattle, and then if need be, allow Charles O. Finley to break his lease at the Oakland Coliseum and move his fading champions who had struggled at the gate for so long to his own backyard in the Windy City. Finley always coveted the White Sox franchise. After he was thwarted by Veeck and Greenberg back in 1959, he prevailed upon Chuck Comiskey to use his influence to gain league approval to buy the struggling Kansas City A's following the death of their owner, Arnold Johnson, in 1960.

The seven-year comedy act in K.C. ended in 1968 when Finley abruptly transferred his ballclub to the Bay Area. The laughing-stock A's of the 1960s captured three world championships in the seventies. But Finley was scorned as an indifferent, absentee owner by Bay Area fans and players alike. The Chicago A's? Finley would have gone for it. And it almost happened.

White Sox fans were spared Finley and his band of angry A's because John Allyn was of the noble opinion that it was important to uphold the traditions and the continuity of the White Sox franchise. He still believed all things were possible, even when the cupboard was bare as it was in 1975. Mr. Allyn waited patiently as Veeck scrambled around the country locating investors and assembling a new syndicate. Mayor Richard J. Daley remained in constant phone communication with Veeck during these trying days, and reportedly tipped him off to potential investors who might be persuaded to come aboard.

The money came from a variety of sources—Lee Stern, the soccer promoter who owned the Chicago Sting was in for $200,000. Ruben Rosen, a Philadelphia businessman chipped in $600,000. Veeck came up with the names of 46 investors in all. It was the trickle-down theory of Veeckian economics. That is, sooner or later the rain barrel fills to overflowing if you leave it outside long enough. Bill Veeck believed that his usual methods of financing (the debenture-common stock arrangement) were still viable in 1975. Such methods were used in each of his three previous purchases of Major League teams. The syndicate raised $4.8 million from private investors, with an additional $3.75 million coming in the form of a loan from the Continental Bank in Chicago.

Veeck believed he was all set, but a two-man owner's committee that included Bud Selig of Milwaukee and Ted Bonda of Cleveland decided that the syndicate was under-financed. Selig advised Veeck that there was no sense in having a meeting since the league would assuredly turn him down. One can only wonder about Selig's motives. This is the same genius who cried poor in 1971 and demanded that the American League transfer his woebegone Milwaukee Brewers team from the Western Division to the East so that they could play more games with their traditional rivals like the Yankees and Red Sox who were a bigger box office draw than the Angels or Royals.

Bud Selig seemed to overlook the natural rivalry that already existed to the South, and the many thousands of Chicago fans who pour into County Stadium each season for the six White Sox games. White Sox rooters continue to make the annual 90-mile trek that annually inflates the Brewer home attendance.

John Allyn was angry that the Sox were compelled to play in the Western Division, but he acceded to the Brewer owner on this issue against his better judgment. And now at pay-back time, Selig was playing hardball with Veeck. Maybe in the back of Selig's mind he was hoping to be rid of the White Sox once and for all and to claim whatever American League market existed in Chicago after the team was safely ensconced in Seattle. That would never have happened. Dyed-in-the-wool Sox fans who are indifferent to the Cubs would not rush toward the County Stadium box office to purchase Milwaukee Brewer tickets no matter how successful the product on the field. Selig was naive if that was his belief.

Whatever the case, the league voted down the Veeck sale 8-3-1, with Kansas City abstaining. Bill Veeck threatened the league with a lawsuit, which forced the hardliners to soften their position. They decided to allow the sale to proceed if Veeck would change the debentures to preferred stock and raise another $1.2 million in working capital. The owners generously gave Veeck a whole week to come up with the additional money. Otherwise. .. "It's Veeck or Seattle." John Allyn was grim, but Chicago fans quickly rallied to the cause. A "Save the Sox" committee was organized by sportscaster Johnny Morris and a number of prominent Illinois politicos, including Governor Dan Walker and Congressman Marty Russo carried the message to league president Leland S. MacPhail, Jr.'s door. The Sox for Chicago! Now and forever! That was the message that was delivered, but was anyone listening?

The fans were asked to send in their nickels and dimes to help Veeck meet his goals. Some 55,000 donations ranging from 20¢ to $1,000 poured in, but when the final results were tallied, it came out to only $11,000, which Veeck later donated to charity.

Somehow, Bill Veeck parted the seas in the next seven days. He scrambled and hustled like he never hustled before. Without hesitation, Veeck relinquished a 10% entrepreneur's fee ($750,000) due him by the original terms of the sale. But in the end it was Cub broadcaster Jack Brickhouse, a gentle soul and baseball purist who lifted the Veeck syndicate over the top. Brickhouse helped secure the final investment money through his associates from the Chicago-based Canteen Corporation, a sports concessions firm.

With Veeck's finances in order, the league owners debated among themselves, but could find no other reason than their own personal malice to vote him down. And that simply wasn't good enough. Bill Veeck was voted back into the lodge by a 10-2 margin, on December 10, 1975. And now Bud Selig had to contend with the unhappy possibility of more and more Chicago White Sox fans pouring into his creaky stadium nestled in a Milwaukee quarry pit.

* * *

Veeck—the alley fighter, the wily promoter, the visionary—the only man in America who dared to enter New York's posh 21 Club without a tie, re-shuffled the White Sox deck in the fleeting hope that he could deliver a miracle team to the Comiskey Park doorstep in 1976.

Sportshirt Bill knew he had a ballclub that was bad going in—but it only got worse after opening day. And that he had not counted on. All the new faces acquired by Roland Hemond during a whirlwind horse trading session at the winter meetings in Florida failed to stave off a last place finish. The new owner had hoped for good weather and a modicum of success on the field to lure the peripheral Chicago fans to the park to witness a dazzling array of promotions (ethnic festivals, beer case stacking contests, Shriner's Day, Farm Night, plus dozens of souvenir giveaways). He got neither.

The tireless Sox leader desperately needed the magical million in attendance to break even, but he fell short of the mark as the team sunk lower and lower in the standings. In 1976, the White Sox played a schedule of games intended for the proposed occupants of the Seattle Kingdome, which is where the Sox would have wound up if the vote had turned out differently.

* * *

Bill Veeck was a little older now, but the fire still burned in his soul and he had not forgotten the essence of baseball promotion. In five Spartan seasons (1976-1980) the old ballyard played host to belly dancers in the outfield, a coven of "anti-superstition witches," frisbee-catching dogs, rock musicians, and an iconoclastic radio disc jockey by the name of Steve Dahl who invited his blue jean legions to help him blow up disco records in the outfield on July 12, 1979. The heavy metal fans went wild in the same pasture where Shoeless Joe Jackson once grazed, which resulted in the first White Sox forfeit on their home grounds since

April 26, 1925 when fans standing in a roped-off section of the outfield raced onto the field with two outs in the ninth inning, thinking the game was over. The Disco Demolition fiasco turned the White Sox into a national laughingstock—a dreadful moment in Sox history that is still hard to live down when you talk to fans in other cities about it—but Harry Caray, who was quickly re-hired by Veeck in 1976, praised Dahl for his box office allure. Nobody knows for sure just how many people were shoehorned into the park that night to share in Dahl's distaste of disco music. One shudders to think what would have happened if this weren't a *peaceful* riot.

Bill Veeck worked harder than he ever did before to make a go of it in Chicago. It is a shame he did not succeed, because the White Sox afforded him that last, golden opportunity to build a ballclub from the ground up and silence his critics who questioned his player development capabilities. He foresaw the self-destructive tendencies of the baseball owners and tried to warn them that modifications to the ancient and unfair reserve clause needed to be made. The players rebelled against this form of indentured servitude during the Brotherhood Revolt of 1890, up through the Federal League war of 1914-1915, and on into the 1970s. As a student of the game's history, Veeck understood that time was not on the owner's side.

Two weeks after Veeck bought the Sox, federal arbitrator Peter Seitz ruled that Dave McNally of the Baltimore Orioles and Dodger pitcher Andy Messersmith were "free agents" after they had played the 1975 season without a contract. The landmark decision effectively overturned the 100-year-old reserve clause, and granted the players the mobility to move from one team to another as soon as they reached their eligibility. Seitz had warned the owners that free agency was coming, but the owners chose to ignore him on this issue. They relieved Seitz from his duties as arbitrator a short time later, as if that futile action on their part could turn back the clock. Had Mr. Seitz ruled *two weeks before* Veeck finalized his purchase agreement with Allyn, the White Sox in all likelihood would be in Seattle now, and the site occupied by the old Comiskey Park, would be a South Side industrial complex.

The Seitz decision ushered in a gold rush era for the players, but at the same time it put the small market teams and financially strapped ownerships like Bill Veeck's group in Chicago on less than equal footing with the league dreadnaughts like George Steinbrenner's Yankees and Gene Autry's California Angels.

It was ironic and unfortunate, because the Seitz decision struck hard at the one owner most sympathetic to the players' cause. Bill Veeck spent his formative years arguing against the inherent injustices of the reserve system with his fellow owners. In his younger days Veeck had studied contract law, particularly as it related to baseball while attending college night classes. He acquired a finite knowledge of the early history of baseball's labor disputes and had about reached the inescapable conclusion that: ". . . it [the reserve clause] was indefensible in law and morally."

In the 1940s, Veeck drafted a letter to Commissioner Landis suggesting in the mildest of terms that it was rather shortsighted to wait until the ownerships were forced into making concessions to the players, as they ultimately would be. "So I don't hear anything back from Landis for six weeks, maybe longer," Veeck related to the author in 1980. "Les O'Connor, the secretary-treasurer, eventually wrote me a letter which I can quote verbatim. 'Dear Bill: Some very bright fellow once said a little knowledge is a very dangerous thing, and you've just proven him to be a wizard!'"

* * *

The legality of the reserve clause was put to a stringent test in 1970 when St. Louis Cardinal outfielder Curt Flood refused to report to the Philadelphia Phillies after being traded for (who else?) Dick Allen. Flood likened the reserve clause to "legal slavery" and sought redress in the federal courts. The Flood case reached the United States Supreme Court, but Justice Arthur Goldberg upheld the lower court decisions that had previously affirmed baseball's unique status as the nation's only exempt monopoly.

Bill Veeck, as an interested observer of the passing scene, was called upon to share his enlightened viewpoints on the subject of unrestricted free agency during one of the Flood hearings before Congress. "The weird part of it is that what I was trying to do was help, not hurt," he recalled. The plan that Veeck submitted seemed reasonable to everyone except the owners and their lawyers. "I wanted to put into effect an equity-type contract calling for scheduled raises, and scheduled option periods. If a player didn't sign, he became a free agent at the end of seven years." In theory, Veeck's blueprint for change was nearly identical to the arrangement that had existed for years in Hollywood between the studios and the actors and actresses under contract. "If a player didn't sign," Veeck continued, "he would become a free agent at the end of seven years in any event. This would have given the players more than they anticipated at that stage of the game and somewhat near what has happened since."

In essence, the baseball owners had only themselves to blame for not acting sooner. The Seitz decision forced Veeck to deal in unwanted "bargain basement" free agents like Tim Nordbrook and Royle Stillman, while the Reggie Jacksons, Joe Rudis, and Catfish Hunters of the world jumped to the teams with the greatest cash resources.

By dint of a long-anticipated court action, Veeck suddenly found himself unable to compete with the rich and powerful teams. The few good players he acquired via the trade route (Richie Zisk and Oscar Gamble) hit thunderous home runs in the memorable 1977 "South Side Hit Men" summer—Veeck's finest achievement since the '59 pennant year—and then were lost to the ballclub in their option year, because he couldn't afford their extravagant salary demands.

The owner held the line; he would not impose long-term debt through deferred contracts on his investment group by succumbing to the temptation of becoming a baseball plunger like Brad Corbett, owner of the Texas Rangers, or Gene Autry of the California Angels. Rumors percolated in the press that Veeck sat on a pile of investor money that was available to pay a Zisk or Gamble. Whether these assertions had any validity is hard to say, but Veeck preferred to sail a prudent course and vest his hopes in injury-prone castoffs who were looking to prolong their careers with the White Sox. The strategy worked fine with ex-Twins third baseman Eric Soderholm in 1977, but failed miserably a year later when Veeck signed Yankee-designated first baseman Ron Blomberg as a free agent.

One could sense the frustration in Veeck's words. You could see it in his face each night in the press box as he gazed down at an unremarkable collection of athletes that *Chicago Tribune* columnist David Israel sarcastically tagged as the "Keystone Sox," for their erratic infield play, spotty pitching, and untimely hitting. This proud warrior exhibited the same low-key levels of emotion, win or lose. During the day, his Comiskey Park office was always open, and his direct phone line was available to White Sox fans who had a beef or just wanted to offer some constructive advice. At game time Veeck never hid in the owner's private box with business clients or prominent local advertisers as most baseball magnates prefer to do. He enjoyed the company of the writers, the team statisticians, and the visiting ballclub's executives, such as Frank Lane, or Cleveland's Phil Seghi, who dropped by Bill's customary seat in the second row of the Comiskey Park press box to pay homage to the philosopher king they had known so well in better days.

If the Sox happened to win the game it was a good day's work, and Veeck would signal his approval by slowly rising from his chair after the last out had been recorded, and clapping his hands together one time before hobbling off to the rickety press elevator down the hall. The quaint, manually-operated conveyance with the 1930s team logo emblazed in the floor tile, was a throwback to the Depression era. It was built for the convenience of the portly J. Louis Comiskey, who like Veeck, struggled with a debilitating physical condition that sapped him of his physical strength in his adult years.

How different it might have all been if Veeck could have only enjoyed the same tax advantages of the other ballclubs who were able to write off a substantial percentage of their contracts based on player depreciation. Bill Veeck's investors had purchased stock, not the hard assets of the corporation, and therefore could not realize tax breaks until the team was able to report a profit. But the Sox were unable to draw the requisite one million gate attendance in 1976, and losses in the first year of the Veeck ownership were pegged at $600,000. Record attendance and a winning ballclub the next season produced only enough revenue to satisfy the previous year's deficit. The Sox were on a slow-moving treadmill to the poor house.

Revenue shortfalls not only hampered efforts to land quality free agents, but they also meant the ballclub was unable to sign its top draft picks in each of the amateur January drafts, 1976-

1979. The signing of outfielder Harold Douglas Baines in 1977 illustrates what the Sox were up against. By virtue of finishing with the worst record in the American League for 1976, the White Sox earned the right to select the best college player in the nation. The top candidates that year included infielder Paul Molitor from the University of Minnesota, catcher Terry Kennedy, whose dad played for the Sox in the 1940s and '50s, and Harold Baines, whom Veeck had personally scouted while the young man played little league baseball along the Eastern Shore of Maryland.

It was acknowledged at the time that Molitor was the highest-rated player in the nation, but his asking price was more than the White Sox could afford. Ditto for Kennedy (who turned out to be a bust compared to the other players coming out that year), so the Sox had to settle for Baines.

Harold put in nine good years in Chicago, but he never quite achieved the superstar status accorded him by Veeck, Chisox manager Paul Richards, and Charlie Evranian, the assistant director of player development who guaranteed a future berth in the Hall of Fame for Baines by the year 2000. The shy and uncomfortably aloof Baines was named to several All Star teams. He held the White Sox career home run record for a few years, and was instrumental in the 1983 division title run. These achievements were largely overshadowed however, by Paul Molitor, who, with Robin Yount, became the heart and soul of the winning Milwaukee Brewer ballclubs of the early 1980s. Molitor will assuredly be given serious consideration for the Hall of Fame someday. Baines will not.

The entire White Sox strategy was geared toward drafting the kid they knew they could sign as opposed to securing the best player overall. This was no way to build from within, or to ever achieve stability and long-term success. Veeck's business manager, Rudie Schaffer, estimated that the White Sox spent $1.9 million annually in player development. But it wasn't nearly enough, as it turned out.

"My ability to keep players has continued to diminish," Veeck said at the time. "In the process I am excluded from competing on equal terms, because I can't sign a [Oscar] Gamble or a [Richie] Zisk. I need money to operate because of the increased salaries, so I then have to sell a [Jim] Spencer or a

[Bucky] Dent just to keep going. I can't afford to keep Steve Stone (who played out his option in 1978 in order to sign with the Baltimore Orioles where he went on to win 25 games en route to a 1980 Cy Young Award), because my club isn't close enough. So when we have fine relief pitchers like Rich Gossage and Terry Forster, we have to use them as starting pitchers, because if we don't they'd never get the chance to pitch."

Seasons quickly unraveled. Though he could not compete with the wealthier teams, outwardly Veeck exuded enthusiasm and looked hopefully to the farm system for the team's long-term salvation. Younger players were rushed to the majors before their incubation period was complete, which wasn't good for their self-confidence or for Veeck's credibility.

Bill Veeck was in the business of selling tickets, and every Sunday morning he took to the WMAQ airwaves to drum roll the new generation of Sox hopefuls. He tantalized Sox fans during spring training with exciting tales of the heroics of a Dewey Robinson, a Harry Chappas, a Larry Doby Johnson, a Mike Colbern, or a Rusty Torres, just a few of the notable failures of the youth program. But when these players and others of their ilk were brought north after opening day it was painfully obvious to White Sox fans that Charley Finley was correct when he accused Veeck of trying to "ballyhoo a funeral."

When the Triple-A Iowa recruits failed to stick, Veeck resorted to gimmickry and publicity stunts like activating 54-year-old Minnie Minoso, and penciling him into the lineup against fireballing lefty Frank Tanana in an attempt to fill the ballpark at the tailend of a losing season. There were other such examples, like sending his team out onto the field one afternoon wearing short pants. A chorus of guffaws awaited the haggard athletes as the umpire signalled 'play ball.'

At the end of his playing days, Chicago Bear quarterback Bobby Douglass was signed to a minor league pitching contract. It was good for a few laughs at any rate. "Bill Veeck was in love with the idea that he was the show," commentator Bruce Levine notes. "He was the best public relations man in the business, but these skills didn't necessarily make him a good owner."

In 1978, venerable shortstop Don Kessinger who had logged 15 years in the big leagues (most of them with the Cubs) was named manager while still listed on the active roster. The easy-going Kess accepted the challenge, but lasted only a half-season before being replaced by Tony La Russa. Disco Demolition and the Kessinger experiment were embarrassing sidelights to the Veeck ownership that underscored Jerry Reinsdorf's initial assessment of the Sox in the late 1970s. "They were the Rodney Dangerfields of baseball," he said. Veeck's whimsy and methods of operating failed to keep pace with the changing realities. One by one the entrepreneurial owners like Veeck, Finley, and the Carpenter family, who gradually supplanted the founding families in the 1930s, 1940s and 1950s now found themselves classified as baseball's out of touch *ancient regime.*

Phil Wrigley passed away in 1977 at age 82. His son, William, who was going through a messy divorce at the time, disposed of the Cubs four years later—a tragedy for Chicago baseball. Charley Finley gave up his Oakland A's in 1980 after a long, bitter struggle to hang on. Charley-O, one of the last great showmen in the Veeck tradition, preceded the feisty Twins owner, Calvin Griffith, out the door. In that same period, Philadelphia Phillies owner Robert Carpenter, Jr., and Veeck's old adversary, John Fetzer of Detroit, joined Finley and Griffith on the ex-owner's unemployment line for much the same reasons as Ole' Will in Chicago. Private entrepreneurship in baseball was coming to an ignoble end. These men were the last of the grazing dinosaurs who faced an impending ice age; phased out by the mega-corporations.

Conventional wisdom says Bill Veeck's decision to put the club up for sale in 1980 had a lot to do with finances. However, this view has been challenged of late by Bruce Levine. "In every situation where Veeck cried poor, he always came out of it making money. He would fit in with what the modern owner is today; that is, someone who holds on to a club for three or four years and then bails out (recent examples: Jeff Smulyan in Seattle and Eli Jacobs in Baltimore). Their ideas of what their baseball profits would be, liquid-wise, were vastly distorted from what they turned out to be," Levine adds. "Whenever they got into trouble in other business ventures and needed to suck some ready cash, what better way to do it than selling their baseball team? Veeck looked at it as a cash business and was able to make it profitable off the books." Bill Veeck took his shots at baseball's "carpetbaggers;" owners who shifted teams at will for the sake of the bottom line.

He raked them over hot coals in his 1965 tome, *A Hustler's Handbook.* "Baseball's greatest asset, whether it knows it or not," he wrote, "is the sense of continuity that comes not only from the record books but from long personal association." Applying these same exacting standards of fair play and sportsmanship then, it stands to reason that Veeck was part of the same hypocrisy he condemned in others when he chose to vacate St. Louis in 1954, and attempted to peddle the White Sox to Colorado interests 26 years later.

The decision to sell the team in 1980 also involved the media and diminishing returns in the press box—not the box office. Despite the losing ways, South Side attendance for 1978-1980 remained fairly robust, all things being equal. Talent-wise, the Chicago Cubs were not much better than the White Sox during years of the Veeck stewardship, but the North Siders continued to receive gold card treatment in both the print and broadcast media. Results of Cub road games were announced ahead of Sox home games by the newscasters. A small detail, to be sure, but certainly noticeable to Sox media watchers. Bill Veeck measured column inches in his two morning papers and arrived at the unhappy conclusion that his ballclub was being short changed. Cub game stories were situated on the front page of the *Tribune* sports section more times than not. At the *Sun-Times* it was much the same.

This is one of the great intangibles confronting the White Sox year in and year out. And no amount of promotion or Veeckian hype can overcome media bias. Bill Veeck was not alone in his opinions. "The Chicago writers liked to dwell on the negative," John Allyn Jr. said. Going back to the time when his dad and Uncle Arthur owned the ballclub: John, Jr. recalls that "In 1967 when the Sox were in first place for most of the year, sportswriters such as Dave Nightingale of the old *Daily News* seemed to devote an excessive amount of column space to dwelling on the problems of going to the South Side, rather than on the fact that the team was competitive and successful."

The urban violence spawned in the mid to late 1960s frightened and discouraged many suburbanites from attending Sox night games in person. Compounding these concerns was the Chicago Police Department's 1961 cost-cutting measure that eliminated a special events task force that had provided internal ballpark security on game days. Despite published statistics showing the 9th District (encompassing the ballpark) to be one of Chicago's safest neighborhoods, the lingering perception was hard to overcome and the team's publicity department simply did not know how to soothe the public fear.

Nightingale and his colleagues probably exaggerated the danger of commuting to Bridgeport, because in other cities the safety issue seemed far less worrisome to fans and media. The Yankees and Tigers played in stadiums located in dangerous, inner-city ghettos, but easily surpassed the million mark in home attendance in that same period. During the height of the 1967 race riots in Detroit, the Tigers were forced to cancel several home games and replay them in Baltimore because of massive civil unrest in the Corktown neighborhood where the ballpark is situated. "The most positive, effusive writing during that period seemed to be about Notre Dame, through *Tribune* columnist David Condon," Allyn said. The Bears, the Cubs, and the Notre Dame Fighting Irish—Chicago's teams, when all is said and done.

Denver oil man Marvin Davis expressed some interest in the White Sox following Veeck's decision to solicit outside bids, but nothing much came of it. For the third time in less than 12 years, the White Sox were in eminent peril of leaving town. Three different ownerships, each with their own agenda for building a successful operation in the Windy City flirted with the possibility of relocation because of adverse conditions in Chicago. Why was that?

Chronic low attendance and the perception that Bridgeport was an unsafe place to travel afflicted Arthur Allyn. Outside business reversals, declining gate revenue in the post-Dick Allen era, and a sub-par TV-radio package hindered John Allyn to the point where he considered Seattle for a new base of operations. In the case of Bill Veeck, free agency and a complicated financing arrangement that prevented him from reaping necessary tax write-offs impeded his ability to operate effectively in baseball's new era.

The woes of the White Sox. And yet everyone seemed to look past the most compelling argument for why the team failed so consistently.

The problem was old Comiskey Park. The team had to adjust its style of play to the size of the ballpark. In the 1960s, the Dead

Ball strategies employed by Lopez and Stanky produced far too many 1-0 and 2-1 scores, and that was boring to the fans, who desired fast-paced action.

Unless the White Sox came up big-time winners like they did in 1972 and 1977, the fans were apathetic, by and large. There had to be more—a whole lot more—to the baseball experience than just the game on the field. Veeck's promotions reinforced this point.

At the very least, a successful baseball enterprise requires pleasant surroundings to support the product on the field. The success of the Chicago Cubs who registered only *two* plus .500 seasons between 1973-1992 illustrates that winning isn't everything when you can play in Wrigley Field. During this 20-year swing, the Cubs lured over two million paying customers to Clark and Addison in eight different seasons. It didn't happen by accident. The late Branch Rickey was on the mark when he said: "luck is the residue of design."

* * *

Having lost interest in the Marvin Davis bid, Veeck next turned his attention to 69-year-old Edward DeBartolo of Youngstown, Ohio, who was one of the wealthiest men in America. DeBartolo's contribution to Western culture in the second half of the 20th-century was the shopping mall. He built 47 of them after buying a strip of Youngstown land at a sheriff's auction in 1950. By 1980, he owned three race tracks and had purchased the San Francisco 49'ers football team for his son Ed. Jr. to play with.

The American League owners were suspicious of DeBartolo. He owned race tracks and that was considered unsavory, even though the owner of the Pittsburgh Pirates stuck his mitts in the horse game years earlier. DeBartolo was of Italian descent, and that conjured up all kinds of dark images of Mafia gangsters mingling among the worthy members of the fraternity. Bud Selig, as usual, was on hand to articulate their concerns. Edward DeBartolo's bid to buy the White Sox was voted down twice by the league.

A disheartened Veeck was then forced into selling to a local group headed by 49-year-old suburban real estate developer Jerry Reinsdorf and his friend and fellow classmate from the Northwestern Law School (Class of 1960), Edward Einhorn.

Jerry Reinsdorf is as low key a personality as one encounters in the ego racket known as professional sports. This former Brooklynite had built the Skokie, Illinois firm of Balcor into one of the nation's largest and most profitable real estate companies. Distant memories of summers spent at Ebbets Field kindled his desire to get into baseball. The lucrative real estate partnerships he had assembled at Balcor over the years provided the means to do so.

His partner Einhorn was the more flamboyant of the two, but Eddie never inspired the same levels of trust among White Sox fans as Veeck. In fact, this former television executive—who foresaw the coming cable TV boom in this country a decade before most Americans ever *heard* of ESPN, or HBO—was perceived to be a brassy Manhattanite. And Sox fans hated Manhattan by nature. The springboard to TV success for Einhorn occurred back in 1956 when he approached Wayne Duke (then the director of the NCAA) about setting up a radio network to broadcast the Final Four Tournament. Such a thing had not been attempted before, but it sounded like a good idea to Duke, who paid Einhorn a modest $100 honorarium plus $25 per affiliate. Eddie provided the play-by-play with ex-DePaul great George Mikan as his color man.

Reinsdorf and Einhorn (Einsdorf, Reinhorn, the pundits had a field day with this one), sealed the deal with Veeck and the 46 partners on January 29, 1981 for $19 million and change. The value of the franchise had increased by nearly $10 million since 1975. Everyone on Veeck's side went home a winner, but judging by Veeck's actions in the coming months it was plain to see that he harbored a great deal of personal animosity toward the new group (a bitterness not so far removed from what was grinding on Chuck Comiskey when the Veeck group came in).

"We represented something to Bill he didn't like," Sox chairman Jerry Reinsdorf said. "It was not being baseball people—we were what he considered corporate types, suit and tie guys. Then Eddie made an unfortunate comment that was not intended in any way to demean Bill, but he took it wrong. At our first press conference after we were approved by the American League somebody asked us what we were going to do. And Eddie said we were going to build a class organization. Bill took that as a slap at him saying he did not have a class organization. All Eddie meant was that *we* were going to have a class organization."

Jerry Reinsdorf had his own ideas about how the goals were to be achieved. He reorganized the front office in a major way by creating additional departments and hiring degreed marketing, accounting, and sports information professionals to modernize the "candy store." These steps were necessary in order to bring the team in line with baseball's new corporate image. Sox purists in the Bill Gleason camp didn't like it very much, but these steps were necessary if the ballclub was going to permanently shed its "Rodney Dangerfield" image once and for all and be taken seriously.

The entire White Sox payroll numbered no more than 175 employees during the Veeck years; 120 of them were players on both the Minor League and Major League levels. Within a year's time, Reinsdorf easily doubled that number and intensified the marketing and promotions end of the business to build a new fan base. His strategy was tied to selling his team as a family-oriented Chicago attraction, not just a South Side curiosity for weekend barroom brawlers. Sales of hard liquor in the park were immediately suspended, and security was stepped up in an effort to curb the unfortunate incidents of drunken rowdiness that earned Comiskey Park the surly reputation of being the world's largest outdoor saloon in the Veeck years.

The spectacle of beefy off-duty cops who doubled as security guards, wrestling with beer-sloshing ruffians in the aisles of Comiskey Park on a Friday night was all too common. "They were right. The new owners *had* to do that," comments Tom Shaer, a talk show host on WSCR-AM and sports anchor at the NBC-TV affiliate in Chicago. "But in so doing they drastically broke with the past and alienated the traditional fan base by force feeding pay TV on the public and by allowing Harry Caray to leave." It was a different management philosophy that Reinsdorf brought to the table, that's all.

"I tried very hard to build bridges with Bill," the owner relates. "I made overture after overture towards him, and he just wouldn't accept it. I tried to pay tribute to him every way I could. I invited him out here. Whenever I saw Bill I was very respectful of him, but he would have none of it."

* * *

Author's Note

The last time I saw Bill Veeck was in the Bards Room of the old Comiskey Park during the 1983 American League Championship Series. The media dining area had been converted into a working press room to accommodate the crush of out-of-town reporters and broadcast people sent in to cover the White Sox and the Orioles. Veeck sat off in a corner of the room by himself banging away at a manual typewriter. He had been asked to write a series of columns about the A.L. playoff games for a Chicago newspaper and was hard at work preparing his copy.

To my recollection, it was the first time he had set foot in the ballpark since selling the team to Reinsdorf and Einhorn in 1981. Veeck's self-imposed exile from Comiskey Park was his way of expressing anger over the current ownership's ill-chosen remarks at the time of the purchase.

No one paid much attention to Veeck. He seemed engrossed in his work. In the press rooms of the nation's ballparks at playoff and World Series time, celebrities like Veeck are taken for granted by the veterans of the fourth estate. To the younger scribes sent up from the small town newspapers and radio stations serving rural America, it is much more of an eye-opening experience.

I watched as a young man with a spiral ring notebook in hand cautiously approached Veeck from behind. In a shaky, uncertain voice he asked for an autograph. The writer from the downstate Illinois paper was violating the iron-clad rule about soliciting autographs in the press area, but he did not know better. He was just a boy from what I could tell, who was imbued with a love of baseball and a quiet reverence for the game's icons, of which Veeck must surely be counted. It was an inopportune moment to be sure, but I kind of hoped Bill would oblige the request just the same.

He did not. In fact, Veeck did not even acknowledge the young lad's presence, which led me to wonder if the former Sox owner didn't hear the question. "Mr. Veeck?" Still no response. The reporter inched closer and asked the question a third time.

"Mr. Veeck?"

It was impossible for Bill Veeck not to notice the kid out of the corner of his eye at that point, even if the general din of the Bards Room at playoff time drowned his words. The writer slipped away. His puzzled expression mirrored the embarrassment he must have been feeling. He glanced from side to side to see if anyone had been watching.

A few minutes later, Veeck was approached by another reporter who was seeking an interview for a low-voltage suburban radio station. Mr. Veeck said nothing. He didn't even look up from his typewriter to say "I'm sorry, I'm busy. Can you come back another time?" He just pounded away at the keys as the reporter's words twisted idly in the air.

Observing these events from across the room, I couldn't help but feel sadness for Bill Veeck. In future years when these two reporters recall their encounter with Bill Veeck, they will not speak of his heroic struggle to make a go of it in Chicago against tough odds, his revolutionary ideas for improving the future of the game, or that his only intention was to make a ballpark outing as enjoyable as possible for the ordinary fan. Instead, they are likely to remember being snubbed by a man who despised pomposity in all forms; a baseball populist the average fan will always revere as a hero of the game and one of their own. Bill Veeck.

I have to believe that Bill Veeck qualifies as a hero if we still measure the worth of such people by the deeds they do and the quality of their character. A thought expressed by author F. Scott Fitzgerald comes to mind when I try to assess the life and times of William Francis Veeck. "Show me a hero, and I'll show you a tragedy."

Bill Veeck (center), his wife Mary Frances (left) and Vice-President Hank Greenberg complete their purchase of the Chicago White Sox in 1959. Beset by health problems, Veeck was forced to give up his ownership in 1961.

The second coming of Veeck's Sox ownership spanned five Spartan seasons (1976-1980) that included belly dancers in the outfield, a coven of anti-superstition witches, frisbee-catching dogs, rock musicians, and the notorious disco-demolition night.

As this 1908 cartoon from the *Chicago Tribune* shows, the Sox's fight for a new stadium has been going on since the turn of the century. Below, Arthur Allyn Jr. holds the plans for his privately-financed South Loop stadium in the summer of 1967. Allyn is joined by his younger brother John (far right), George Halas Jr. of the Chicago Bears (far left), and William Heymans of the Chicago Cubs (second from left).

Chapter
— Ten —

Fight for a Stadium . . .
a Bit of History

His face blackened by sooty smoke, Fire Commissioner Robert Quinn peered down at the twisted steel and smoldering debris of a public building that until now had joyously celebrated the can-do of post-war Chicago.

In the cold, gray morning hours of January 15, 1967, McCormick Place, Chicago's massive lakefront exposition center was destroyed by fire. Hours earlier a gloomy Mayor Richard J. Daley pronounced the hall a total loss after being roused from his bed. Daley advised that the city's lucrative convention business worth $4-5 million in yearly rental and an additional $5 million in labor contracts would have to seek other accommodations in the foreseeable future unless McCormick Place could be rebuilt on a superhuman scale.

In the dubious annals of Chicago history, the McCormick Place conflagration was the city's costliest blaze since the great fire of 1871. The building carried a hefty $40 million-dollar price tag. Nothing before had even come close. The loss of McCormick Place in 1967 also had a ripple effect on the Chicago White Sox and their quest for a new stadium to replace the increasingly inadequate Comiskey Park.

Chuck Comiskey had some business to attend to in the Loop, and like many other motorists driving in on Lake Shore Drive that morning, found traffic was an impossible snarl. The Old

Roman's grandson pulled off the roadway and parked his car in a lot belonging to the R.R. Donnelley printing company, not far from the scene of the fire devastation. Comiskey pushed his way past the police cordon—Charley caught up with Bob Quinn, a Chicago baseball fan who touched off a city-wide panic in 1959 after flicking on the city air raid sirens moments after the Sox clinched the pennant, and asked the chief for an assessment of the damage. In the back of Comiskey's mind he had an inkling of what the likely consequences were to be for the stadium project that had been kicking around the City Hall corridors and the White Sox board room for the better part of a decade.

"Well Charley, I can tell you this," Quinn sighed. "I just bet this will take care of your new stadium for a while."

* * *

Skyscrapers, sprawling super highways, new housing stock, and a world class airport; these things Mayor Daley had delivered to Chicago's doorstep during his first decade in office. The mayor subscribed to architect Daniel Burnham's now famous 19th century credo: "Make no little plans. They have no magic to stir men's blood." It was a record of unparalleled accomplishment for any big city mayor. Chicago, The City of Big Shoulders, was looked up to by other municipalities as a model of civic efficiency.

As Daley looked ahead to the new year in 1967 and the upcoming mayoral election, he had every reason to believe that he could revive his dormant stadium plan, which had been lying fallow for the last three years. Daley wanted it very badly, and he believed that Chicago sports patrons deserved the very best in luxury accommodations. He was firm in the belief that a spacious multi-purpose stadium housing the Cubs, Bears, and White Sox under one roof was in the best long-term interests of the city. Thus far, Mayor Daley's reach exceeded his grasp.

The idea took root in the early 1950s when the first rumblings of discontent emanated from the sports ownerships across town. "The costs of maintaining our individual stadiums for 105 days a year had changed since the 1920s and 1930s," Comiskey explained. "It was important to have a unified stadium; a place where we could all play and share expenses. That was the trend back then, and it made sense."

Charley Comiskey's baseball mentor, Phil Wrigley, also complained of structural problems in his ballpark. Work needed to be performed in the lower rightfield area and the restrooms needed upgrading; similar to the problems the Comiskeys were experiencing in their own bailiwick. After contemplating the joint tenancy proposal (that was originally put forward by Mayor Martin Kennelly and endorsed by Comiskey), the Cub owner said he would support the measure—with reservations. The Cubs would agree to play 18-20 night games in the new park that was to be situated along Madison Street; a run-down Skid Row section west of the central business district. (Other sites were considered. Years later Daley suggested a stadium in the lake for the Bears, but the idea was rejected by the baseball owners and lakefront preservationists.) Daytime baseball would continue to be played in Wrigley Field. That was the only condition Phil Wrigley attached to the plan.

Chicago Bears owner George Halas heard the steady drone from National Football League executives who wanted him to expand the seating capacity of Wrigley Field to 50,000 in order to conform to N.F.L. standards. Sharing a facility with the Wrigleys proved to be an unsatisfactory arrangement all around for the Bears ruling family but they had to live with it. At one point "Papa Bear" Halas offered to buy up half of the stadium bonds in order to move the project off the dime. "George Halas was all for it," Comiskey said. "He had to make a move."

* * *

What happened to Chicago's beloved Cardinals (founded in 1898, they were pro football's oldest franchise from a point of service), is a textbook case that illustrates the tenuous hold a city has over a sports franchise when a combination of mismanagement, media apathy, stadium neighborhood problems, and a powerful cross-town rival drive down revenue and force an embattled ownership to shop for new markets. Cardinal misfortunes in the post-war period provide an eerie parallel to the fate that nearly befell the White Sox beginning in the late 1960s and continued up through the 1980s.

The Chicago Cardinals were well established by the time George Halas solicited the approval of their owner, Chris O'Brien to move his struggling Decatur Staleys to Chicago. O'Brien consented (his mistake), and in 1922 the Halas team (re-christened the Bears) arrived in the Windy City. Within a few years, Halas emerged as the National Football League's big cat. Chris O'Brien, a South Side plumbing and painting contractor, eventually sold his interests to Chicago physician Dr. David Jones, and then eventually Jones sold to Charles Bidwell.

The Cardinals paid the Comiskey family a leasing fee for the right to play their home games in the South Side ballpark. The Bears entered into a similar arrangement with the Wrigley family for the use of Wrigley Field during the Sundays of autumn. These were the days when the N.F.L. desperately struggled to gain national acceptance, and pro football was viewed as an off-season diversion for the hot-stoving baseball fanatic.

George Halas was a smart and resourceful owner who realized that in order to survive and profit in Chicago, sooner or later one of the two teams had to depart, and it sure wasn't going to be the Bears. The Cardinals, meanwhile, had been sold twice in a three-year period ending in 1933.

Their third owner, Charles Bidwell, Sr., assembled what many veteran redbird watchers considered to be the greatest Cardinal football team in history—they captured a league championship in 1947, and advanced to the N.F.L. title game a year later.

The senior Bidwell was a respected, pro-active, nurturing owner who waited patiently for the tree to bear its fruit. He died of pneumonia shortly before the Cards were dealt their first championship in the modern era, and after his death, things quickly soured. Bidwell's widow, Violet, inherited the club and served as the chairman of the board of directors. She placed Ray Bennigsen, a popular and trusted associate of her late husband in charge of the team, but relations deteriorated in the front office. Bennigsen resigned four years later amid rumors of growing dissension and family strife.

Mrs. Bidwell married team executive Walter Wolfner in 1951 and granted her new husband complete control over the Big Red as its managing director until the time her two sons, William and Charles Jr., "Stormy," (who is the present owner of Sportsman's Park Racetrack in Cicero, IL.), were old enough to have a say in the decision-making process.

The financial health of the Cardinals endured another serious setback when the N.F.L. callously shifted the team into the weaker Eastern Division in 1950, depriving them of gate revenues from the added attraction of a second game with their hated North Side rivals, the Bears. It was a maneuver not unlike the poorly thought out 1969 baseball realignment that dumped the Sox in the Western Division with the two expansion teams and West Coast ballclubs.

Great individual accomplishments by such South Side gridiron stalwarts as Charley Trippi, Elmer Aangsman, Ollie Matson, and John David Crow failed to stave off a string of losing seasons. The Cardinals became the N.F.L. also-rans of the 1950s, and a local laughingstock by decade's end. Throughout the 1950s there were persistent rumors that the Cardinals were on the verge of skipping town. One city after another stepped forward to claim the franchise for its own—Miami, Denver, Dallas, Houston, Minneapolis, St. Louis, and Buffalo—but Wolfner kept assuring jittery Cardinal fans that such talk was nothing more than rumormongering by a hostile press.

For years, Walter Wolfner (who was calling all the shots subject to Violet's final, sanctimonious approval) pestered Comiskey for concessions on the lease agreement and stadium enhancements he felt were necessary for the team's survival. The South Side worked to the detriment of the Cards, as it would the Sox, once they fell out of contention in the 1960s. In an effort to stave off insolvency, Wolfner opened negotiations with Northwestern University in Evanston for the rental of Dyche Stadium—a football facility with ample parking only a few blocks away from a CTA elevated transit line connecting the northern suburb to Chicago.

The Cardinals were stopped cold. After it appeared that the university was ready to accommodate the Big Red, George Halas invoked a little-known clause in the N.F.L. agreement signed on August 27, 1931, that expressly forbade the Cards from playing anywhere north of Madison Street without the permission of the Bears' owner. "Everything we did seemed to go against us," Wolfner said later. "I thought if we could have moved into Dyche Stadium in Evanston, we could have really drawn." Wolfner filed suit in Superior Court on September 26, 1958, to declare the ancient contract null and void, but was stymied. The court upheld the validity of the agreement signed between Halas and (then) Cardinal owner, Dr. David Jones nearly 30 years earlier.

After the 1959 lease negotiations with Comiskey stalled, Wolfner moved the operation to palatial wind-blown, Soldier Field along the Chicago lakefront with two of their home games scheduled for Metropolitan Stadium in Bloomington, Minnesota. The Big Red was guaranteed a substantial advance by Minnesota backers seeking a tenant for their refurbished stadium in the coming N.F.L. expansion. Wolfner explained at the time that the Cards' only desire was to test the Minnesota market for the league, and to expand their meager television coverage with these two games beamed back to Chicago. (Similar arguments were given by Art Allyn in 1968 to justify his reasoning for wanting to play 11 home games in Milwaukee.)

The final say as to whether the Cardinals would remain in Chicago after 1959 rested with Violet Bidwell Wolfner, who had abandoned all hope of achieving parity with the Halas-led Bears after her attempt to move to Dyche Stadium was thwarted. When a St. Louis brewer guaranteed the sale of 25,000 season tickets and provided assurance that a new 50,000 stadium would be erected Mrs. Bidwell-Wolfner happily accepted. Right up to the very last minute, when the reports of the move flashed across the wires, Walter Wolfner kept denying and denying. "The Chicago Cardinals will remain the Chicago Cardinals."

Then came the usual apologies and excuses. "My wife only attended three games in Chicago last fall because the situation was deteriorating so much," Wolfner explained moments after the transfer of the franchise was confirmed on March 13, 1960.

The Cards were given a final ignominious shove out the door by George Halas and the Columbia Broadcasting System who agreed to split the $500,000 fee paid to the Wolfners for the exclusive TV rights to the Chicago market.

Chicago's oldest professional football team was an annoying gnat to George Halas and the new N.F.L. commissioner, Pete Rozelle, whose five-year strategy was tied to opening additional geographical markets with regional teams who would build their fan base across a vast multi-state area via television coverage. With two pro football teams in town, it was a moral certainty that when the Cardinals or Bears were playing at home TV coverage of the away game back to Chicago was blacked out. The departure of the Cardinals assured greater TV exposure for the Bears, since their road games could now be beamed back to Chicago on Sunday.

Professional sports is a predatory business and only the strong can emerge from the economic war zones unscarred. "Papa Bear" Halas was one such survivor. In 1971 he moved his team into Soldier Field. The inadequacies of that aging structure, which made it unsuitable for the Bidwells in 1959, were given immediate attention by the Chicago Park District and Mayor Daley who compromised with the opponents of the new lakefront stadium, and decided instead to renovate Soldier Field to Halas' satisfaction.

George Halas was never the same sleepy, crossed-paw dog that his landlord Mr. Wrigley had been when it came to maintaining a friendly rivalry with a competitor from across town. He knew how to throw his weight around and get necessary things done. Given the chance to drive a stake into the hearts of the dwindling numbers of Cardinal fans and the few remaining writers in town like Bill Gleason who still cared, Halas did so—with relish. The city did not act fast enough to resolve the Cardinals' stadium dilemma; that was the underlying issue. But there were other intangibles. The Cards offered a blueprint as to why a pro team fails in a given market. If the media had anything at all to say about the Cardinals, it was usually harsh and judgmental. According to one veteran city photographer who covered both the Bears and Cards, George Halas was in the habit of granting free tickets and complimentary passes to the reporters who said nice things about his team. On the other hand, the sportswriters who showered praise on the Cardinals often found themselves omitted from the Bears' pass list, come Sunday afternoon.

More significantly, the Big Red was accorded secondary status in a league that had not yet attained the overwhelming levels of popularity that were to come in the early 1970s. If the Bidwell family had given Chicago half a chance and hung on a few more years, it is likely that they could have survived and maybe even prospered in this city. All they lacked was that undefinable virtue called patience. Today Bill Bidwell and his heirs are operating in Phoenix; they moved to the Southwest in 1988 because of growing dissatisfaction with the limited seating capacity of Busch Stadium in St. Louis, which they shared with the baseball Cardinals. Up until the last few years, Bidwell charged among the highest ticket prices in the N.F.L. for a product that, after 45 years, has yet to demonstrate a level of competence on the playing field sufficient to sustain the necessary fan support.

*   *   *

The changes in American sport were slow to arrive in Chicago, but the mercenary tactics employed by Halas, the TV network, and the Bidwell family in 1960 offered final convincing proof that the days of candy store proprietorship were over in sports. During the next four years, interest in the new multipurpose stadium withered on the vine.

Bill Veeck was noncommittal and seemed satisfied with his arrangements at Comiskey Park during his first ownership. Mr. Wrigley decided to invest his money in refurbishing his own ballpark, leaving George Halas as the only local sports mogul to keep the issue prominent before the politicians.

In other cities however, the moment was at hand to replace the aging urban ballparks of Dead Ball era. The appeal of a traditional baseball-only stadium crafted along the lines of a Camden Yards in Baltimore lay far in the future. Implementing dazzling Space Age gadgetry, unobstructed sightlines, waterfalls, exploding scoreboards, and electric light shows were the main concerns of 1960s stadium designers seeking to emulate the Houston Astrodome in their own bailiwicks. The Dome was the world's first all-weather, multi-purpose indoor ballpark. It was hailed as the eighth wonder of the world when it opened for business on April 9, 1965.

The up-to-date luxuries of the Astrodome were impressive when measured against the drab concrete structures that had gone before. Never again would an ownership lose revenue to the elements—baseball in the summer, football in autumn, and concerts, rodeos and tractor pulls in between. In fact, such modern stadiums actually maximized the profitability of an enterprise that by and large was *never* profitable to a city or management team. Moreover, modern technology was what the public *expected* from the new megastadiums built for their pleasure in the 1960s and 1970s. Only recently, when the memory of the earlier imperfect diamonds lodged in high-crime inner-city neighborhoods began to fade, did the public outcry for their preservation (or re-creation) begin.

"If Chicago wants an all-sports stadium, which George Halas of the Bears certainly does, I would suggest that we proceed with a carbon copy of the Houston edifice . . . "wrote *Sun-Times* columnist Dick Hackenberg on August 3, 1964. It was never a question of whether Chicago was to build a new stadium, the question was how soon can we get it done? Rival cities like St. Louis, Cincinnati, Pittsburgh, and Philadelphia already had a leg up on Chicago. They had committed massive amounts of public money and had floated bond issues to construct roofless circular cookie-cutter Dome clones that took into account the local football team as well as the baseball tenant.

Chicago American columnist Bill Gleason predicted that the lakefront super structure Daley envisioned would be ready for the 1966 Armed Forces Football Game, if not sooner. The South Side scribe showed resounding support for the goldfish bowl concept when he wrote on August 10, 1964: ". . . [when] a town like Anaheim, California, which for years was nothing more than a throw-away gag line on the Jack Benny radio show is planning a $20 million stadium to provide a home for the little lost Angels of baseball, it is time for Chicago to get moving."

Leaving no room for doubt as to where he stood on how this new sports palace should look when completed, Gleason added: "The bowl unquestionably is the real architectural form for a new stadium, and a stack of bowls (two or four) would insure maximum use of space and put every spectator reasonably close to the action. A sports fan doesn't object to being high above the action. All he demands is the illusion of proximity."

* * *

In the Spring of 1964, Mayor Daley appointed a blue-ribbon citizens' committee to conduct a feasibility study for a municipal sports facility to be financed by revenue bonds. According to Comiskey, a balsa wood model featuring a retractable roof was developed by the Charles Murphy architectural firm. But Daley had expressed skepticism about domed stadiums and sliding roofs—concerned that such stadiums might not be economically practical or even do-able.

"So I said Mr. Mayor: 'If we can get three ballclubs in an outdoor stadium it would pay for itself,'" Comiskey advised. "Our fans are a different breed of cat. They're accustomed to sitting out in the weather, and besides, we had the Amphitheater and Chicago Stadium for the Ice Capades and circuses."

Outside experts such as Edward Magee, who oversaw Pittsburgh's campaign to build Three Rivers Stadium for the Pirates and Steelers warned against the likely cost overruns of a dome.

Magee told the commission that his colleagues first considered a remote site for the Pittsburgh stadium "...in a cow pasture, but that would have eliminated city participation, land clearance, and some phases of finance. Then we came to the only conclusion: that it had to be in the downtown area to produce new and continuous business for the central city. It is the only thing that will keep the area strong for many, many years to come."

At issue in Chicago was whether the new stadium should be financed by taxpayer money or independent capital, since it was a foregone conclusion that the "Daley Dome" would either be built on lakefront property or in the tenement district adjacent to west Madison Street. If a local sports magnate even considered for a moment the remote possibility of relocating to the suburbs, Daley would have prevented them from taking the good name of Chicago along with them.

Such was the case a decade later when a disgusted George Halas threatened to vacate Soldier Field and sign a 30-year stadium lease with the city of Arlington Heights, northwest of Chicago. "You just don't leave a great city behind," snorted an angry Daley. For probably the only time in his life, George Halas blinked first in what amounted to a pissing match between two cagey public figures. The Bears would remain in Soldier Field for the time being.

The immediate beneficiary of a new stadium, besides Halas would have been Arthur Cecil Allyn Jr. On the surface there seemed to be a greater urgency for the Sox to have a new stadium than the Cubs. But in 1964, a year or two away from the racial violence that engulfed the South Side and spurred the white backlash that contributed to the precipitous drop in White Sox attendance later in the decade, Art effectively killed any lingering hope for a municipal stadium. He bluntly informed the mayor that he would oppose any publicly financed construction project that would put the city on credit and eliminate competitive bidding when he could build the same state-of-the-art park with private venture capital for 60%-80% of the cost.

Without White Sox participation, Mayor Daley knew that a Bears-only stadium would be a hard sell, and in fact, a political impossibility when the nationwide trend of that period emphasized the long-term profitability of a shared facility. Private individuals no longer built sports palaces on the scale of what Daley had in mind. History was not on Art Allyn's side as he began tinkering with the notion of constructing his own megastructure using corporate monies.

Since the opening of Yankee Stadium in 1923, there had only been one privately financed baseball park to arise in the U.S., and that one belonged to Walter O'Malley in Chavez Ravine, near the tree-lined Elysian Hills of Los Angeles. If not for the determination of Mayor Norris Poulson and other city officials to lure the Dodgers to L.A. in 1957 by dangling a vacant parcel of land reserved for an undetermined public use before the crafty O'Malley, it is a dubious assumption that Dodger Stadium could have been built at all without a tax appropriation.

"I am against any new stadium built with taxpayer money for private enterprise," Mr. Allyn reiterated. Arthur's media posturing won him the gratitude and admiration of a segment of the voting public in Chicago. But all the editorial support in the world failed to induce Chicagoans to come out to Comiskey Park and support the ballclub, as the ledger sheet statements proved.

The Daley Dome never went beyond a conceptual rendering. Then came the McCormick Place fire and all bets were off. The issue was finished for the time being at least, as the Mayor worked feverishly to salvage the city's convention business by rebuilding the exposition hall as quickly as possible.

Art Allyn's acrimonious dispute with the Mayor over public finance did not necessarily mean that he intended to remain in Comiskey Park because he considered it a grand and historic place to play. The financial health of his own corporation was jeopardized if he remained on the South Side much longer. Allyn wanted out of Comiskey almost as badly as George Halas desired to vacate Wrigley Field.

* * *

In the early months of 1967, Allyn and his compliant younger brother applied the final brush strokes to their own modest proposal; a privately financed $46 million-dollar sports complex with three separate arenas to house the White Sox; the Mustangs soccer team belonging to John; and a third facility nearby for the Chicago Bulls and Blackhawks, should they care to partake.

In customary fashion, the artist's drawing of the Allyn multiplex was unveiled in a whirlwind press conference at the Sheraton-Chicago Hotel on June 14, 1967—just 12 hours after the other sports owners around town first received their information packets from Arthur. Because he had a plane to catch the following morning for a long-awaited Roman holiday, Arthur gave reporters the brush when asked to explain his secretiveness. "When a lot of people start finding out about a big project, it's no longer possible to keep it quiet," he explained. "I didn't want any story about my negotiations blowing up in the faces of either Mr. Halas or Mr. Wrigley."

Mr. Wrigley and Mr. Halas offered polite encouragement to Allyn, but were disinterested in working with the Sox owner after he had poisoned the well for them all three years earlier. Black Hawks owner Arthur Wirtz was more to the point. "Why should I become someone else's tenant when I have my own building?"

* * *

The stadium was to occupy air rights *over* a 53-acre railroad yard just south of the historic Dearborn Street train station in the South Loop, which at the time belonged to the Chicago and Western Indiana Railroad Company. Allyn pegged the completion date for 1971. When no action was taken after the first year, the timetables were pushed back to 1972. And then ultimately . . . oblivion.

Financial arrangements were not adequately explained. A lease agreement for the air rights was never signed with the railroad, and the degree of participation by the other professional teams had yet to be determined. Nevertheless: "I am moving the White Sox from Comiskey Park whether the others come in or not," Allyn barked.

As for the old Comiskey Park, it was expected that the Illinois Institute of Technology would claim the site for re-development, or sub-lease the property to private concerns as an industrial park. So much for baseball's glorious South Side traditions.

Arthur Allyn dropped the proposal into the Mayor's lap with the expectation that Daley would help guide it past the Chicago Plan Commission and the City Council. But Hizzoner had more important issues on the table than pandering to the self-interests of the curmudgeonly White Sox owner.

The prime South Loop real estate with its many abandoned rail depots and junk yards was an area that would remain in dispute for many years to come. No one was exactly sure if this garbage-strewn industrial weed patch should be re-developed for low-cost housing (residents of the dangerously overcrowded Chinatown to the immediate south had petitioned the city time and time again for consideration but were largely ignored), or retail and commercial space. The Chicago Central Area Committee (CCAC) was formed in 1956, and began taking a long, hard look at this property as a future site for upper-income housing. The upscale town houses were built much later, in the early 1980s. But as the urban planners of the late 1960s looked ahead to the 21st century, there were so many questions still unanswered. Whatever the outcome of all this, Daley's pocket veto of the 1967 stadium plan was the final kiss of death for Art Allyn's rising hope for a new stadium to be ready by opening day 1971.

Even at that, the Allyn complex might have stood a better chance of breaking ground if only the White Sox owner had succeeded in his original plan to bring an A.F.L. team to Comiskey Park in the mid-1960s. Art Allyn was thwarted by powerful interests within the N.F.L. who blocked the rival league from entering Chicago and competing with the Halas monopoly. It was not the intention of the Bears owner to allow an interloper back into town who would usurp his TV market after he had fought so hard and so long to drive the Cardinals away for these very reasons.

* * *

Speculative talk of a tax payer-friendly South Loop complex had a soothing effect amongst the editorial writers of the day who applauded Allyn for his remarkable foresight and for giving Chicagoans "something to glow about." Allyn's happy talk was mere conjecture and it didn't cost his company a dime, since no spade of dirt had been turned, nor a dollar committed. Summing up the likelihood of the Allyn arcade actually being built, nationally known sports commentator Brent Musburger (then attached to the staff of the *Chicago American*) predicted that: ". . . the stadium dilemma won't be resolved 10 years from today, this despite the rather curious proclamation by Allyn . . . " The date: May 20, 1968.

Opening to great acclaim in 1910, the Baseball Palace of the World had ceased being one of the city's attractions by the late 1930s.

The opening of the Dan Ryan Expressway in 1962 and the convenience of the El train running by the stadium (above) prolonged the demolition of Comiskey Park that ultimately came in 1991 (below).

Mark Fletcher

200

NAME _____

AFFILIATION _____

AMERICAN LEAGUE

SOX

1983 AMERICAN LEAGUE
CHAMPIONSHIP SERIES
COMISKEY PARK

LOCATION Aux. Press Box

SEC. 239 ROW H SEAT 5

WORKING MEDIA
(Admit to Press Box,
Field, Interview Room)

№

Not Transferable
Subject to Conditions on Reverse Side
Not For Use By Anyone Under 18
THIS PASS MUST BE WORN IN A
VISIBLE PLACE AT ALL TIMES

| GAME 3 | GAME 4 | GAME 5 | GAME X |

ENTER AT PRESS GATE

MEDIA

CHICAGO WHITE SOX

1993 SEASON PASS
MUST BE DISPLAYED AT ALL TIMES

NAME _____
(NOT TRANSFERABLE)

AFFILIATION _____

FULL ACCESS

CHICAGO WHITE SOX
1985 MEDIA COURTESY PASS
ENTER COMISKEY PARK VIA PRESS GATE (#9)
GOOD FOR ADMISSION TO: PARK ONLY

NAME _____

AFFILIATION _____

Chapter
— Eleven —

Press Box Evenings: The Biases of the Sportswriters Considered

Jerome Holtzman, the sagely regent of Chicago's literary fourth estate, and midwife to baseball's modern save rule, decreed a long time ago, that there shall be "no cheering in the pressbox." In Comiskey Park and elsewhere, Holtzman's time-honored custom is sacrosanct. Decorum must always be observed. The press dare not cross the line of impartiality and be made to look foolish in front of their peers with an outrageous show of emotion on behalf of the home team . . . but sometimes it is impossible for these literary bravos of the fourth estate to set aside their biases toward one or the other of the local baseball teams in the name of objective reporting.

Holtzman is a columnist for the *Chicago Tribune,* a recent inductee into baseball's Hall of Fame, and the Paine-Webber of the Chicago sports fraternity. That is, his ruminations about the players, owners, and administrative personnel whom he has known intimately since the early 1940s are usually on the mark. Jerome is a link to the vanished era of Underwood typewriters, fat, aromatic cigars, and inked letter presses. People respect him for his years of experience, and will usually listen to what he has to say.

As a columnist, he is exempted from attending the games in person. Talk show hosts, feature writers, and the WGN sports staff on the radio side are other birds of prey rarely seen in the

Comiskey environs, unless it is opening day, the playoffs, or management calls a press conference. To the paying customer who loves this game so dearly, what greater job could there be than to sit in the press box each night, munch on free hot dogs and peanuts, and observe the baseball ballet?

However, to the current generation of scribes, the ebb and flow of the national pastime is more of an unpleasant daily grind than a poetic rhapsody. A three-hour game at Comiskey is not quite up to the excitement of a tennis final, the Master's Golf Tournament, or the prestige attached to covering an unfolding political drama. By the fifth inning of a meaningless contest with the Detroit Tigers on a drizzly, mean-spirited night in late April, the bone-weary reporters start to grumble about the time the game is likely to end. A Carlton Fisk-caught game—when the "Commander" directed the field with the aplomb of a symphony conductor—only delayed their departure from the ballpark. Baseball fans who love the game are unphased.

Below the press box sit the shivering masses, huddled in woolen blankets and sipping watery hot chocolate purchased from the concession stands. They are just happy to be here to watch baseball, and if the game is close, they frankly don't care what time it will end. They "ooh" and "ahhh" every time a fly ball is lofted high into the air, breathlessly anticipating that this will be the shot that will clear the fences.

Upstairs some of the radio guys are snickering at the fans' inability to differentiate between an ordinary fly ball and the home run. The fans are stupid they say.

If Jerome were here tonight, he would light his cigar and gaze thoughtfully across the spacious, comfortable room at a changing world. When Jerry was a young reporter beginning his career in 1943, there were still five daily newspapers in town and a reverence for the game that is all but absent today. There was a time in ancient memory when the word of the sportswriter still carried weight in this town. There was a time not so far removed when fire burned in a journalist's belly, and he possessed the courage of his convictions. Wendell Smith of the *Chicago American* put his neck on the line in the waning days of the "Jim Crow" era, in order to draw attention to the plight of the black player forced to sleep in flea bag motels many miles from the spring training camps in Florida. Wendell Smith was an African-American reporter of great renown. His hue and cry echoed throughout Florida and Chicago—eventually forcing White Sox owner Arthur C. Allyn to purchase his own hotel in Sarasota in order to circumvent the archaic segregation laws that still existed in the south during the early 1960s.

* * *

From the earliest days of the game, baseball and the big city newspapers were ideally suited to each other. The box scores and play-by-play descriptions of late afternoon contests (starting at 3:00 p.m., and ending by the evening commute) appeared side by side with the stock market quotes on page one. Baseball helped bolster the circulation of the evening papers and provided the moguls with an invaluable source of free publicity. In this happy, bygone era, the profit motive and greed factor—the real under-pinnings of the game when you get down to it—were less a public issue than they are today. A firm alliance was forged between players, reporters, and fans for the mutual betterment of this national treasure known as baseball.

Before the modern age of sound-bite journalism, lap-top P.C.s, faxes, and jet travel, the game moved at a more leisurely pace. During the all-night poker games in the club car of the New York Central, writers and players kibitzed with each other as the train raced across the Midwestern flatlands bound for Cleveland, Detroit, and points further east. There was a bonding process at work here, and the feeling that "we were all in it together," since the writers made only slightly less than what the average rookie player was pulling down at the time.

The fans of Chicago were blessed with a rich cadre of beat writers; and the fresh insights of an Arch Ward, a John Carmichael, or a Warren Brown, were readily identifiable by their newspapers and signature columns. These men were innovators in the truest sense of the word, and their colorful newspaper careers extended back as far as the antiquarian days of baseball. Arch Ward, for example, conceived baseball's first All-Star Game, the International Golden Gloves, the All-Star Bowling Classic, and the Silver Skates competition during his thirty years in the trenches. Mr. Ward observed a simple credo regarding sports that seems sadly out-of-date today. "We hear a great deal these days about the importance of preserving democracy," he stated during the height of the Cold War era, "but where else than in sports do you actually see democracy in action? Everyone knows that when contestants go into action all that matters is their own strength, their own skill, their own determination."

Alas, if it were still only so . . .

While these writers might not have cheered lustily for the White Sox (the same rules applied in those days as well), they appreciated the special significance of the Comiskey family's ties to their loyal South Side flock. The Old Roman, son Lou, and daughter-in-law Grace could count on receiving a fair shake from the media even in the leanest of times. It is not that way today, and there are no more Jerry Holtzmans, John Carmichaels, or Warren Browns coming over the ridge anytime soon.

Warren Brown was a Latin scholar, author, wordsmith of tremendous repute, and the proprietor of the widely acclaimed "So They Tell Me" column for many years. Brown associated with such legendary figures of the fraternity as Grantland Rice, Westbrook Pegler, and Damon Runyon, whose columns all appeared in syndicated form in the Chicago dailies at one time or another.

In his formative years, the budding scribe once batted the horsehide around the sandlot of the Telegraph Hill Boys Club in San Francisco, with one Charles "Swede" Risberg—even then, very much the "hard guy." During his college years, Brown teamed up with "Dutch" Ruether on the St. Ignatius nine. Years later, Brown's vivid recollections and anecdotes of his rough and tumble West Coast days entertained and delighted the scores of listeners he addressed along the banquet circuit.

The spring of 1913 found the St. Ignatius college boys paired up against the barnstorming White Sox who happened to be training on the coast at the time. The nucleus of the brilliant, but tragically flawed 1919 Black Sox squad was already in place, and on a typically cool afternoon in the Bay area, the raw talents of these budding young stars were on display.

Going into the ninth inning of that long-ago game, Warren Brown, a gangling first baseman of exceptional speed and agility, was savoring the prospect of upsetting the Chicagoans. St. Ignatius was clinging to a precarious 2-1 lead. In the final frame, the White Sox rallied. Buck Weaver whacked a two-run homer off of the kid

Ruether to emerge victorious by a 4-2 count. Afterward, Brown shook hands with Ray Schalk, the peppery White Sox catcher who was beginning his first full year in the big leagues.

And so began a life-long friendship between the two men that lasted well into the 1960s, when the world they had known markedly changed. After Schalk's name was submitted to the Veterans Committee of the Hall of Fame years later, Chairman Warren Brown provided his pal with the necessary boost. The doors of Cooperstown that otherwise might have slammed shut on a .253 lifetime hitter, swung open to Schalk as a consequence of Warren Brown's influence within B.B.W.A. circles.

At the height of an era when Brown's influence over the newspaper-reading public (from the mid-teens up through the post-World War II period), his musings on the passing sport scene were right up there with Carmichael's column, and Arch Ward's "Wake Of the News" offering in the *Tribune*. Warren Brown was a versatile reporter, who was at home interviewing politicians, and covering the so-called hard news stories as well as a horse race or All-Star baseball game, or track and field event. (The same talents can be ascribed to Jack Brickhouse and the late Bob Elson in the radio-television realm.)

Brown was a gentle teetotaler who wagered the boys in the newsroom one day that he could churn out a book-length manuscript over the course of a weekend. Borrowing heavily from Gus Axelson's 1919 biography of Charles Comiskey, Brown produced the first team history of the White Sox in 1952. The boys in the newsroom cheerfully covered their bets, or so the story goes.

Once, baseball was all that mattered to the sports fanatic, and the liveliest debate in town could be heard in the cozy intimacy of the corner barber shop. In this princely realm of tall stories and idle chatter, a baseball fan could receive a haircut, a shave, and a preview of the latest *Police Gazette* containing all the breezy news of the day from the four corners for two bits. It was the gift of blarney that made a man stand out among his peers as he awaited a haircut and a shave on a high humidity afternoon in July.

As a youngster growing up in Madison, Wisconsin, John Peerless Carmichael got to know the barber shop regulars. He dwelled on their every word as they spouted off about the neighborhood plug uglies, the pugilists down at the gym, local politicians . . . and the ballplayers. Mr. Carmichael dearly loved baseball. He became an American League enthusiast, and un-abashedly so. Stepping off the train in Chicago in 1927, John was fortunate enough to find work on the copy desk of William Randolph Hearst's *Herald & Examiner*, where he was shown the ropes by his editor Warren Brown. Seeing little chance to unseat his mentor, whose pious sobriety ran against the grain of the profession in those days, Carmichael crossed the Madison Street bridge and joined the staff of the *Daily News* in 1932. He opened his "Barber Shop" column just two years later, and finally the White Sox and American League partisans knew where they could go to hang their hats.

A spirited rivalry soon developed between Mr. C. and Lloyd Lewis; author, raconteur, and a Chicagoan to the bones, who also happened to be a Cub fan. As the proprietor of the "Voice of the Grandstand" column, Lewis deflected Carmichael's spirited anti-National League, anti-Cub salvos as best as he could. Perfect editorial balance in a newspaper.

For a time, sports editor Lewis enjoyed a slight edge. Up until 1938, the Cubs were winning pennants on three-year cycles. But in the off years, the White Sox prevailed. They so thoroughly demoralized the Cubs in the annual City Series played for bragging rights, that the post-season contests became *de rigueur*, until they were called off for lack of interest in 1942.

The bell rang for these two on opening day. The good natured ribbing reached a fever pitch by the All Star Game, and climaxed at World Series time with the inevitable Yankee triumph. On the eve of the 1936 World Series as he was packing his bags for New York, Mr. Lewis told his readers that he would enjoy watching: "Mr. Junior Carmichael's face remirror all the emotions it suf-fered when he and I were together in Boston in July (for that year's All Star game won by the Nationals), watching Mr. Carl Hubbell toy with the "terrifying" sluggers from the American League." (Author's note: The New York Yankees won the '36 Series.)

A year later, Lloyd Lewis guaranteed sudden death for the White Sox in their City Series wrap-up with the Cubs. But as usual, the Sox K.O.'d the Cubs in a seventh-game grudge match, leading Carmichael to gloat: "For Mr. Lewis it has indeed been a perfect year from the day last April when the same Sox beat the same Cubs in the spring series on through the All-Star Game in

Washington, into the World Series of 1937 when the Giants should have stayed in bed and so to the last gasp at Wrigley Field."

The Cub fans agonized over Carmichael's good-natured heckling. Couldn't something be done to curtail the opinions of the Yankee-loving, White Sox-rooting curmudgeon from tweeking the nose of the Cubs? "I can't help it getting in the paper," Lewis replied. "I never see the column before it goes to the printer. He steals in at night and hands it to the typesetter much as Eugene Field, another *Daily News* man, once did. I thought I had him on this World Series—thought I could take him with me on the train to New York and give him a long talk about the shortcomings of the American League. But he outwitted me."

The next year, 1938, the Cubs advanced to the World Series and the American League lost the All Star Game. It was a pretty grim year all around for Carmichael. The day after the A.L. dropped a 4-1 tilt to the Nationals, the Barber Shop column consisted of a white space with a solitary notice appearing at the bottom, penned no doubt, by Mr. Lewis. "Mr. Carmichael has nothing to say to his constituents today."

* * *

John Carmichael, a witty, urbane toastmaster, consummate story teller, and social drinker, retired from the news business in 1972 and went to work for the White Sox as a community relations speaker. It was not such an uncommon career move. Howard Roberts and Ed Short of the newspapers and radio respectively, went to work for the Sox. Jim Gallagher, another press veteran joined the Cubs.

It was fitting perhaps that in later years Lloyd Lewis' "Voice From the Grandstand" column should be handed down to *Daily News* man John Justin Smith, (via Harry Sheer in the *American*), who administered it in partisan manner on behalf of the White Sox fans at a time in the late 1960s, when the Pale Hose desperately needed all the free publicity they could possibly muster.

When John Justin Smith, the scion of an esteemed literary family, was afforded a glimpse of the red ink in Art Allyn's ledger book, he decided (not without some pre-existing American League bias I'm sure), to balance the scales, fearing perhaps, the exodus of the franchise from the city due to diminishing fan support. But when Smith became the travel editor of the *Chicago Sun-Times*, one of the last spokesmen for White Sox fandom in the media was lost.

Today the media's attitude toward the Sox runs the gamut from tedium to apathy. This was true even after "Barnum" Bill Veeck waltzed into town for the second coming in 1975. After surveying the situation after a year's time, Veeck concluded that the White Sox would never get a fair shake against the WGN/Cub axis. The Sox owner was so fed up with the print media in town, that he began measuring column inches in the morning papers.

Is there a pro-Cub bias in Chicago sports reporting? The press corps maintains it is all nonsense. A chicken and egg issue. "It may have been true at one time—but it is not anymore and people should stop whining about it," complains Tom Shaer, WSCR sports talk show host. "I prefer to live in the present." Shaer and his colleagues will deny these allegations until eternity, but most Chicago baseball fans sense it. There is a ring of truth to the charge. Simply because the media chooses to brush aside these allegations does not mean there is no pre-existing Cub bias.

If Bill Veeck, the beloved showman could not conjure up enthusiasm for his team in the press, what then did that say about the future of the franchise in Chicago? It is clear that there is a correlation between sagging attendance, declining advertising, TV ratings, and a lack of press coverage. Mike Veeck has confided that his father arrived at the painful conclusion that Chicago was no longer viable as a two-team city for these reasons. If not for the breakdown in discussions between Marvin Davis and Bill Veeck after Veeck had flown to Denver to commence negotiations, it is likely that 1980 would have been the last year for a White Sox franchise in Chicago.

Veeck was right about the media. The Sox marketing department can win the sniper skirmishes with the Tribune Company, but they realize that in order to do so, they must occasionally revert to gimmickry to enchant the press, work that much harder, and pray that the baseball organization can field a competitive team—if they are to have even a fighting chance.

Case in point: In 1983 there was limited euphoria around town when the White Sox won Chicago's first-ever baseball divisional title. The next year, Pandemonium reigned supreme when the Cubs captured the National League East. According to Tom Shaer, WBBM-TV, the CBS affiliate in Chicago, lavished $400,000 on travel expenses, sending reporters on the road to cover the Cubs during the team's title quest. When the White Sox were in the hunt a year earlier, all the Chicago TV stations spent a *combined* half-million in travel expenses. That should tell you which way the wind blows in this town. The Cubs will *always* be the big story in the print media and on the sports call-in shows until they bow out of the pennant race; a rite of summer occurring on or about July 1 of every year. By then it's almost time for the Chicago Bears pre-season camp to open, which means that until the conclusion of the baseball season in October, the Sox are likely to be eclipsed by news of free agent signings, hamstring injuries, draft picks, and other items of interest to the media guys covering the goings on at Halas Hall.

* * *

Just who is this media that at times has worked to the detriment of White Sox ownerships going back to the mid-1960s when the last of an old and venerable breed—Warren Brown, Edgar Munzel, Wendell Smith—and a John Carmichael, departed the scene?

Most people will concede that Chicago is a Cubs town and has been a Cubs town for many, many years. This process of transformation to a Cub town was slow to evolve, but evolve it did, and in some ways the Sox brass have no one to blame but themselves.

A convincing argument can be made that the Old Roman voluntarily surrendered control of the media to the Cubs after the Black Sox scandal, when, in failing health and broken spirit he sequestered himself away in his North Woods retreat. His Woodland Bard camp followers were rarely invited to join him on this lonely sojourn to Mercer. Comiskey's only comfort in his declining years was his grandson Charley, and memories of the pearl-button era when he was still the "Noblest Roman" of them all.

Since the 1930s, the Sox have seemed to enjoy playing the role of the squeamish underdog, justifying their yearly failures to an inability to compete with the cash-rich franchises like the Yankees, Red Sox, and Cubs. While the Sox hunkered down behind the barricades in the thirties and forties, the Cubs energized Chicago fandom with a winning ballclub, and "beautiful" Wrigley Field; a clever marketing ploy engineered by William Veeck Sr., and his son Bill, who was already demonstrating the promotional genius that was to make him so popular with fans in the years to come.

Vines and ivy, and wholesome outdoor fun in the sunshine of Wrigley Field was offered in stark contrast to cavernous Comiskey Park, an imposing structure that cast a long shadow over a shabby neighborhood threatened by racial divisions and a gradually deteriorating economic base. These neighborhood fears only compounded the White Sox misery and they dated all the way back to World War One.

The strategy of selling the fans on the ballpark was a variation of a successful theme originally employed by the Old Roman decades earlier. When Comiskey Park was new, the owner lured thousands of casual fans to his gleaming stadium because he successfully touted it to a generation that still marveled at technological innovation and the "largesse" of society, be it a new skyscraper, or an "unsinkable" ocean liner that dwarfed everything that had come before. Here in Chicago the fans could visit the showplace of modern baseball; the biggest, the best . . . the South Side Palace. And it worked to perfection until the Wrigleys realized that societal tastes were slowly shifting, and that a case could be made for charm and intimacy in a sports stadium.

Minimal attention was paid to marketing technique by the Sox. Breaking even became the obsession of Grace Comiskey, J. Lou's widow who kept the team in the family out of respect for her late husband and three children. To surpass the break-even point it was necessary for the White Sox to draw a million— 500,000 on the road—and 500,000 paying customers into the park each year. The goal was accomplished twelve times between 1930-1950.

Grace's austerity programs, which often meant slashing player salaries in the lean years, coupled with the novelty of night baseball, helped keep the White Sox above the water line through the forties, but more importantly, they had already lost a generation of new fans to the Cubs who trotted out a winning team and all that beautiful ivy.

Beautiful Wrigley Field . . . indeed.

Charles Comiskey, and to a lesser extent George Halas and Bill Veeck, understood that the fans' loyalty could be bought cheaply. The succeeding Comiskeys, however, neither had the resources nor inclination to revive the Woodland Bard hunting and fishing tradition. J. Lou was a sickly man beset by scarlet fever for much of his adult life and could hardly be expected to tramp around the North Woods in pursuit of deer and grouse. Grace was the family matriarch. Charley was too young, and Dorothy's only ambition was to be a good housewife to her husband; the ex-pitcher, John Dungan Rigney.

Too bad really, because the Sox lost their competitive advantage. Beginning in the late 1960s and early '70s, a new generation of college-bred sportswriters, weaned away from alcohol binging and night-clubbing, took their place in the press box alongside the holdovers from the New Deal era. Some of them toted microphones for suburban radio stations. Many more arrived fresh from the sunbelt states of Arizona, Florida, California, or the journalism schools east of the Mississippi.

If they had no biases for either team, all this began to change when they compared the visual charm of Wrigley Field to the cold environs of Comiskey Park, and the clientele that patronized the respective stadiums. Cubs Park was woven into a pleasing urban tapestry that included day baseball, friendly saloons and restaurants nearby, the vines, Bleacher Bums in hardhats, young professionals out slumming, and Ernie Banks who symbolized Cub baseball. On the *other* side of town, where the neighborhoods were gutted by poverty, despair, and white flight, there stood an empty stadium, colorless Bob Elson behind the microphone, a losing team, and an unpopular owner in Arthur C. Allyn.

The new breeders (as I shall refer to them henceforth) who arrived without any pre-set loyalties or commitment to either team, settled on the Cubs as their ballclub of choice for much of these same reasons. The new breed came of age during the Watergate era when the admissions offices of the nation's prestigious journalism schools were clogged with new applicants. Everyone wanted to be the next Bob Woodward, Carl Bernstein, or Red Smith, at least those who were fortunate enough to afford the steep tuition.

Their arrival on the scene coincided with the maturity of the late baby boomers whose happy TV memories of early childhood included the popular kid's show, Bozo's Circus on WGN. "Joel Bierig (former *Chicago Sun-Times* reporter) once wrote a column where he said that the profile of a White Sox fan was a man over 35 whose son was a Cub fan," Jerry Reinsdorf recalls. "And he said that was because the kid had grown up watching the Cubs on WGN - you couldn't see the White Sox after 1967."

* * *

The earliest impressions of the game for this new generation of fans were nurtured by WGN, the pied piper of Wrigleyville. Bozo the Clown, Hall-of-Fame broadcaster Jack Brickhouse— they were the catalysts of this new movement. Call it what you will. The Sox had just lost a *second* generation of fans to the Cubs in this century. Why? Bad judgments and poor marketing technique. Nobody was watching the Allyn-Sox on the Chicago UHF outlet that the team had unwisely chosen to broadcast its home and away games in 1968. In order to beam into the WFLD-Channel 32 signal, homeowners had to first go out and purchase a decoder box for $30 to pick up the often fuzzy signal.

Unlike New York, which had two powerful independent stations in WWOR and WPIX, the F.C.C. granted Chicago only one: WGN, and very quickly WGN fell into the National League camp. Cub day games were ideally suited to WGN's broadcast schedule, and did not conflict with the station's nighttime programming. Consequently, Phil Wrigley's team profited from greater exposure than the cross-town White Sox.

"Most people didn't have the UHF signal in their houses back then," Reinsdorf adds. "The biggest mistake the team ever made was going off of WGN in 1968." The second biggest mistake, Jerry Reinsdorf neglects to mention, was the poorly thought out marketing decision that forsook free TV for Sportsvision, the cable-TV fiasco the club vested its long-range hopes in back in 1982.

* * *

The legions of Cub admirers in the media swelled in the late 1960s and on into the seventies as the Cubs gained national momentum via their expansive cable operations. Busloads of freshly minted Cub fans from downstate Illinois, Iowa, Wisconsin, Indiana, and Michigan—all who watched the team on their WGN cable—padded the yearly attendance figures at Wrigley to the exclusion of the White Sox. This was a market the South Siders were never able to tap into because the UHF stations representing them all these years barely penetrated the outer reaches of suburbia! The only out-of-town fans of consequence that attend Sox games are Detroit Tiger fans from Southwestern Michigan.

* * *

The Sox have had few advocates in the Chicagoland media since the 1950s. One of them, though, is Bill Gleason, perceived to be one of the blue collar heroes whose South Side Irish roots run very deep. Sadly, Gleason's perceptions of reality are obscured by his wistful longing for the late Bill Veeck. Consequently, the tandem of Reinsdorf and Einhorn became the bogeymen for Gleason's diatribes. These owners were cancerous to all good South Siders, to hear Gleason tell it.

"Gleason has opposed us constantly," Reinsdorf complains. In 1983 he said that: ". . . we would sell after we had owned the team for five years because we were just in it for the tax breaks. He's been constantly wrong, but he's not a factor. He's a bitter old man who was fired from the *Sun-Times* and he writes for a couple of little newspapers and nobody cares what he says or what he thinks about anything."

As the complex issues surrounding the construction of a new stadium evolved, Bill Gleason's simplistic, unacceptable bombasts against the owners only served to inflame community-based opposition and polarize Sox fans who were searching for something more than gut-level emotion from their only advocate in the press. Bill Gleason is now attached to the staff of the *Southtown Economist*, and grumbling loud enough for anyone along press row to hear, that the new park "is the best money can buy."

It is a never-ending wonder how the White Sox managed to survive the late 1980s to become as successful as they are.

Eddie Gold, another *Sun-Times* man who is fond of Mickey Mouse tee-shirts, stale poetry, and the immortal ex-Cub "Swish" Nicholson, was an editor at the paper for many years. He is an unswerving Cub fan who eschews the Sox for different reasons than his former cell mate at the *Times*. One way that Eddie got under the White Sox skin was his habit of running his own portrait above his Sunday trivia column. Eddie is seen wearing a Cub floppy hat in the picture. It was no trivial matter to Sox executives in 1987, who threw up their hands in disgust and said "Now do you see what we mean?"

* * *

Media apathy is one thing; that can be overcome in time. You have to really wonder, though, what you're going to do when the press starts inventing news. Hostile, panic-peddling news.

By now almost everyone in Chicago has heard the ugly rumors that sharp shooters in the upper floors of the Robert Taylor housing projects across the way from the new park were taking dead aim on the box seats in the upper deck. The rumor was first circulated by Jonathon Brandmeier, an FM disc jockey in Chicago known for his on-air puns and biting satire. The rumor was repeated in the newspapers a few weeks later by nationally syndicated columnist Mike Royko.

"When the story first broke, we checked every seat and every inch of this ballpark and we found nothing," explains Tim Romani, then the assistant executive director of the Illinois Sports Authority, who oversaw construction of the new Comiskey. "It ended up being a story that somebody put out there as a nuisance factor."

WMAQ sports anchor Tom Shaer was dispatched to the park to check out the rumors, but could find no compelling evidence to suggest that shots had been fired from the Taylor homes nearby. "I told Tom I was being honest, and I had nothing to hide," Tim Romani recalls. There were no bullet holes. Period.

"My coverage of the story was professional start to finish," Shaer wants it known. "There were rumors flying all over town about this, but the fact is we decided not to put it on the air." WMAQ anchorman Ron Magers wisely decided not to legitimize irresponsible reporting from a disc jockey whose stock and trade is the outrageous. A story like this, which plays on some deep-seeded, dangerous, and long-standing racial fears, refused to go away, however. The more it escalated into a three-ring circus, the more likely it became that individuals within the housing project would be inspired to place the lives of the construction workers in eminent peril by firing real bullets.

In fact, two months later, a shot *was* fired and the bullet was imbedded in the back of the new scoreboard. "The truth of the matter is, the scoreboard *wasn't erected* when Tom Shaer was here the first time," Romani said. "There was no physical, possible way there could have been bullets in the back of the scoreboard or anywhere else at that time."

* * *

There is a pecking order to the pressbox. Where they sit has everything to do with their importance and what media they happen to represent at the moment. The beat writers from the *Tribune, Sun Times, Daily Herald*, and *Economist* pound away at their portable P.C.s from a reserved seating area in the center of the long, narrow room. They are flanked by statisticians, public address announcer Gene Honda, official scorer Bob Rosenberg, out-of-town media, and various front office employees who are solicitous of their every need.

At the opposite ends from the media command post directly above home plate, the by-play between the fringe players on the cusp of greatness is spiced with anecdote, cynicism, and ribaldry. The normal rules governing pressbox decorum do not apply to the irascible part-time reporters from the A.P., U.P.I., the small weekly newspapers, the wire services, or the radio stations of low voltage that dot suburban Cook County and downstate Illinois.

In old Comiskey Park, these reporters who occupied space in the upper tier of the press box liked to refer to themselves as the "Third Row Rats," with all due respect to their well-heeled peers in the first row. Though rats they may be, their shared experiences and free-wheeling love of sport sets them apart from some of the well-paid counterparts from Chicago and the other Major League cities who consider baseball a colossal bore.

* * *

It is the fifth inning of a budding no-hitter. Toronto Blue Jay hurler Todd Stottylmyre is mowing down the White Sox batters with alacrity, and the crowd is restless. Up in the Peanut Gallery the cynics are making penny-ante wagers on which Sox batter will shatter the young pitcher's premature dreams of mound glory. Such little faith in humanity they possess. But like the young moundsman whose no-hitter is likely to be ruined at any moment, the Peanut Gallery journalists have experienced a similar kind of heartbreak; the realization that the clock is ticking on their fading careers.

Whatever hopes and aspirations they once held for a rewarding career in a profession that has thus far seen fit to exclude them, there comes the time when they must do other things and cultivate new job skills in order to survive in the real world outside the axis of professional sports.

In the Peanut Gallery, they are safely out of earshot from the new breeders and the Sox executives who grant them their press box privileges during spring training. Each year there are new restrictions foisted on the media by the Sox, and several of them who like to think they are also a part of the "working press" nervously speculate as to whether or not their names will be lopped off the credentials list come next season. The media room is rarely filled after opening day. In fact it is often half empty. But security is tight and access is closely monitored.

Todd Stottylmyre's performance this evening conjures up moss-covered stories of Cub no-hitters of the past. Memories of the Leo Durocher era in Chicago, and Kenny Holtzman's blanking of the Cincinnati Reds two decades ago are revived by new-breed Cub fan Les Grobstein of WMVP. In the 1970s, Les was a frequent target of the acerbic disc jockey Larry Lujack's mirthful satire when he was with the AM-radio powerhouse WLS. Grobstein, a seasoned veteran of the wars took the barbs of Chicago's first "shock jock" in the spirit they were intended.

Between innings, Les trots out his tape recording of former Cub manager Lee Elia's expletive-deleted tirade against the Chicago fans for the benefit of his Peanut Gallery colleagues. The Rats have heard the censored recording dozens of times since the incident occurred more than ten years ago. Now Les fills us in on what we didn't hear. Some laugh. Others roll their eyes. Is this still a Sox game we are watching? The no-hit tension mounts. "Who's got Thomas in the eighth?" Grobstein demands. "Someone's got Thomas in the dollar pool. Who is it?"

The radio people like Bill Motluck of WCGO, Chicago Heights, and WLS' Joe Rozanski, one of the best producers in the business, must now figure out a way to pry original quotes out of Stottlylmyre in the post-game interview if indeed he pulls it off. Players are notorious for hiding in the trainer's room—off limits to the press—if they do not wish to be interviewed.

This is crunch time; when you have to dash to the elevators with a Radio Shack tape recorder in hand and pull the good material out of the ballplayers who want to shave, shower, and depart the premises as quickly as the traffic congestion outside the park will let them. Are the batteries still good? Will I be able to get to Stottylmyre?

"Harold Baines was always a lousy interview," the Grobber intones. "The worst!" The Peanut Gallery agrees. Grobstein has no use for the former White Sox home run king, and wonders what possessed Jerry Reinsdorf to retire the uniform number of this sullen, withdrawn athlete when others are far more deserving. "Harold could have owned this town, if he wanted to," Grobstein declares.

Now comes the eighth inning. Bill Motluck, who works full time as a real estate agent in the south suburbs calls his station to report that a no-hitter is in progress. Bill is here each night, faithfully lining up program material for his half-hour call-in show on WCGO. After attending Lewis University in Chicago, Bill went to work in the minor leagues in Texas. Such jobs do not pay very much, and the chances of making it to the big leagues are minimal. Those who aspire to baseball administration are usually disappointed, or find themselves living on the edge of poverty. Fine when you're single, 22, and have the wanderlust in your soul. Not so good later on.

Returning to Chicago some years later, he proposed a real-estate talk show that he would write, edit, and host. It was a comfortable arrangement for Motluck and the station. And after a brief gestation period, they allowed him to cross over to sports. Bill is happy, because he has no grandiose expectations. There comes a point when age creeps up on you in this business. Accept it, because very often there is no choice.

One out in the eighth inning. The Sox are on the short end of a 9-0 count. The real South Side die hards filed out of the park after the seventh inning. These stout-hearted devotees of White Sox baseball do not want to stick around and experience the shame of the Sox succumbing to a no-hitter. They take it person-ally. But the new breeders in the press box do not get it. This kind of spiritual commitment between a team and its fans strikes them as patently ridiculous.

Up steps the ex-Yankee Dan Pasqua, whose injury-plagued year has sent his batting average plummeting. Pasqua, as they like to say, is on the bubble. But with one out in the bottom of the eighth, the burly Sox first baseman drives a wicked shot to right field that sails over the Toronto right fielder's head. End of the dream for this kid pitcher. There is a spattering of applause, accompanied by a mass exodus for the gates. The remaining fans have seen enough misspent history for one evening.

Upstairs, as the press scurries to their phones and P.C.s to record the disappointing news, Les Grobstein is fuming. He has lost the bet . . . and a dollar . . . despite his reporter's intuition about such things. "Pasqua! I knew it would be him!" Just like he knew that the Sox weren't moving to Florida at a time when the politicians had written them off. Les says he was the only reporter in town who never doubted it for a second.

"Pasqua!" He spits the name out one more time before packing his gear away. And then the game drags to an ignomini-ous end. The new breeders, the Peanut Gallery, and the visiting press clamor for the elevators, leaving behind empty Styrofoam cups, hot dog wrappers, cigarette butts, and dog-eared game notes for someone else to clean up. The press box is all but deserted now except for a handful of the White Sox suits and Joe Pinoti, the soft-spoken Andy Frain usher who has a kind greeting for everyone.

Joe has worked old and new Comiskey Park since time immemorial, and well remembers sneaking into the park to watch Babe Ruth play. He has witnessed generations of players pass in review, and front office people come and go. But his enthusiasm for the job never wanes. God willing and his health permitting, he will be here next year and (we certainly hope) many more years after that. His smile is radiant. Joe is a Comiskey Park treasure who always makes the little guy feel welcome. But for now, Joe waits patiently in the copy room for the Sox statisti-cians to deliver the postgame statistical summaries. He cannot go home until he has photocopied multiple sets for handouts.

That is the nightly drama, the politics, and the pathos of the press box. Much has changed, and sadly, only a few traditions have lingered since Warren Brown and John Carmichael looked down at the throngs from the Comiskey Park crow's nest.

But hopefully there are still some writers and broadcast people out there cut of a finer timber who desire something more from their craft than a paycheck and the ego perks that come with name recognition. I am encouraged by the banter of the Third Row Rats. They represent something in short supply nowadays: a refreshing idealism for an honorable profession that is not so much a job but a way of life. Their more fortunate colleagues whose names are better known to wider audiences have inherited a noble legacy. But do they realize it?

The three tiers of the Comiskey Park press box host Chicago's Fourth Estate. This picture was taken moments after the final out of the last game at old Comiskey Park on September 30, 1990. Public address announcer Bob Finnegan (lower left) called his last game that day.

Along with his partner Eddie Einhorn, Jerry Reinsdorf (above) purchased the White Sox in 1981. Since that time, Reinsdorf and Einhorn have endured an avalanche of criticism as they built the Sox into a World Series contender.

Chapter
— Twelve —

Crisis Years at Comiskey (1981 - 1988)

Talk of a South Loop sports complex, a carpeted, air-conditioned dome, and a private stadium club emanating from the House of Comiskey subsided in the 1970s, a time of economic restraint and retooling.

There was less urgency on the part of management to replace the aging, neglected stadium after it was demonstrated in 1972 that Sox fans would return to the neighborhood to support an exciting, competitive team.

Before dismissing Art Allyn's rationale for a new stadium, however, it is important to remember that the average Major League salary in 1972 was only $34,092. By the time construction began on the new Comiskey Park in 1989, it had risen to $512,804—a staggering 2,599% increase over 1967 figures—obscene by anyone's standard of fairness.

It was still possible for an embattled ownership in the late 1960s and early 1970s to slide by in an outmoded stadium like Comiskey or Tiger Stadium, offering a limited number of choice box seats and zero skyboxes. Ticket revenues coupled with local advertising, and TV income sustained most professional teams provided the product on the field was good and was supported by the media and the fans.

Conditions changed later in the decade after Marvin Miller and the Player's Union gained free agency and salary arbitration for their members. Player salaries, which had climbed slowly but steadily in the 1960s, skyrocketed overnight, forcing owners to take a second look at their ballpark's revenue-generating capacity.

Even the great social egalitarian, Bill Veeck, made token gestures to baseball's changing economics in 1977 by converting the unused Cardinal pressbox overlooking third base into a private party room serving 40 guests. The upper deck suite came complete with a wet bar, caterer, and food server, and was rented for the sum of $400 per occasion. The conversion of the pressbox was Chicago's first experiment with private skyboxes and a tacit admission on the part of Veeck that in order to operate successfully in the modern era one needed additional revenues over and above ticket sales.

* * *

Millionaire real estate developer Edward DeBartolo spent six fruitless months in 1980 trying to buy the White Sox. During the negotiations he hired structural engineers to conduct tests and evaluate the condition of the ballpark. The engineers concluded that there was "nothing substantially wrong" that couldn't be fixed with minor expenditures. Bill Veeck offered DeBartolo's report to Reinsdorf as convincing proof that there was nothing wrong with Comiskey Park that a dab of paint and a little sprucing up wouldn't cure.

Based on Veeck's guarantees, Reinsdorf projected his first-year operating expenses on the assumption that he would spend no more and no less on ballpark maintenance than his predecessor did in 1980.

In his modestly appointed office inside the new Comiskey Park—a sparse working space that belies his status as one of the game's most influential owners—Jerry Reinsdorf paused to light his cigar before reconstructing the sequence of events that dropped the curtain on the old park. "I don't think we saw any problems in those next couple of months," he relates. "But certainly by the end of the 1981 season we realized we had significant problems." Reinsdorf's recollection of these events follows:

* * *

Fall, 1981

The White Sox observed and monitored deterioration in the lower deck concrete slab extending around the bases from the left field to right field foul line. The concrete was determined to be 1910 vintage.

Upon completion of the strike-shortened 1981 season, a comeback year for the Sox sparked by the key free agent acquisitions of perennial All Star catcher Carlton Fisk, and Detroit Tiger outfielder Ron LeFlore, the new owners spent $1.4 million in the initial wave of renovation. By the end of the 1988 season, the total repair bill for old Comiskey Park zoomed to just under $20 million, equalling the *entire* amount paid to Veeck for the team and the stadium.

* * *

Fall 1982 - Spring 1983

Thirty-three private skyboxes were installed in the upper deck area between first and third bases highlighting phase two of Comiskey renovation. The super suites were greeted with a mixture of skepticism and outright hostility by a vast majority of White Sox fans who were accustomed to the easy manner and informality of the previous Veeck ownership. The fan reaction was predictable, but what the patrons of the cheap seats did not understand: "The building of the suites wasn't done as a revenue generator, but rather as a way for us to raise enough money to do other repairs to the ballpark." Reinsdorf explained that the team borrowed $6 million dollars in the form of revenue bonds that year. "We used $3 million of the six to construct the suites and the other $3 million for general improvements to the plant. When we built the suites, we had no idea we were going to have to build a new ballpark."

During the structural examination of the upper deck in preparation for the suite installation, George A. Kennedy & Associates (the engineering consultant) detected truss member separation just behind home plate. "In building the suites, the engineers had to do a much deeper inspection than had ever been done before on this park to make sure the stadium could support skyboxes. Had we not gotten into this project, within a very short period of time, the entire upper deck behind the plate would have collapsed." Carpentry and structural repairs ($215,000); plumbing ($92,500); painting ($170,000); and electrical work ($136,500); cost the Sox $615,000. This does not include a new Diamondvision scoreboard erected in centerfield for the fans' convenience. From his office in Ohio, Edward DeBartolo later told a newspaper reporter: "There's nothing wrong with the park structurally. We had engineers who checked *everything* out."

* * *

Fall 1983

A season of perfect team play culminating in a record setting Western Division championship ended on a somber, heart-tugging note for Sox fans when shortstop Jerry Dybzinski's baserunning gaffe in the seventh inning of the decisive fourth game of the American League playoffs snuffed out all hope of a Chicago team advancing to the World Series. The "Dybber" was hung out to dry between second and third base in a scoreless contest with the hated Baltimore Orioles. The shutout loss to the Orioles (a haunting nemesis of the White Sox since the 1959 pennant year), was a cruel ending to the remarkable "Winning Ugly" season that witnessed the Pale Hose claim the division by 20 games over runner-up Kansas City.

Dybzinski offered no excuses or apologies to the fans or media in the postgame interviews. He was poised, cool, and, unmindful of the suffering he had inflicted on a generation of Sox fans who toughed out 24 long and disappointing seasons since the last time the sirens wailed on the South Side.

* * *

Postseason maintenance resumed. Rust and deterioration of the outfield light standards demanded immediate attention. The light towers were re-lamped because low light areas in the playing field made it difficult for outfielders to track fly balls. The White Sox were advised that the light fixtures were so old that replacement parts were no longer available.

* * *

May 1984

An informal meeting with representatives of the engineering firm in Executive Vice-President Howard Pizer's office was convened in order to review the yearly inspection reports. "We went over all the things that had to be done to the park, and I remember saying to the engineer, 'When is this shit going to get to the point when it will level off or recede?'" The consulting engineer looked at Reinsdorf quizzically. "You've got to understand that the ballpark is nearing the end of its useful life." Jerry Reinsdorf turned to Pizer with a look of disbelief registering on his face. "It was like somebody had dropped a block of granite on my head. I had no idea what we were going to do. We certainly didn't have the resources to build a new stadium, but we had to come to grips with it."

* * *

Tony La Russa had emerged as one of the finest young managers in the game after he was hurriedly summoned to Chicago by Bill Veeck to replace Don Kessinger in August 1979. The team steadily improved under Tony's patient guidance to the point where many considered them the best team in the American League. The fans, and most of all, the front office, expected no less than a World Series appearance from the ballclub in 1984. However, fifth place was to be their final resting spot in this oddball season. "Eighty-four was a year I'll never forget," Reinsdorf said. "We were making plans in the spring for how we were going to handle the playoffs in the fall. Everybody in the organization, including the players, thought all we had to do is show up and we'll win the division."

The Cubs were the larger story in 1984. By winning the National League East they reclaimed Chicago's baseball market temporarily lost to the Sox in 1982-1983, and in the process Wrigley Field had become the "world's largest outdoor fern bar." It was without question the place to go to see baseball—and to be seen. No one was exactly sure of what the greater attraction was for the wealthy young urbanites who patronized the Halls of Ivy. Was it the Cubs, or the novelty of transacting stock deals in the grandstand?

In '84 a gust of ill wind blew in from the North Side for dismayed White Sox fans.

* * *

Spring 1985

The bell began to toll for old Comiskey Park in this the 75th anniversary season of its gala grand opening. Site evaluations and extensive demographic analysis were conducted by team officials over the winter. Marketing research confirmed old suspicions. The highest percentage of Sox fans attending games in person neither walk to the park, nor do they commute by public transportation from the immediate adjoining city neighborhoods. They come by car from the suburbs. A full 50% of season ticket holders reside outside of Chicago. An astonishing 75% of *all* fans attending games at Comiskey Park are suburbanites.

"An overwhelming high percentage of our fans came from the West, the Southwest, and South Suburbs," Reinsdorf said. "Let's suppose you draw a circle, and at the center of the circle is 35th and Shields. Using a 30-mile radius you'll find that 40%-50% is in Lake Michigan. Another large segment of that pie falls within the African-American neighborhoods to the south and immediate east of the ballpark. Blacks don't go to baseball games. They just don't come . . . " the owner adds with emphasis. "Meaning . . . that if you draw the same circle 30 miles to the west in Addison, Illinois," where the team owned a piece of undeveloped land, "you find that many more people live in the suburbs and suddenly we're much closer to the people who come to baseball games. That would have been the best place to go, but our first choice was to stay in Chicago, because we didn't want to hurt the city."

Over the next several months, the White Sox received a number of unsolicited proposals suggesting various site locations across the city, including a 40-acre rock quarry on the South Side, and the Goose Island industrial area on the North Branch of the Chicago River, a stone's throw from Wrigley Field. These alternative locations would have entailed substantial governmental assistance and costly infrastructure improvements.

* * *

Governor James Thompson was first apprised of Jerry's dilemma in a closed-door session with Einhorn and Reinsdorf at the ballpark prior to 1985's opening day ceremonies. Thompson knew Jerry and Eddie, but not in a baseball sense. "They were one year behind me at Northwestern Law School," Thompson relates. "I was Einhorn's editor on the *Journal of Criminology and Police Science.*" With a twinkle in his eye, the Governor recalls that: "We weren't really social friends in law school because they spent their time playing bridge in the basement. They were downstairs in the company of the really bright guys."

Kidding aside, the Sox owners laid it on the line to their old classmate. They told the Governor that the White Sox investment group did not have the resources to build a stadium with private funds. State assistance would have to be there if a new stadium was to be in the cards. "And then he told us something very prophetic," Reinsdorf said, his voice lowering. "He said I'll work with you, but in the end I don't think you're going to get it done *unless they think you're going to move* the team."

Thompson adopted the moniker Big Jim early on in his political career. It was a designation given to him by the press. The Governor was a product of Garfield Park; a West Side immigrant enclave that brought forth some of Chicago's most clever and canny politicians of the Depression era; the power brokers of the Chicago Democratic machine. The WASP-ish Republican Governor was somewhat of a political anomaly among his peers: a two-syllable orator preaching in the land of Democrats, but whose speeches had an air of resonance and poetry to them.

Thompson was comfortable within his element when it came to cutting deals with the high priests of the Chicago Machine. And if history had taught Big Jim anything, it's that you can't expect to win an alley fight playing by the Marquis of Queensberry rules.

* * *

July 9, 1985

One month after *Crain's Chicago Business* revealed that a movement was afoot to acquire a South Loop property to build a $200 million retractable-domed multi-purpose stadium, the White Sox sat down with developer Dan Epstein to analyze financing and possible sites. According to Reinsdorf: "The South Loop location in reality never had a chance because the site was too expensive. It would have cost tens of millions of dollars to do infra-structure work. That's what we were told by [Mayor Harold] Washington's administration, and we had to do it with the Chicago Bears because the city wasn't going to do anything for the Sox alone."

The White Sox were willing to work with the football team. The Bears as usual, were not interested in talking to the Sox. Bears President Michael McCaskey (the eldest grandson of George Halas) expressed his preference for a football-only facility to replace Soldier Field. Saddled with an onerous lease that locked the Bears into Soldier Field until 1999, McCaskey stood to gain the most by moving in with the White Sox, if he could squirm out of the lease.

The Sox temporarily shelved their West Suburban Addison plan to sign a letter of intent to occupy the South Loop site, contingent on McCaskey's willingness to commit the Bears to the project. Bob Wislow, a prominent local developer and chairman of U.S. Equities, Inc., had come up with a futuristic design concept that moved entire sections of grandstand on a slow-moving track, making it possible for a 45,000-seat baseball park to convert to an 80,000-seat football oval within hours. "Al Johnson and the people representing Mayor Washington insisted on making the deal with us first," Reinsdorf said. "And I kept saying why don't you contact the Bears and find out if they're willing to do it." The Chicago Bears, even with the might of WGN Radio and the Tribune Company behind them, are essentially a family-owned business lacking the financial reserves to build a stadium with private capital. Culminating a year-long effort to revitalize the disputed South Loop property for the sports teams, Mayor Washington introduced Bob Wislow and Dan Shannon, President of G.S.I., Inc., as his point men to move the plan off the dime and keep the White Sox in Chicago.

South Loop stadium plans were ultimately dashed, but why? Community activist William Wendt traces the blame to a 1956 urban renewal plan originally formulated by First Ward real estate developers and the Chicago Central Area Committee

(CCAC), which desired to integrate the South Loop with townhouses, and mid- to high-rise condominiums. The plan afoot was to "put 100,000 Yuppies" in upscale housing as Wendt argued before members of the Illinois Sports Facilities Authority. The South Loop plan also failed because of prohibitive infrastructure costs and Mr. McCaskey's intransigence in dealing with the White Sox. The Bears' first preference, if they had been able to escape their lease with the Chicago Park District, would have been a suburban stadium. Mike McCaskey, " . . . wouldn't play with a baseball team, but even on the off chance he ever would agree to play with a baseball team it would have to be the Cubs because the Bears had a natural affinity to the Cubs."

The cold war between McCaskey and Reinsdorf stemmed from Eddie Einhorn's effrontery in trying to place a U.S.F.L. football team in Comiskey Park a year or two earlier. There was just no way the Halas family was going to open up the Chicago market to Eddie Einhorn, or anyone else after driving out the Cardinals and fending off Art Allyn two decades earlier. Einhorn had been foolish or naive if he believed that the fledgling football league could gain a toehold in Chicago without McCaskey mounting a furious protest.

* * *

December 23, 1985

Jerry Reinsdorf received a communique from American League President Dr. Bobby Brown, cautioning the Sox ownership of the league's growing impatience with the slow progress of stadium negotiations in Chicago. Brown wrote:

> I am writing to express the interest and the concerns of the American League over your plans for Comiskey Park and/or a new stadium. It has become apparent to all that despite the excellent job of continual maintenance that you afford Comiskey Park, the time is rapidly approaching where that structure will no longer remain viable as a big league park. I know that you have been exploring the various alternatives, having considered other park sites in addition to having meaningful discussions with Chicago governmental officials about the construction of a new multi-purpose domed facility. We wish to encourage you to pursue these alternatives with all deliberate speed.

What we fear and wish to avoid is a prolonged delay over finalizing plans for either a privately owned baseball park or a city/county ownership of a domed facility.

We are not anxious for you to sink into a quagmire of indecision brought about by a lack of conviction or authority on the part of local government officials. The American League would like to set a one-year time limit for you to make a definite decision as to which choice to take—either a cooperative effort with the city or a private or public effort at a location in metropolitan Chicago *but not within the confines of Chicago.* We would like to set a three-year time limit for site selection, drawing of plans, and beginning of construction. We feel that by the 1992 season the White Sox should be in a new facility.

I also feel it would be worthwhile to remind you of some of the criteria set down by Commissioner Peter Ueberroth for new stadium construction. Ideally it would have a capacity of 35,000 to 45,000, be primarily a baseball stadium with natural turf, and be privately financed. It should have excellent ingress and egress, ample parking, and be readily accessible to major thoroughfares and rapid transit. If the facility was the result of a cooperative effort with a municipal or county government *the terms of the lease would become all important.* The Commissioner's office and the American League *would not sanction a long-term lease that would bind the White Sox for decades to come.* A very reasonable rent, tax structure, and share of concessions and parking revenues should be realized. A prohibition on an admissions tax and exclusive scheduling rights and control of the facility would be other mandatory conditions. In summary, we feel that a well-run Major League baseball franchise is a tremendous asset to any community and should be treated accordingly.

If private construction becomes unattainable, and if negotiations with the city, county and state officials could not be satisfactorily concluded, *the final alternative of moving the franchise might have to be addressed.* Chicago, obviously, is a large enough market to support two Major League franchises and the long tenure of both the White Sox and Cubs attests to that fact. If however, *conditions become so unpalatable to the White Sox that a move was necessitated, the fact that Chicago still had a remaining franchise would remove much of the onus from such a transfer.*

We would like to have official progress reports from you at six-month intervals, and the league stands prepared to assist you in all ways possible to bring your negotiations and plans to a successful conclusion.

Whose head was the gun held to? The city or the White Sox? If it wasn't already obvious, the message was made clear to the Sox in '85. Get a new park—or leave town.

* * *

January-February 1986

The sense of urgency attached to Bobby Brown's letter forced the White Sox to step up the timetables, and establish "12 minimum criteria" that must be met by city officials. The team demanded a rent-free, baseball-only facility with 100% of concessions, parking, and advertising revenues retained by the team. Eddie Einhorn termed the proposal "very reasonable."

Speaking under the condition of anonymity, a city developer told a *Chicago Tribune* reporter that the 12-point agenda is "onerous" and predicted that it would be impossible for the city to meet the conditions. On February 4, the Mayor's project team asked for a one-month extension of the February 7 deadline agreement set forth by the White Sox. The developers are still working with two hopeful scenarios: an open-air baseball stadium and a baseball stadium with an adjacent arena.

* * *

March 1986

The Mayor's development team decided that a new Chicago sports stadium would not be economically feasible with just one tenant. Further negotiations between the team and the city were suspended for one month.

March 21, 1986

Peter Krallitsch, Vice-President of George Kennedy & Associates, the engineering firm responsible for monitoring the physical condition of Comiskey Park in the last few years advised Jerry Reinsdorf of the continuing decline of 76-year-old Comiskey Park:

". . . we were very surprised at the rapid deterioration that has occurred in Comiskey Park since the extensive renovation project just three years ago. Unfortunately, we foresee the likelihood of significant expenditures on an annual basis to keep the park in safe and usable condition through the 1989 season. Beyond that there are no realistic

long-term solutions, since the deterioration is irreversible. Simply put, Comiskey Park is nearing the end of its useful life."

The so-called "Krallitsch Report" was not a report at all, but an advisory letter from the consulting firm to their client. Much was made of the fact that Reinsdorf did not release the contents of this document to the press and the community-based group opposed to razing the stadium. In so many words, S.O.S. spokeswoman Mary O'Connell branded Reinsdorf a liar for asserting that Comiskey Park could not be saved.

Mary's opinions were expressed to the Illinois Sports Facilities Authority (ISFA) in a public hearing aired August 5, 1988. "You know, my mother raised me to tell the truth, and I'm always amazed at the way that other people get away with telling lies," she said. At the heart of the matter was Reinsdorf's mystifying reluctance to publish the letter supporting his position. It was his first tactical error. "They kept looking for a document that didn't exist," he explained. "There was that letter showing what had to be done for that particular year—there was no other report."

An in-depth report was filed after the State of Illinois approved the funding package for the new stadium. An exhaustive structural analysis and laboratory tests with conclusions and recommendations were submitted to the Authority, which cleared up any lingering doubts about the condition of old Comiskey. An abstract of the report handed in by the Bob D. Campbell & Co., engineering firm of Kansas City, Missouri summarizes their findings.

"Site observations revealed that great amounts of deterioration have occurred, and deterioration appears to be continuing in spite of ongoing maintenance efforts. The results of this study indicate that renovation of the current facility into a "state of the art" Major League baseball stadium is neither practical nor economically recommended, and that reconstruction either on this site or on another site (perhaps nearby) is most prudent."

Even if it were possible to renovate the Baseball Palace of the World to the satisfaction of the S.O.S. skeptics, there were two unresolved issues. Where would the team play during the two-year renovation? Point two: a renovated Comiskey Park would have bore little resemblance to the beloved stadium where Walsh, Appling, Fox, and Baines cavorted for so many years.

A quick tour of the new and "improved" Yankee Stadium in the South Bronx bears this point out. The post-modern "House

That Ruth Built" re-opened after a two-year renovation in 1976. It is an embarrassment to Yankee history and pin-stripe traditions. And in this instance there are many who believe that it would have been far more desirable for George Steinbrenner and the Yankee ownership to break with the past and build a new stadium rather than tarnish the memory of the old one with a cheap makeover. Steinbrenner has arrived at that same conclusion, apparently.

"You could have waved a magic wand over the old Comiskey Park and made it brand new and in mint condition, and it still wouldn't have worked," Reinsdorf adds. "Because the economics of baseball had changed so much since 1981 when we had a $3-million payroll. Last year (1993) we had a $37-38 million payroll. You couldn't generate revenue out of the old park even if it could have been made brand new."

* * *

In early June, Jerry and Eddie toured Denver's Mile High Stadium and evaluated the facility as a possible new home for the White Sox in the event that negotiations with the City of Chicago broke down completely. In the coming months, the pair visited sites in Miami, Orlando, New Orleans, St. Petersburg, and several locations in Northern Indiana.

* * *

July 8, 1986: The Press Conference
High on the list of things Jerry Reinsdorf would likely want to change if he could, was the poorly thought out decision to convene a press conference at Comiskey Park putting the city on notice that the ballpark was crumbling and the team intended to pursue a suburban location as their first choice for a new home. "I would not have stood up and told the truth," he said. "I would have leaked it out." In hindsight, that was the *only* strategy that could have worked.

In December 1984, the White Sox purchased 140 acres of undeveloped property in West Suburban Addison, Illinois for the sum of $7 million. Located 30 miles west of the Comiskey crossroads at 35th and Shields, the Addison site was attractive to

Sox officials because of lower construction costs—infrastructure repairs alone in the South Loop would have run in excess of $54 million. It would have cost half that amount to develop Addison. More importantly, the DuPage County site was desirable because that's where suburban White Sox fans could be ideally served.

The fans and media alike mistrusted the motives of Eddie Einhorn, but he was on the mark when he observed: "the situation was not created by the present administration of the City of Chicago," hastening to add that: "the problem should have been addressed earlier. Chicago has needed a new sports facility for a long time." The Chicago Stadium, home of the Blackhawks and Bulls, opened in 1929 and was the newest of the sports facilities within city limits.

Fans were critical of Einhorn's cable-TV package that withdrew the Sox from free television in 1982. They blamed the ownership for losing Harry Caray to the Cubs after the 1981 season; for firing Harry's popular sidekick Jimmy Piersall; for tightening security at the stadium; for removing Bill Veeck's centerfield shower; and for installing the skyboxes that brought to the park the corporate elements and the hated North Side Yuppies. The perception lingered that all Eddie and Jerry cared about was the almighty dollar. Public relations experts advised Eddie to assume a lower profile, which he did . . . in time.

The fans were frustrated and angry at the Sox owners for many reasons. The rapid disintegration of the 1983 "Winning Uglies" exposed the organization to a torrent of criticism. Even Tony La Russa, the incumbent manager who heard an unrelenting chorus of boos from the fans for much of his duration in Chicago, basked in a sympathetic glow when news of his firing leaked out in June.

It was the worst of times to announce to a skeptical public that Comiskey Park was falling down, coming as it did on the heels of the La Russa fiasco.

With a grim look registering on his chairman, Jerry Reinsdorf ominously warned: "Time has forced the White Sox to act. White Sox management has concluded any further delay will jeopardize its ability to develop the Addison site, which could result in a need to leave Illinois."

Echoing the sentiments of many White Sox fans, Mayoral advisor Al Johnson remarked that the city "is shocked and disappointed."

* * *

July 11, 1986
Peter Krallitsch informed Reinsdorf and Pizer that the structural beams holding the upper deck in place were rusting away and could not be repaired. Because much of the rusting steel was encased in concrete or masonry, sufficient repair work could not be completed without first ripping away the structure above it.

That same day, Chicago Aldermen Bernard Stone and Fred Roti demanded the closing of Comiskey Park because of safety concerns. The White Sox agreed to provide an engineering inspection report three times a year to the City of Chicago, updating officials on the structural integrity of the park.

* * *

October 5-6, 1986
The White Sox opened an office in the Addison Commons Shopping Center to stir up local support among DuPage County residents who were unenthused about the arrival of a baseball team in their tranquil suburban bailiwick. A *DuPage County Magazine* survey showed that 68% of its respondents opposed the stadium.

Local civic boosters, who were undismayed by these reports, predicted that the White Sox stadium complex would pump $100 million a year in added revenue into the local economy and create 2,500 temporary construction jobs. They urged voters in Addison and Bloomingdale Township to vote yes on an advisory referendum in the November election, less than 30 days away.

Community opposition to the Addison White Sox ran much deeper than the usual reasons put forth by the politicians and their constituency. Traffic congestion, noise pollution, and the spoilage of 22 acres of wetlands—wetlands that resulted from previous owners stripping the topsoil from the site—were smoke screen excuses. The real issue lurking just below the surface in this affluent, mostly upper-middle class Caucasian county carried with it strong racial overtones. "Opposition to Addison was predicated on several things," Reinsdorf related. "One was racial. There was a fear that our being there was going to bring blacks into DuPage and that was expressed to me by a prominent politician. The fact of the matter is, he should not have had that concern. But I wasn't about to convince him he shouldn't be a bigot. That wasn't my goal."

Jerry's goal was tied to winning legislative support for a measure that made perfect sense to the ownership, to league officials, and an increasing number of fans whose only concern was keeping the Sox in Northeast Illinois. Whether it was Chicago or a suburb was only incidental at this point.

"There was not enough public support through the public referendum. It is not what people in that area wanted," commented Democrat Phil Rock, who completed a record-breaking 14 years as President of the Illinois State Senate in 1993. "People in that area did not want crowds from Chicago and all over Cook County. Some of it was fear of minorities," he conceded.

* * *

A gloomy, depressing season on the field marred by considerable front office intrigue quietly ended in the Hubert H. Humphrey Metrodome, when Minnesota Twins left hander Frank Viola shut out the White Sox on just two hits. Tony La Russa's sullen departure in late June, and the new general manager Ken "Hawk" Harrelson's futile efforts to make due with a ballclub shorn of its talent on the minor league level, failed to stave off another fifth place, 72-90 finish. Interest in the White Sox and their home attendance at the imperiled South Side landmark continued to free fall.

* * *

November 4, 1986 - Election Day

The non-binding Addison referendum failed by a 43-vote margin (3,744 or 49.7% for, 3,787 or 50.3% against). The inconclusive results discouraged some Addison officials who wanted to see the White Sox continue to pursue efforts to build in their locale. Village President Anthony Russotto pledged his continued support for the stadium project, but just two months later Jerry Reinsdorf placed the 140 acres at Swift Road and Lake Street on the sale block. Asking price: $15 million.

* * *

November 21, 1986

Chicago officials returned to the bargaining table with the White Sox shortly before the Thanksgiving Holiday. Governor Thompson informed the ownership that they must find a site other than Addison because the Republican leadership loyal to Senate Minority leader James "Pate" Philip of Wooddale was opposed to a DuPage County stadium. "The referendum lost," Philip tells the *Addison Press*, "We ought to go with the majority, should we not? I'm not convinced the White Sox should move from Chicago." Pate's role in the Addison debate was "passive," according to Phil Rock. "When he found out there was little local support, he provided none." According to Rock, Senator Philip is "responsive to his constituents." However, a highly-placed source within the White Sox organization traced the blame for the Addison defeat to the powerful DuPage Republican faction led by Pate Philip.

* * *

December 1, 1986

Jerry and Eddie reached an accord with the City of Chicago. Mayor Harold Washington, a lifelong Sox fan with fond remembrances of Luke Appling and Minnie Minoso, expressed his preference for a baseball-only stadium to be built across the street from old Comiskey in South Armour Square, a low-income residential community containing much of Bridgeport's pre-1910 housing stock. Mayor Washington was committed to keeping the White Sox in Chicago. They are a South Side institution and should remain a South Side team. That was his final say on the matter.

South Side history and deeply rooted traditions notwithstanding, there were more compelling economic factors that made South Armour Square a desirable location from the viewpoint of city officials: (1) Washington believed there would be little or no opposition to a new Sox stadium from within the community; (2) he anticipated no legal problems when the city moved to acquire the land under the law of eminent domain or the "quick take," delineated in the Code of Civil Procedure. Under these terms, the stadium authority is empowered to acquire private land for public use and reimburse the owners of the 116 dwellings comprising South Armour Square only *after* they had been secured by the city and state; (3) compared to the infrastructure improvements necessary before construction of a downtown location could begin, the amount of work to be performed in South Armour Square was minimal and cost effective.

Eddie Einhorn, who had stated that he did not want it inscribed on his headstone that he was the man who moved the White Sox out of Chicago, endorsed the proposal with reservations. The next day Mayor Washington announced an agreement in principle with the Sox owners that the team had committed its resources to playing in Chicago. Team officials and mayoral advisors proceeded to the State Capitol in Springfield to lobby the legislature to create a seven-member stadium authority empowered to issue $120 million in municipal bonds to finance and oversee construction. The bonds would be backed by a 2% increase in the city's hotel and motel tax, but the lodging industry cried foul. This latest tax increase would place Chicago at a competitive disadvantage among the other major convention cities in the U.S., the hoteliers argue.

Insiders predict that the White Sox would have a hard time selling the package to the lawmakers in the closing hours of the 84th biennial session of the Illinois General Assembly.

* * *

December 5, 1986

Having been bedridden with a sore back, Governor James Thompson hobbled into the General Assembly to champion the White Sox legislation and another measure to re-build the fire-damaged Arlington Park racetrack located in the Northwest Suburbs of Chicago. Support for both measures fell within traditional party boundaries. Suburban Republicans favored appropriation to rebuild the racetrack, but expressed doubts about funding a new Comiskey Park. State Senator Jeremiah Joyce among others, characterized Sox Chairman Jerry Reinsdorf and his partner Einhorn as a pair of New York hustlers.

Chicago Democrats were more inclined to support the ballpark, but say no to Arlington Park, which was tied together with a controversial proposal to expand off-track betting in the metro area.

The stadium proposal failed by six votes in its first go around on the House floor, but James Thompson was most persuasive in his arguments. Resurrected by a parliamentary procedure, it was approved by a 64-33 roll-call margin. The bill called for the creation of the seven-member authority (the Illinois Sports Facilities Authority) to administer the construction and operation of the stadium. Three members are to be appointed by Thompson, three by Mayor Washington, and the seventh by the governor, subject to mayoral approval.

The eleventh-hour wheeling and dealing brought a significant victory to the people of Illinois, despite stern opposition from many downstaters and some Chicago legislators. The media, however, was generally supportive. "A new stadium near Comiskey Park will help energize a rundown, stagnant part of Chicago and eventually produce a net tax gain that will help the state treasury as well as the city," commented the *Chicago Tribune* in a published editorial.

Jerry Reinsdorf promised to sign a binding lease, and in a moment of rare humor noted: "We don't know a lot about politics, but we know a lot about winning close ballgames in extra innings."

* * *

April 10, 1987

Opening day of another calamitous losing season. The ex-Angel connection pilots the controls in '87; Jim Fregosi was in the dugout and the new General Manager Larry Himes (replacing Ken Harrelson who was elevated to the front office for one disastrous season, in the vain hope that his fan popularity would score points against the Cub-*Tribune* juggernaut of the mid-1980s), occupied the swivel chair upstairs, promising to guide the Sox from "Point C" (or is "Z" a closer approximation?) to Point "B."

The White Sox and their fans scored no points either on or off the field in 1987. Things got off on the wrong foot just before the ceremonial opening pitch when Mayor Washington refused to join in the pre-game pageantry to celebrate the city's and state's commitment to building the new Comiskey Park. Earlier in the day, Governor Thompson incurred Harold Washington's wrath by announcing attorney Thomas Reynolds, a long-time friend and political fund raiser who owned a piece of the Sox back in the early 1960s, as his choice for the chairmanship of the Illinois Sports Facilities Authority. Thompson violated protocol by neglecting to consult the Mayor. "The Governor got up there with his guy and said to the rest of us, 'go fly a kite,'" complained mayoral aide Jacky Grimshaw. "You can't describe Reynolds as even-handed between the city and the state. His pre-disposition is to be a representative of the state."

Which was true . . . Jim Thompson never denied it. "Since I was the Governor and representing the whole state, my feelings were very strong that since they're asking the state to put its credit on the line, since they're asking the state to do infrastructure work, and all the other things that go with it, the state is going to run it. It was that simple." The Governor characterized his imbroglio with Washington over the appointees as a political "turf war," and downplayed the seriousness of it. "Harold fought me for a while . . . sure." A smile crossed Thompson's face as he recalled his past disagreements with the Chicago mayor. "He would put a facade on something in order to make a position. I'm sure that Harold Washington thought my naming Tom Reynolds as the chairman made perfect good sense from my standpoint . . . and ultimately from his."

A six-month stalemate between the State House and City Hall followed, which endangered not only the fragile legislation, but placed the franchise in greater peril of leaving Chicago. The White Sox began contingency negotiations with Mayor Robert Ulrich and Assistant City Manager Rick Dodge from the City of St. Petersburg who believed that their involvement with the Sox would only serve to enhance their visibility in bringing Major League baseball to the newly completed Sun Coast Dome. "I was never in the camp that said these guys wanted to go to St. Pete." James Thompson chuckled as he recalled the absurdity of a team called the Florida White Sox. "They're Chicago guys. Not Florida guys. Its like the threat Mike McCaskey made a few years back to move the Bears to Charlotte, North Carolina. The Charlotte Bears? That's crazy."

"But could I have sold the Sox stadium deal *without* St. Pete in the picture? As a politician I'd like to think I could have, but to tell you honestly, I just don't know."

* * *

Opening Day '87 was unremarkable. A section of concrete overhang crashed into the lower deck seating area in right field just before the ballpark opened. The grandstand was closed for several weeks until repairs were completed. Later, the Sox endured a depressing 11-4 loss to the Detroit Tigers.

The few remaining "Winning Ugly" holdovers on the 1987 roster hobbled to the finish line in fifth place, eight games under the hallowed .500 mark—the benchmark achievement for baseball success in Chicago, according to the South Side sage Bill Gleason.

* * *

July 1987

Jerry Reinsdorf on "the Book."

"I used to hate Walter O'Malley for moving the Dodgers out of Brooklyn. But after I read Neil Sullivan's *The Dodgers Move West* I didn't hate Walter anymore."

Far from being the single-minded, putative villain commonly portrayed in standard baseball histories, Professor Sullivan of Baruch College (City University) in New York persuasively argues that Walter O'Malley desired to keep the Dodgers in Brooklyn if only city officials had shown their willingness to meet him half way in his intentions to replace cramped Ebbets Field with a modern structure closer to the rail lines connecting the borough with Manhattan and Queens. Ebbets Field was miles from the closest expressway and public transportation to and from the ballpark was a hit or miss proposition.

O'Malley played in a decaying inner-city Brooklyn neighborhood perceived as unsafe by the greater majority of ticket-buying Dodger fans who fled to the distant suburbs of Long Island and New Jersey for the same immutable reasons as the blue-collar immigrants who lived within five to ten miles of Comiskey Park, or any of the other older inner-city ballparks in the post-war era. Walter O'Malley had to have a new stadium. There was no question. And now O'Malley's problem had suddenly become Jerry Reinsdorf's problem.

"So I went to see Harold Washington and I said to Harold: 'Read this book. All you have to do is change the names of the politicians and you have Chicago.'"

* * *

October 22, 1987

The political standoff between the mayor and the governor formally ended when Harold Washington dropped his opposition to Thomas Reynolds. In return for the mayor's bi-partisan support of Thompson's guy, Washington got to name 37-year-old Peter C.B. Bynoe to the $100,000-per-year post of Executive Director of the Illinois Sports Facilities Authority. The Harvard-educated Bynoe was a staunch ally of Washington, and his presence on the board assured fair allocation of minority contracts during the bid process. "I assumed that was one of the reasons Peter was there," Thompson said. "Washington had picked him, and I got Reynolds and Tim Romani, and life went on. So there wasn't a lot of talk about that [minority hiring] because I assumed Bynoe was the enforcer."

Representing Mayor Washington and the City of Chicago on the ISFA board was Joan Hall, a partner at the law firm of Jenner & Block, and an expert on commercial litigation; Andy Athens, president of Metron Steel, and prominent local fund raiser for Democratic candidates; and Al Johnson, a South Suburban Cadillac dealer, mayoral troubleshooter and point man during the Bears-Sox stadium negotiations.

The Thompson appointees included Attorney Perry Snyderman from the law firm of Rudnick & Wolfe; Gayle Franzen, a political protege of the governor and former director of the Regional Transportation Authority (R.T.A.); and Gerald Stillman, president of Mid-Continent Builders. They were all bright, ambitious, upwardly mobile public servants, each with their own political allegiance and separate agenda. And yet, despite the obvious potential for political gridlock, members of the ISFA Board were in complete accord on most issues, and together they worked in harmony in the difficult months that lie ahead.

Over the next two years, 300 votes were cast by the board to resolve matters of policy and every vote taken was unanimous. "That was due to the leadership of Tom Reynolds," Tim Romani believes. Reynolds outlined the ground rules early on, and one of them was his absolute insistence that grievances be aired privately—away from the glare of the TV cameras. "Everyone on the board came in and agreed that we had to pull this thing off. No one in this room wanted to be associated with failure."

* * *

November 25, 1987

Mayor Harold Washington suffered a massive coronary attack in his City Hall office and was rushed to Northwestern Memorial Hospital. Prolonged efforts to resuscitate the Mayor failed. Harold Washington died at age 65.

The tragic, startling death of Chicago's first African-American mayor dealt a major setback to the delicate stadium negotiations and pushed back the timetables for construction by at least six months to a year. The acting Mayor, Eugene Sawyer, designated State Senator Richard Newhouse and Representative Carol Moseley-Braun as his liaisons to the ISFA. Newhouse and Moseley-Braun were only lukewarm to the project and indicated that they might or might not support the measure when it goes back to the General Assembly for an added appropriation in 1988.

* * *

December 14, 1987

The ISFA convenes its first meeting. Board members commissioned an independent engineering study to determine if Comiskey Park could be saved despite the fact that the funding legislation mandates the Authority to build a new stadium.

* * *

March 11, 1988

With the selection of Hellmuth, Obata, & Kassabaum (H.O.K.) as the project architect for new Comiskey Park, the ISFA went a long way toward soothing the impatience of senior White Sox officials concerned about the repeated delays—and a second cryptic warning from baseball's governing powers. This time Commissioner Peter Ueberroth sounded the drum roll of alarm by notifying the White Sox that he had placed the team on his "watch list" of endangered franchises; a list that also included the Seattle Mariners, the Pittsburgh Pirates, and the San Francisco Giants. Ueberroth writes: " . . . the White Sox are on the top of my list now. I think they are going in the right direction on the field. I think they're going to have an exciting, young, get-your-uniforms-dirty club this year and for years to come. Off the field, though, they are a concern. They need a new stadium either in the city or in the suburbs. If they exhaust all possibilities to get one as I'm convinced they are, and they still don't get it, the Commissioner will not stand in their way."

* * *

The H.O.K. Sports Facilities Group is an architectural firm devoted solely to the planning, design, and implementation of sports stadiums. For the past five years they had worked in an advisory capacity for the White Sox and had developed the preliminary design for the ill-fated Addison stadium.

In the 1980s, the Kansas City corporation emerged as a heavyweight among the nation's engineering firms involved in the building of sports stadiums. The jewels of the H.O.K. crown (through 1987) were Miami's Joe Robbie Stadium, and the Sun Coast Dome in St. Petersburg. According to Rick deFlon, H.O.K. Senior Vice-President and design specialist, "The new stadium is being designed to fit into the fabric of Chicago and may reflect the character of the old ballparks, such as Comiskey Park and Ebbets Field."

* * *

March 29, 1988
Chicago Tribune columnist Jerome Holtzman revealed in his column that a "significant number" of the 86-member White Sox investment group had "second thoughts" about the practicality of building a new facility on the South Side of Chicago, and they would not rule out the possibility of relocating the franchise elsewhere. "A new stadium would be an attraction," an unnamed source told Holtzman, "a curiosity for two or three years. Then what happens? What have we got? We're still in the same

neighborhood. It'll be the same as before. Chicago is a Cub town. I've always known that. I've lived here all my life. But today the Cubs dominate more than ever."

Holtzman predicted that if the White Sox indeed decide to leave town, "a replacement franchise should not be expected."

* * *

April 28, 1988

Jerry Reinsdorf and Eddie Einhorn met privately with Governor Thompson to explain to him that economic conditions have substantially changed for the White Sox since the original stadium package was approved in December 1986. The Sox owners pressed the Governor for a revision of terms to accommodate 1988 conditions.

In light of the Florida Progress Corporation's generous offer of a $10 million loan to defray the team's moving expenses to St. Petersburg, Jerry and Eddie sought additional concessions from the State. Reportedly they demanded a reduction of the annual $4 million rent they were scheduled to pay the ISFA for the privilege of playing in the new park. Governor Thompson expressed his concerns and promised to get back to the Sox owners soon.

* * *

May 1, 1988

James Thompson assigned Deputy Governor James Reilly to mediate and facilitate lease negotiations between the ISFA and the White Sox three days after Senate Minority Leader James "Pate" Philip reversed his earlier opposition to the proposed DuPage County Stadium. Philip declared, somewhat surprisingly: "I've always been a White Sox fan. I would do everything in my power to help them."

* * *

A bed-sheet banner draped over the left field wall at Comiskey Park reminded the Sox brass and the foot-dragging bureaucrats that the forgotten fans had a stake in this too:
ST. PETE SOX? GOD HELP US!

May 12, 1988

Jerry and Eddie were in Tallahassee, Florida to confer with Governor Bob Martinez, Florida House Speaker Jon Mills, and Senate President John Vogt to discuss contingency arrangements and to publicly reiterate that the team's first preference is to remain in Chicago.

"They said to us: 'look, you've been honest, but the only chance we have to get a team is with you. And we understand you might end up staying there, but at least you'll put us on the map,'" Reinsdorf said. "At no point did we *want* to go to St. Pete, but we were prepared to go. It wasn't a fake threat. Had we not gotten the stadium we would have gone, and the reason we would have gone is that we could not have survived [here]."

* * *

May 18, 1988

State Senator Greg Zito proposed that the State of Illinois purchase the White Sox for an estimated $55 million. The Illinois Department of Commerce and Community Affairs would then offer the public 5.5 million shares of White Sox stock at $10.00 per share. Predictably, Governor Thompson reacted with anger. "The answer is no to buying the White Sox! No! N-O! Keep me out of it, okay? The state's got other things to do than buy a baseball team."

* * *

June 7, 1988

Four hours of fruitless lease negotiations between the White Sox and the ISFA concluded with no clear-cut resolution. Afterward, Jerry and Eddie flew to Springfield at Thompson's behest to lobby the legislature. In Florida, a $30 million funding package to complete construction work on the Sun Coast Dome sailed through the State Senate. While Illinois politicians wrangled and bickered, the Floridians were gearing up for the anticipated arrival of Major League baseball in 1989.

Mike McClure, the Senior Vice President of marketing and broadcasting for the White Sox was in the Sunshine State laying the groundwork for a statewide TV-Radio network for the ballclub beginning in '89. McClure was part of an increasingly outspoken White Sox front office cabal who believed that Chicago could no longer sustain two teams in light of Cub dominance in the local media. There are only four professional sports teams within 500 miles of St. Petersburg. Within a similar 500-mile radius of Chicago, there are 27 pro teams competing for fan loyalties. Looking at it from strictly a merchandising and broadcasting standpoint, Florida made the most sense if revenue potential was the bottom line.

* * *

June 11, 1988

Forty dedicated volunteers collected 6,000 signatures outside Comiskey Park to demonstrate support for keeping the White Sox in Chicago. Mary O'Connell's Save Our Sox (S.O.S.) group grudgingly accepted the help of Northwest Siders John Pontikes, Attorney George Skuros, and their friends Jeff Bolker and Jens Lauesen during the petition drive.

S.O.S. hoped to save Comiskey Park at the expense of the team. Philosophical differences between the O'Connell group and Pontikes and his friends, who were more worried about the White Sox leaving Chicago unless the funding package was approved, resulted in a permanent schism in grassroots organizing efforts. The fight to keep the Sox in Chicago was complicated by strong community opposition from the mostly elderly African-American residents of South Armour Square who had been guaranteed replacement housing in the Gap, a historic landmark neighborhood not far from Comiskey Park. Frustrated and alarmed by the angry words and negativity aimed squarely at the Sox owners by the S.O.S. activists, Pontikes initiated his own Save the Sox campaign headquartered in Skuros' law office on the outer reaches of Chicago's Northwest Side (Cub country). Skuros was a 31-year-old dyed-in-the-wool Sox fan who inherited his love of baseball and the ballclub from his grandfather, a Greek immigrant who owned a small South Side grill.

Attorney Skuros provided Pontikes and a small staff of volunteers access to phones, a copy machine, and typewriters so they could get the word out to downstate legislators who were about to consider the matter in the General Assembly. John

Pontikes managed an Osco Drug store when he was not at the ballpark rooting for his Sox. He was a burly, soft-spoken, second-generation Greek who did not understand all the subtle political intricacies standing in the way of a new White Sox stadium. Politics was less interesting to him than the larger drama unfolding on the diamond. But John and his fellow Sox Fans On Deck members worked quietly, effectively, and with little media fanfare for something they happened to believe in.

S.F.O.D. was convinced that a new stadium was in Chicago's best long-term interests; it would spur job creation, help redevelop the South Side, and pump added tourism dollars into the local economy. These were the points Pontikes tried to articulate to the fence-straddling Chicagoans who complained about tax increases and greedy owners, but the politicians—and the voters—just weren't listening.

* * *

June 16, 1988

The *Chicago Tribune* was still championing a combined White Sox-Bears facility on the West Side, while Mike McCaskey and clan were in the State Capitol blowing smoke about a new facility for their team.

Mayor Sawyer up until now had been hedging his bets, as he tried to build support for his administration among the remnants of the former Washington coalition. The Mayor finally declared the 35th Street location as his preferred choice for the stadium and established October 1 as the deadline for the ISFA and their attorneys to take control of the site through condemnation proceedings.

James Thompson was puzzled and frustrated by all the political bantering coming out of the Windy City. "Let's pick a site and get it done!" the Governor snarled. "For Heaven's sake, you change the site every week! Pretty soon they'll be playing in mid-air and the only people displaced will be the robins! That's crazy. Let's get with it!"

* * *

June 17, 1988

White Sox backers sponsored an all-day petition drive and pep rally in the Daley Civic Center Plaza across the street from City Hall. Opportunistic politicians from the County Building and the Ward offices wandered by the tables to convey messages of support to S.F.O.D. volunteers gathering signatures in the plaza during the noon hour. "We're with you baby!" said one woman.

Later in the day, the 30,000 signatures were presented to State Senator Bill Marovitz during an informal ceremony attended by local sports celebrities, Loop office workers, fans, and media. Marovitz promised to deliver the message to his Springfield colleagues amid a mood of fatal pessimism. The crucial vote was less than two weeks away, and the outlook for the White Sox was grim to say the least.

* * *

June 24, 1988

Fourth Ward Alderman Timothy Evans told the *Chicago Sun-Times* that displacement of the South Armour Square residents need not be the final price of a new stadium. Evans was gearing up for a run at Gene Sawyer in the Spring Mayoral election and was courting the votes of these elderly South Siders likely to lose their homes during condemnation.

Evans urged the White Sox to consider an alternative site immediately north of the ballpark in Armour Square Park. The baseball diamond, Field House, and recreational play lot within Armour Square Park were owned by the Chicago Park District and had been mentioned in discussions numerous times by architect Phil Bess, a knowledgeable baseball fan with a fine appreciation for history. Bess envisioned a classical urban ballpark arising on the South Side along the lines of Fenway Park in Boston. He named his cozy, intimate-looking stadium Armour Field.

The young architect spoke with the courage of his convictions, and his conceptual rendering was imaginative and innovative in every sense. However, Armour Field was consigned to the trash heap of good ideas that never stood a chance. The existing Park District fieldhouse on Shields Avenue was erected in 1904 by Daniel Burnham and had been declared a historic landmark by the city, meaning that it could not be sacrificed for neighborhood re-development. By the terms of the ISFA agreement, Park District land, Board of Education property, Chicago Housing Authority buildings, and City of Chicago properties are all exempt from quick take condemnation proceedings. And that was a loss for Chicago, because Armour Field would have added luster to the already existing neighborhood ambience of old Bridgeport.

* * *

June 27, 1988

Beads of perspiration formed on Governor Thompson's brow as he addressed the concerns of some 200 White Sox supporters who arrived in the State Capitol early on this morning to plead for the stadium bill, which was on the General Assembly's agenda just before the scheduled adjournment in three days.

The mood of the junketing Chicagoans was positive and upbeat; there were a lot of senior citizens, children, and curiosity seekers in the bunch with time on their hands, or simply looking for a pleasing diversion on a warm summer afternoon. Promoters of the Springfield trip had to literally drag people off the downtown streets in order to fill the two busses. Again we must ponder the question: how many people would an event like this have attracted if it were the Cubs who were facing extinction?

Somebody paid for the bus ride to Springfield, the free hot dogs, soda pop, and the Irish folk band humming traditional South Side saloon songs. The question is whom? "A high-level Sox investor," was the back-of-the-bus scuttlebutt. Oak Lawn organizer Jimmy Richards refused to reveal the identity of this White Sox guardian angel, but the show of solidarity, however modest, shored up sagging support for the bill and went a long way toward convincing legislators that at least *some* White Sox fans still cared about the team's destiny.

* * *

Governor Thompson and House Speaker Michael Madigan disagreed on many points of law, but they held out a unified hope that the White Sox would make everyone's job easier by signing the damned lease before the bill came up for a vote. "If the White Sox want to stay in Chicago they have it within their power to do that by signing a lease," Thompson explained to the fans who had gathered on the Capitol lawn. "If they're not interested in that they should tell us that, and the waiting should end."

* * *

June 30, 1988

The final day of the legislative session. The end? Or a new beginning? State Senator John Daley, who had accompanied his father, the late Mayor, to ballgames at Comiskey Park from the family's Bridgeport bungalow, was not at all confident. "The income tax [measure] had to be there. But it is not and Florida is going to get the White Sox. I think the Sox deal is dead."

And then came the resurrection.

Former Governor Jim Thompson's eleventh hour politicking pushed the new stadium bill through the Illinois legislature and sealed Thompson's place in Sox history as the man who laid the bricks and mortar of the new Comiskey Park.

Mark Fletcher

On September 30, 1990, Sox fans left old Comiskey for the last time.

New Comiskey Park under construction, May 22, 1990.

Chapter
— Thirteen —

Re-inventing a Field of Dreams

With the legislative mandate squarely in place, the ISFA now faced the formidable task of acquiring 64 acres of land (100% of the commercial properties, 80% of the residential homes) by October 15, 1988, which gave them just under 12 weeks to reach an amicable accord with the apprehensive residents of South Armour Square.

The early rounds of negotiation between the ISFA and the homeowners were conducted in a climate of suspicion and mistrust. The notable absence of White Sox officials—who appeared unwilling to go before the community and the ISFA to plead their case for a new stadium—sparked old resentments. "We, the residents, have not been contacted about anything," complained Helen Hamilton, who lived in the neighborhood for 45 years. "It's as if we do not exist as a neighborhood, and we are supposed to just sit by and let our homes be taken from us. And we as residents have our demands also. We would like economic development, replacement housing, rehabilitation of public housing, employment, businesses, health care for our elderly and disabled, and improved city services and recreation for our young people" (ISFA hearing, Apr. 8, 1988).

The residents pooled their resources and founded the South Armour Square Coalition to address these very serious concerns. It was a bewildering predicament these people found themselves in; forced to abandon their homes and a way of life for a baseball team; a non-essential public-private enterprise.

Minus the direct participation of the Sox ownership in the public forum, it was up to Peter Bynoe to personally address their concerns about displacement and relocation. Mr. Bynoe came up with what he believed to be a reasonable remedy within the tight deadlines imposed on his agency by the legislature.

At first, the homeowners were offered a modest $45,000 cash buyout for their buildings. (The typical assessment of a South Armour Square dwelling in 1988 fell within in the $5,000-$7,000 range.) When the preliminary offer proved unsatisfactory to members of the Coalition, they hired Attorney Mary L. Milano from the mega-firm of Baker & McKenzie to negotiate an equitable settlement. It eventually allowed residents a choice of two options: (1) a straight cash buyout; the appraised value of the building plus $25,000 or (2) a new home in the Gap.

Neighborhood renters who did not own property in South Armour Square were promised a moving allowance. The settlement also included a $200,000 consulting fee earmarked to the entire Coalition. Following many tough and heated bargaining sessions, a deal was struck and a spirit of accord was finally achieved. Attorney Milano appeared before the ISFA on August 5, 1988 and eloquently expressed the sentiments of a substantial portion of the Coalition:

> "It is very difficult to trust people who are about to take your homes away. It is very difficult to do that. Likewise, it is very difficult to trust people who have said we will stop your project. It is very difficult to do that. But what happened, I think, in the hours after June 30, was that the community said 'Come to us over the water Peter. Come to us.' And what the Authority said was, 'Come to us over the water folks. We can walk on it together. You don't believe it but we can do it.' And I saw people sit down and trust one another when they had no reason to do so, no reason other than their abiding trust in human nature and the God that guides us. Hope. Who hopes for what he can see? For hope that is seen is not hope."

Forty-seven individuals qualified for replacement housing in the Gap. Nineteen families elected to take the new houses; twenty-eight accepted the cash buyout. Many of the residents had already signalled their support of the ISFA proposal by appearing before the board in T-shirts bearing the inscription "We Want the Gap," but more often than not their voices were drowned out by the angry residents of the T.E. Brown Apartments and the Wentworth Gardens housing project nearby; home to many elderly and disabled people who would be forced to remain behind, next door to a baseball stadium.

They accused the city, the White Sox, and the ISFA of a long-standing pattern of racial discrimination, and solicited the help of veteran community organizers to plead their case before the board. The short-lived goodwill existing between the ISFA and the Coalition was rapidly dissolving. "They wanted everything from us," Tim Romani recalls. "They wanted us to solve as many problems as they could come up with. Ultimately we *did* solve a lot of them."

The ISFA floated an $8 million loan to the Chicago Housing Authority (C.H.A.) to help them renovate the ramshackle Wentworth Gardens constructed on the site of the original home of the White Sox, the 39th Street Grounds in the early 1950s. But the C.H.A. refused the money, because they could not guarantee repayment of the loan.

A private roadway was paved for the convenience of the T.E. Brown residents, and the ISFA agreed to pay a cash subsidy to help defray the added electricity costs resulting from prolonged air-conditioner use during the summer months of ballpark construction.

The Progressive Baptist Church demanded a wheelchair van for the congregation, which the ISFA was more than happy to provide at no charge. But the church refused delivery, saying that their acceptance would be an admission on the part of the community that what the White Sox were doing was fine with the community, when it was not. The wheelchair van was later donated to the C.H.A., which was more than happy to receive it.

The White Sox agreed to adopt the neighborhood grammar school; the ISFA committed its resources to resolving the lingering issues of noise pollution, street parking during games, ballpark security, and other problems associated with having a 43,000-seat stadium in one's backyard. But the re-tooled South Armour Square Community Development Corporation, by and large, was not receptive to ISFA overtures and Attorney Milano had long since left the group.

A lawsuit was filed against the team, the city, and the ISFA, accusing them of perpetuating a continuous and historic pattern of racial discrimination against South Side African-Americans dating back nearly 40 years when the initial plans were being drawn up for the Dan Ryan Expressway (I-94), an east-west artery slicing through miles of residential and commercial neighborhoods. The lawsuit is still pending in the courts six years later, and in all likelihood will take many more years to resolve.

Meanwhile, the South Armour Square residents who were relocated to the Gap appear to be satisfied with the quality of their housing and the pleasant surroundings of an inner-city neighborhood on the upswing. "Those are wonderful homes," Romani wants ISFA critics to know. "They are all very happy. I know those people. I talk to them regularly." Which is more than the White Sox appeared willing to do during the critical stages of negotiation.

*   *   *

Official ground-breaking ceremonies for the new Comiskey Park were conducted in a relaxed atmosphere on Sunday, May 7, 1989. Local dignitaries filed past a fair-sized assemblage of fans to take their place in a reserved seating area to hear speeches and witness the Old Roman's great-great grandson throw out the ceremonial first pitch. Not surprisingly, Comiskey's toss was an errant one.

It was a day of sentimental reflection and unbridled optimism for White Sox fans who looked forward to the dawning of a new decade and a winning tradition. The 1980s had begun so promisingly, but were about to end with the sting of defeat and the usual off-the-field intrigues that overshadow much of the history of this franchise.

The jubilation felt by members of Sox Fans On Deck, and others who had fought long and hard for passage of the 1988 bill was interrupted by a small, but noticeable faction of protestors; some white, some black, who had joined hands in a circle to pray for the soulless corporation and the greedy bureaucrats whom they believed had conspired to lay waste to a neighborhood. A familiar lament. But they were largely ignored.

* * *

As the new ballpark rose from the dust like a phoenix, the team playing across the street posted 94 victories in the farewell season. It was a remarkable 25-game improvement over the last-place finish in 1989. An outstanding nucleus of young talent developed at the minor league level by Larry Himes had come of age even as Himes was being fired by Reinsdorf over personal differences. Jerry never lost a minute's worth of sleep over his decision, either, and he believes he will be vindicated when his new general manager Ron Schueler guides the White Sox past that treacherous "Point B" (the Playoffs) and on into the World Series.

Robin Ventura, Jack McDowell, Frank Thomas, and Alex Fernandez were top draft picks under the Himes regime; a "kiddie corps" of talented young players who sparked a renewal of interest in White Sox doings and provided an early winning tradition for the new Comiskey Park. More than anything, this new ballpark had to offer something more than a pleasing sightline in light of the belated nostalgia accorded old Comiskey by the preservationists.

On the very day the wrecking ball made its first pass at the forlorn hulk standing on the north side of 35th Street, a fan on the street admitted to a reporter covering the event that he never quite found the time to attend an actual game in person, but he thought that the demolition of old Comiskey was a terrible tragedy all the same.

There are many, many Chicagoans who will say the same thing. Maybe if these good people who complained the loudest in the closing days of Comiskey had attended more games during the lean years—when the foundering team and the ballpark desperately needed a solid show of support from the fans in order to pay the salaries of players and to fund the cost of ballpark maintenance—this day of reckoning might never have come to pass.

* * *

Peter Bynoe and his staff of three delivered the new Comiskey Park—on time and under budget—to the City of Chicago on

April 18, 1991; Opening Day of Year I. The 45,000-seat, open-air stadium represented a cooperative venture between two construction firms and 28 labor unions who agreed to a no-strike clause in return for a promise from the Authority that only union men and women would be retained for the project. It was a fortuitous decision; one that the ISFA made even before the unions presented their demand, because two major labor strikes closed down every other construction project going on in Chicago during the time Comiskey Park was being built.

The bid submitted by the Gust Newberg and Dugan & Meyers (joint venture) construction firms called for a final delivery price of $119,373,000. (The opening bid was $129,887,000, but the ISFA managed to shave $10.5 million off the top through a "value engineering process" of downgrades that did not detract from the aesthetics or functionality of the stadium.)

"We actually had a budget of $137 million; that was our target price from day one, and the only people that knew this were Peter, Tim, and our Board of Directors," Romani reveals. "If you let the world know that you have $137 million, the contractors are going to find a way to spend it. So we identified $18 million as our comfort zone. We ended up spending $15.5 million *over* the contract price submitted by the two firms, but actually we were $2.1 million *under* our budget."

* * *

The single-purpose stadium was designed by Rick de Flon and Joe Spear of H.O.K., but the end result conformed more to the guidelines set forth by the White Sox planners and the ISFA who forsook the urban ballpark revival for a facility that leans more heavily toward the shopping mall culture. The White Sox had to choose between state-of-the-art amenities or creating a glitzy 1990s version of Ebbets Field. They decided to draw the line closer to the mall continuum, emphasizing a spacious concourse featuring a gallery of revenue-generating souvenir shops, food courts, and a White Sox museum.

Governor Thompson, who took no formal position as to the design and layout of the plant, was nevertheless pleased with what emerged. "I have people say to me, 'oh gee, why didn't you do what Baltimore did? Build a new stadium, but make it look like an old stadium.' Well, frankly, Camden Yards wasn't around as a role model then. But to me this looks like a modern baseball stadium. That's what I was after. We have Wrigley Field on the North Side. The best of both worlds are in Chicago."

* * *

The new Comiskey Park enjoyed a short, sweet honeymoon with the public. A week after the festive unveiling on April 18, 1991, *Time* Magazine lauded the modernistic design as a pleasing blend of "art and commerce" that "can sometimes mix. This was a park *made* for baseball." That seemed to be the consensus of opinion in 1991. By the middle of the second year, however, the critics changed their minds. The traditional Camden Yards design symbolized popular tastes in the 1990s—the desire on the part of consumers to return to a simpler and more virtuous era; the 1950s presumably, before the vintage ballparks were doomed to obsolescence.

To re-create a Forbes Field, Ebbets Field, Fenway Park, or even the Polo Grounds in New York, seems to denigrate the memory of these earlier structures whose unique configurations were dictated by zoning restrictions or physical barriers that prevented the architects from building a symmetrical plant. As pleasing as a Camden Yards or the new Cleveland Gateway Center may seem today, there are no sure-fire guarantees that they will retain their unique appeal when popular tastes change in the next 25-50 years as they surely must. One need only recall the early praise for the Houston Astrodome, Three Rivers Stadium in Pittsburgh, or any of the other circular concrete slabs arising in the late 1960s and early 1970s to understand how fickle public opinion can be.

This is not to whitewash the flaws of the new Comiskey Park or suggest that the modest structure reflects a visionary's preview of the 21st Century. There are problems. Serious problems that are likely to imperil the franchise at some future point.

Beginning in 1992, a chorus of criticism was directed against the architects for constructing an upper deck sloped at 35 degrees. (The elevation of old Comiskey Park was a modest 27 degrees by comparison.) "No one can say anything good about the open upper deck," commented Bill Granger in the *Chicago*

Tribune. "It is even worse than being stuck behind a pillar in the old Comiskey Park. To get an idea of what it is like in the higher elevations of the upper deck, think of Glacier National Park and think Himalayas." However, if the Addison plan had been approved by public referendum, the West Suburban Comiskey Park built on that site would have afforded Sox fans a better view from a closer angle. There was more available land to build the stadium outward—as opposed to 35th Street, where the existing constraints forced architects to construct the upper deck on a higher elevation.

The unsightly billboard advertising and the ear-shattering cacophony of rock music bombarding the ballpark between innings are distractions that detract from the gentle rhythms of baseball. Many White Sox fans do not need to be mesmerized by blaring, non-stop music, cartoon characters cavorting on the scoreboard, and a steady stream of product advertising to accompany it. Older Sox fans resent this unwelcome intrusion upon the senses, and will say that Nancy Faust's pleasing organ renditions are sufficient between-innings entertainment.

"The in-park entertainment is something that stirs great debate on both sides of the coin," counters Rob Gallas, Senior Vice President of Marketing and Broadcasting. "There are many fans who would prefer to go back to the days of light organ music between innings. However, there are even many more fans who like the fast-paced entertainment—anything from rock music to scoreboard messages. This is something we measure all the time through our fan surveys and we certainly would not continue to offer rock music unless the vast majority of fans like what we give them."

And of course the White Sox are locked into the South Side. Paul Jensen, the P.R. Director of the Phoenix Cardinals, points out that if it were the Bears playing in Comiskey Park in the 1950s, the epitaph of the Monsters of the Midway would have likely been written long ago. We might be talking about the Phoenix Bears today, if the situation were to be reversed. The Sox, experiencing a similar set of problems were lucky. The Cards were not.

The new Comiskey Park has failed to spur economic re-development along the commercial district west of the stadium. The ballpark is an island surrounded by parking lots, the Dan Ryan expressway, and housing projects. Once the game is over, the fans are in their cars streaming toward the interstate highway. There is a school of thought that the White Sox and the residents of the 11th Ward prefer to keep it that way. The absence of a cozy neighborhood saloon and street level restaurants on 35th Street will hurt the White Sox in the long run. The urban collage of Wrigleyville is one of the pleasing aspects of going to a Cubs game in person and certainly one reason why the National League team will continue to outdraw the White Sox even in an exceptional year like 1993, when the Pale Hose gave it their best effort and brought home a Western Division championship. Governor Thompson favored a plan to re-build McCuddy's Tap—a community landmark since 1900—inside the new ballpark but was stopped cold by legal barriers. The loss of McCuddy's has been a setback for the ballclub, whether the marketing department cares to admit it or not.

"Comiskey Park has become a *destination*," Gallas adds. "Everything is inside the park, and there for the fans to have a good time. What we have done is make the park fit its surroundings." Meaning—the residents would not sanction another Wrigleyville, and consequently liquor licenses are hard to come by in this part of town.

Some of these issues will hopefully be resolved in good time. Otherwise, it is likely that down the road the White Sox will encounter a parallel set of problems with a hauntingly familiar 1960s refrain, if the ballclub cannot sustain its winning ways. Dwindling attendance. Fan apathy. Neighborhood complaints. All are constant themes running the gamut of White Sox history.

These worrisome issues loom on the distant horizon and should not be construed as a threat to the wonderful success of the "Good Guys In Black," who won in '93 with their tried and true formula of stellar pitching, just enough hitting, and an adequate defense. Add to the mix one Frank Thomas, a 1993 M.V.P., who is the most potent offensive presence to grace a South Side diamond since Shoeless Joe Jackson—without question—and the prospects for the *immediate* future seem very promising indeed. Interest in Sox matters ran high in 1993-1994, as Bo Jackson's triumphant comeback from hip-replacement surgery proved that there is still something wonderful about this game. Bo's comeback and Michael Jordan's 1994 tryout illustrate the indomitable hold of baseball, even over our most successful, highly visible athletes.

The team is back on WGN-TV for a limited number of games, and this will cultivate a national following and a younger generation of fans with a clever marketing campaign featuring local celebrities in humorous skits. The WGN exposure may even bring a few busloads of Cub fans in from Iowa if everything goes according to Rob Gallas' master plan.

The Sox of white were on a roll in the early 1990s. Ken "the Hawk" Harrelson returned to the TV booth in 1990, and with his sidekick, Tom Paciorek, a tradition of excellence in White Sox broadcasting is maintained. Over the years, the team has been very fortunate to have its games telecast by some of the very finest, most astute announcers in the business.

Sales of team paraphernalia soared from 18th place in 1990 to number one among all Major League teams the next two seasons after the marketing department acceded to years of fan pressure and resurrected Chuck Comiskey's Old English "SOX" logo design. The color scheme of the uniform was changed to a crisply styled white and black combination. The results are telling.

Through the first three seasons of its short life, the new Comiskey Park has returned in excess of $10 million to the city and state. It has been a smart investment all around, and the local lawmakers who went out on the limb for the ballclub in 1988 should feel vindicated. A city attendance record not likely to be broken as long as the Cubs continue to inhabit Wrigley Field was established by the White Sox in 1991 when 2,934,154 fans passed through the turnstiles. A competitive ballclub and the "halo" effect of a new stadium continued to attract consistently large crowds in 1992-1993. The White Sox remained well above the two-million "comfort zone" necessary for a team's financial survival in the 1990s, and are ranked among the top three franchises in profitability. Only the Baltimore Orioles and Toronto Blue Jays outpace the White Sox revenue-generating capabilities. Quite a reversal of fortunes.

"What this park has done, among other things, is given us a higher fan base, because I believe there are more people who will come here just to watch a ballgame than would go across the street," Reinsdorf explains. An examination of the attendance figures of the last 20 years of the old park proves this point. The White Sox drew 2,136,988 fans in 1984, coming off a division championship to establish an all-time record for the old Comiskey Park.

"When you really cut through it, the old ballpark was a lousy place to watch a game. The new Comiskey Park generates far more revenue and it enables us to be competitive," said Reinsdorf.

* * *

How well the Sox can sustain these levels of success depends a lot on the fluctuations of player salaries, free agency, and the ability of General Manager Ron Schueler, Director of Baseball Operations Danny Evans, and others in the baseball organization to consistently develop quality young talent to replace veteran players. The short-term success of the 1982-1983 "Winning Uglies" disguised the inadequacies of a ruined farm system that continued to yield a bitter harvest through much of the 1980s. The dearth of promising rookies in the high minors unfortunately coincided with the most serious crisis in team annals since the Black Sox Scandal.

As amusing as Jerry Reinsdorf's "moving from Point B to Point A" analogies may have seemed to the illustrious members of the press corps in the last few seasons, the '93 mini-pennant demonstrated that the franchise stood on higher ground than at any time since the mid-1950s when the Comiskey family was still in control.

Jerry Reinsdorf and his partner Eddie Einhorn have absorbed much unfair criticism in their 12 years at the helm. Both men have often been compared to Walter O'Malley as insensitive, nickel-nursing owners out to fleece the public. O'Malley's sin as Neil Sullivan reminds us, "was to remove the fig leaf from baseball," and "display what others had camouflaged in rhetoric." Reinsdorf on the other hand, spoon fed a 1990s philosophy of sports management to a ballclub and a city wedded to a 1940s way of doing things. Are the old ways necessarily a bad thing? They are, if an ownership entertains notions of competing on a championship level in the modern era.

The threat of leaving for St. Pete as a leveraging tactic—and tacitly encouraged by certain elected officials—in order to muster support within the Illinois General Assembly established a new precedent for other locales seeking stadium funding. These tactics also raise interesting questions about the proper role of government when a city is threatened by the relocation of a sports franchise. Though desirable, it may no longer be possible to build a stadium with private venture capital and the limited support of a municipality in helping secure title to a piece of land, as was the case when the Dodgers moved the operation west. Escalating costs of labor, materials, and infrastructure improvements will preclude 100% private investment in a 45,000-seat facility.

Conditions in the free market economy suggest that this era has already passed. If the industrial cities of the Northeast and Midwest desire to retain their teams when challenged by a Sunbelt interloper, they must re-evaluate the role a sports franchise plays in the local economy. They must decide for themselves whether the added tourism dollars and the prestige of being known as a "big league town" are strong enough inducements to subsidize a stadium. If not, there will *always* be another city who will not regard the issue in the same provincial terms. These are disparaging economic times we live in, and it is a bitter choice for state legislatures who are coping with the aftershocks of a serious recession, high unemployment, and school funding miseries to justify construction of a sports facility for a private enterprise.

But it is also important to remember that Brooklyn was a big league city once, but no longer. The city never recovered from the loss of the Dodgers, and the most serious problems of urban decay set in *after* the team moved to L.A.

Is a baseball team an extension of the public trust; similar to libraries and recreational parks? If so, then Jerry Reinsdorf is correct when he points out that the city and state must begin to take an active role in assisting the club when circumstances threaten its survival. On the other hand, if a baseball team continues to remain a private venture subject to normal business fluctuations—and the state refuses to intervene when that business is threatened—then ownership should not be impeded from relocating to more commodious surroundings.

These issues engender angry, emotional debate, and the precedent set in Chicago was copied by the Atlanta Falcon ownership, which dangled Jacksonville, Florida before a hotel tax was passed in 1989 to help fund the $200 million Georgia Dome. Such tactics will likely be re-enacted in Milwaukee when Bud Selig makes his final pitch for a new County Stadium to replace the current aging structure, which is devoid of the all-important skyboxes. Detroit will likely face the same dilemma when Tiger owner Mike Ilitch demands concessions similar to what Walter O'Malley expected from the city fathers of Los Angeles. That is, O'Malley was given title to Chavez Ravine and the necessary infrastructure work was performed on the site in return for a promise to commit his resources to the city in a privately financed stadium. Ilitch hopes the Michigan legislature will do the same for him, with a neglected property in downtown Detroit.

Whether Ilitch can actually realize his dream of a privately financed stadium remains to be seen. But either way, you can be sure that an appeal to civic pride, the battle cry of the preservationists, and minority interests will be loud and robust, and the presence of a warm-weather city like St. Petersburg lurking in the background will eventually factor into the debate before the State of Michigan takes final decisive action. Ilitch will likely prevail and receive his new stadium before the century turns. On the other hand, Bud Selig may eventually be forced to abandon Milwaukee, because the demographics and limited TV market simply do not add up to sustained financial prosperity in the 1990s for his ballclub. The state of Wisconsin has indicated its willingness to assist the Brewers in their plans to build a nostalgic, turn-of-the-century stadium featuring a retractable roof. However, a substantial portion of non-property tax revenue is needed to augment the private monies owner Bud Selig has already committed to the project. One solution, which Illinois politicians never considered, is to pass a sports lottery to help defray construction costs. But even with a creative funding package in place, and a receptive legislature backing the project, the new stadium—should it ever be built—may only be a stop-gap measure to ward off the likely exodus of the franchise from Milwaukee. Given the attractiveness of the Milwaukee market to Art Allyn only a generation ago, the irony of the situation is all too apparent.

When Jerry Reinsdorf and Eddie Einhorn completed their purchase of the White Sox in 1981, they inherited an economically obsolete stadium that should have been replaced decades earlier. A movement was afoot in the 1950s and 1960s, but local politics and changing priorities killed a plan of action. Jerry Reinsdorf did what he had to do to achieve his final objective— which was tied to anchoring the White Sox to Chicago in such a manner that they would be able to compete in the coming era.

It was Jerry's other great misfortune to succeed Bill Veeck as the headline act on the marquee—a tough act for anyone to follow, least of all an introspective self-made Jewish guy with Brooklyn roots.

There is no Machiavellian motive attached to what Jerry Reinsdorf hopes to accomplish as a baseball owner responsive to both the fans of Chicago and the American League. From day one, the Sox Chairman of the Board has preached fiscal responsibility to a group of owners who at times act like nine-year-olds marching into the toy store with a Visa Card. If Jerry Reinsdorf has erred in his judgments over the years, it is because he did not hire a better P.R. firm to polish his image before the public during the early rounds of stadium negotiations.

"This is not a franchise that is owned by people that can pour tens of millions of dollars into the operation like the Kansas City Royals," Reinsdorf adds. "So we will not do things that are financially stupid in order to win. But every penny of profit is committed to this ballclub and the fans should know that our one and only goal is to win—and I would rather win and break even than finish second and make $20 million."

Don't expect to see any "for sale" signs draped over the old candy store—for now.

Through its first three seasons, the new Comiskey Park has returned in excess of $10 million to the city and state coffers. During the 1991 season, a record 2.9 million fans came through the turnstiles.

Index